LEARNING AND TEACHI
AROUND THE WORLD

M000023897

Learning and Teaching Around the World is a wide-ranging introduction to diverse experiences, practices and developments in global primary education. It explores different contexts for children's learning, and methods and purposes of primary education, in settings across Africa, Asia, Europe, the Americas and Australasia, and addresses wider issues such as the rise of refugee learners and large multigrade classes.

With an explicit focus on comparative and international studies and improving the knowledge, understanding and practice of effective pedagogies for children's learning, this book reflects on key issues such as:

* Standards for learner-centred education
* Patterns of inclusion and exclusion
* Defining 'teacher professionalism'
* The impact of global education agendas
* Language policy for schooling and assessment

Learning and Teaching Around the World is an essential text for those wishing to develop a critical understanding of the experiences of primary teachers and children around the world. Aimed at both undergraduate and postgraduate education studies students, the scope of this book will support all students in developing knowledge of primary education and of the diverse needs of learners in an era of global movement of children and families.

Kimberly Safford is Senior Lecturer in Primary Education at The Open University, UK. She contributes to the university's International Teacher Education and Development programmes in India and Africa, authoring Open Educational Resources collaboratively with academics and practitioners. She also writes OU courses and OER for UK teachers, classroom support staff, and for the wide range of education staff in the Third and Cultural Sectors.

Liz Chamberlain is Senior Lecturer in Primary Education at The Open University, UK. She is a member of the International Teacher Education and Development team and contributes to in-country fieldwork in Uganda and Zimbabwe. Liz authors the module *Comparative and International Studies in Primary Education* and is co-author of an Early Reading Badged Online Course for teachers in Africa and a MOOC, making teacher education relevant for 21st century Africa.

This book forms part of the module 'Comparative and international studies in primary education' (E309), in the Open University BA (Hons) Education Studies (Primary) qualification. This is an innovative practice-focused qualification for people working in or planning to enter the early childhood or primary educator sector anywhere in the world. The Education Studies (Primary) qualification prepares students for postgraduate study and research, and for careers in teaching, the cultural education sector, teacher education and international education and development.

Details of this and other Open University modules can be obtained from Student Recruitment, The Open University, PO Box 197, Milton Keynes MK7 6BJ, United Kingdom (tel. +44 (0) 300 303 5303; email general-enquiries@open.ac.uk).

www.open.ac.uk

LEARNING AND TEACHING AROUND THE WORLD

Comparative and International Studies in Primary Education

Edited by Kimberly Safford and Liz Chamberlain

LONDON AND NEW YORK

First published 2019
by Routledge
2 Park Square, Milton Park, Abingdon, Oxon OX14 4RN

in association with The Open University, Walton Hall, Milton Keynes, MK7 6AA, United Kingdom

and by Routledge
711 Third Avenue, New York, NY 10017

Routledge is an imprint of the Taylor & Francis Group, an informa business

© 2019 compilation, original and editorial material, The Open University

All rights reserved. No part of this book may be reprinted or reproduced or utilised in any form or by any electronic, mechanical, or other means, now known or hereafter invented, including photocopying and recording, or in any information storage or retrieval system, without permission in writing from the publishers.

Trademark notice: Product or corporate names may be trademarks or registered trademarks, and are used only for identification and explanation without intent to infringe.

British Library Cataloguing-in-Publication Data
A catalogue record for this book is available from the British Library

Library of Congress Cataloging-in-Publication Data
Names: Safford, Kimberly, editor. | Chamberlain, Liz, editor.
Title: Learning and teaching around the world : comparative and international studies in primary education / edited by Kimberly Safford and Liz Chamberlain.
Description: Abingdon, Oxon ; New York, NY : Routledge, 2019. | Includes bibliographical references and index.
Identifiers: LCCN 2018008926| ISBN 9781138485204 (hbk) |
ISBN 9781138485211 (pbk) | ISBN 9780429491498 (ebk)
Subjects: LCSH: Education, Primary—Cross-cultural studies. | Education, Primary—Aims and objectives. | Education, Primary—Social aspects. | Comparative education.
Classification: LCC LB1507 .L48 2019 | DDC 372—dc23
LC record available at https://lccn.loc.gov/2018008926

ISBN: 9781138485204 (hbk)
ISBN: 9781138485211 (pbk)
ISBN: 9780429491498 (ebk)

Typeset in News Gothic
by Florence Production Ltd, Stoodleigh, Devon, UK

Cover photo by Martin Crisp.

CONTENTS

ACKNOWLEDGEMENTS

Our thanks are due to the following publishers and authors for permission to reprint edited and abridged versions of their material in this text:

Australian Journal of Teacher Education:

Simoncini, K. M., Lasen, M. and Rocco, S. (2014) Professional Dialogue, Reflective Practice and Teacher Research: Engaging Early Childhood Pre-Service Teachers in Collegial Dialogue about Curriculum Innovation. *Australian Journal of Teacher Education*, 39:1.

Elsevier:

Reprinted from *Procedia Social and Behavioral Sciences* 9, Demirkasmoğlu, N., Defining Teacher Professionalism from different perspectives, 2047–2051 (2010) with permission from Elsevier.

Peter Lang:

Ongoing exclusion within universal education: Why education for all is not inclusive by John Parry and Jonathan Rix. Republished with permission of Peter Lang Publishing Inc, from *Inclusive Education Twenty Years after Salamanca*, Kiuppis, F. and Hausstätter, R. (eds), (2014); permission conveyed through Copyright Clearance Center, Inc.

SAGE Publications:

Ringarp, J. and Rothland, M. (2010) Is the grass always greener? The effect of PISA results on education debates in Sweden and Germany. *European Educational Research Journal* 9:3, 422–430. © 2010 by Sage Publications Ltd. Reprinted by permission of SAGE Publications Ltd.

Dryden-Peterson, S. (2015) Refugee education in countries of first asylum: Breaking open the black box of pre-resettlement experiences. *Theory and Research in Education* 14:2, 131–148. © 2015 by Sage Publications Ltd. Reprinted by permission of SAGE Publications Ltd.

South African Journal of Education:

Donohue, D. and Borman, J. (2014) The challenges of realizing inclusive education in South Africa. *South African Journal of Education* 34:2: Art. #806, 14 pages, https://doi.org/10.15700/201412071114

Springer:

Ansell, N. (2015) Globalizing Education from Christian Missionaries to Corporate Finance: Global Actors, Global Agendas, and the Shaping of Global Childhoods. Adapted by permission from Copyright Clearance Center: Springer, *Geographies of Children and Young People 8* by N. Ansell et al. (ed.) © 2015.

Taylor & Francis Ltd books:

Kivunja, C. and Sims, M. (2016) Demystifying misperceptions and realities about the efficacy of monograde and multigrade pedagogies: Africa's response to globalisation of education. In Shizha and Diallo (Eds), *Africa in the Age of Globalisation: Perceptions, Misperceptions and Realities*. Abingdon: Routledge, pp. 203–218.

Schweisfurth, M., The Gambia: The intersection of the global and the local in a small developing country. In Schweisfurth, M. (2013) *Learner-centered Education in International Perspective: Whose Pedagogy for Whose Development?* Abingdon: Routledge, pp. 75–85.

Taylor & Francis Ltd journals:

Andrea S. Young (2014) Unpacking teachers' language ideologies: Attitudes, beliefs, and practiced language policies in schools in Alsace, France. *Language Awareness*, 23:1–2, 157–171, www.tandfonline.com.

Azuara, P. and Reyes, I. (2011) Negotiating worlds: A young Mayan child developing literacy at home and at school in Mexico. *Compare: A Journal of Comparative and International Education*, 41:2, 181–194 © British Association for International and Comparative Education, Taylor & Francis Ltd, www.tandfonline.com on behalf of British Association for International and Comparative Education.

Bray, M. and Kwo, O. (2013) Behind the façade of free-free education: Shadow education and its implications for social justice. *Oxford Review of Education*, 39:4, 480–497 Privatisation, education and social justice, www.tandfonline.com.

Mills, K., Davis-Warra, J. Sewell, M. and Anderson, M. (2016) Indigenous ways with literacies: transgenerational, multimodal, placed, and collective. *Language and Education*, 30:1, 1–21, www.tandfonline.com.

Slesaransky, G., Ruzzzi, L., Dimedio, C. and Stanley, J. (2013) Is This the Right Elementary School for My Gender Nonconforming Child? *Journal of LGBT Youth*, 10, 29–44, www.tandfonline.com.

Smyth, G. (2016) What languages do you speak? A reflexive account of research with multilingual pupils and teachers, *Language and Education*, 30:2, pp. 143–157, www.tandfonline.com.

Wiley:

Wyse, D. and Ferrari, A. (2015) Creativity and education: Comparing the national curricula of the states of the European Union and the United Kingdom. *British Educational Research Journal* 41:1, 30–47. © Wiley.

NOTES ON CONTRIBUTORS

Lina Adinolfi is Lecturer in English Language Teaching in the School of Languages and Applied Linguistics, The Open University, UK.

Mikayla Anderson is an Indigenous Australian educator. She has taught in urban and remote Indigenous schools in Australia, supporting students to learn through culture.

Nicola Ansell is Professor of Human Geography at Brunel University London. Her research focuses on social and cultural change in the lives of young people in the Global South, and the role of global processes in the production of policies and practices that shape their experiences.

Patricia Azuara is Assistant Professor, College of Education and Human Development, Department of Bicultural- Bilingual Studies, University of San Antonio, Texas, USA. Her research interests focus on literacy development of bilingual children.

Juan Bornman is actively involved in the disability field as a researcher, trainer and scholar, advocating especially for the human rights of persons with significant communication disabilities.

Mark Bray is UNESCO Chair Professor in Comparative Education at the University of Hong Kong. He was previously Director of UNESCO's International Institute for Educational Planning (IIEP) in Paris.

Alison Buckler is Research Fellow at The Open University, UK, where she convenes the International Education and Development research group. She works and researches with teachers, particularly in Sub-Saharan Africa, and is on the executive committee of the British Association of International and Comparative Education (BAICE).

Liz Chamberlain is Senior Lecturer in Education at The Open University, UK. She is Programme Leader for the Education Studies (Primary) qualification and is Co-Director of Children's Research Centre. She is a Trustee of the United Kingdom Literacy Association and is Chair of its International sub-committee.

Martin Crisp lectures in Education at The Open University, UK, and is a Maths specialist. He works in teacher development programmes in India, Sierra Leone and Zimbabwe.

He has a particular interest in the contribution of teaching assistants to children's learning.

Alison Davies is Associate Lecturer in the School of Education, Childhood, Youth and Sport, The Open University, UK. Her research focuses on the voices of young people from Black, Asian and minority ethnic backgrounds, in collaboration with Peterborough Racial Equality Council in England.

John Davis-Warra is a community Durithunga member and has been involved in varied Indigenous education approaches across regional and urban schools in Australia.

Nihan Demirkasımoğlu is Associate Professor at the Department of Educational Sciences at Hacettepe University, Ankara, Turkey. Her research interests include argument culture, abusive supervision, public service motivation, emotional labour and organisational principles.

Joan Dickie is an education consultant in the UK and Kenya, specialising in languages and literacy teaching in the primary age phase.

Connie DiMedio is Head of School at the West Hill School in Pennsylvania, USA. As an adjunct professor she trains and mentors student teachers at university level, and mentors and trains new and in-service teachers.

Dana Donohue is a developmental psychologist. Her research interests include culture and risk/resilience factors for academic achievement. She was postdoctoral fellow at the University of Pretoria, South Africa and is Senior Lecturer at Northern Arizona University, USA.

Sarah Dryden-Peterson leads a research program that focuses on the connections between education and community development, specifically the role that education plays in building peaceful and participatory societies. Her work is situated in conflict and post-conflict settings and with diaspora communities. She is on the faculty at the Harvard Graduate School of Education.

Elizabeth J. Erling is Professor of English Language Teaching Research and Methodology at the University of Graz, Austria.

Anusca Ferrari is Project Manager for European Schoolnet, supporting European projects that focus on entrepreneurship, digital skills and employability.

Charles Kivunja is Associate Professor in Pedagogy, Educational Leadership and Research Methods in the School of Education, University of New England, New South Wales, Australia. His recent research has explored the potential of multigrade pedagogies to achieve global primary education goals.

Ora Kwo is an Associate Professor at the University of Hong Kong. She is known for her work on teacher education and teachers' lives.

Michelle Lasen is Associate Professor and Head of Teaching Quality and Student Success in the Division of Academic and Student Life, James Cook University,

Queensland, Australia. She works with stakeholders across the university to promote evidence-based teaching and assessment practices, and approaches to student retention and success.

Roda Madziva is Assistant Professor in the School of Sociology and Social Policy at Nottingham University, England. She has conducted research on forced migration and family separation, highly skilled migrants, refugee integration and access to services, and the links between migration, human-trafficking and contemporary slavery.

Kathy A. Mills is Professor of Literacies and Digital Cultures at the Learning Sciences Institute Australia, Australian Catholic University, where she leads research on Indigenous ways to multimodal literacy for primary school students. Her *Handbook of Writing, Literacies and Education in Digital Cultures* won the 2017 Divergent Award for Excellence in 21st Century Literacies.

John Parry is a Senior Lecturer in Education (Early Years and Inclusion) at The Open University, UK. His latest book *Special Needs in the Early Years* explores the most effective ways of supporting children and implementing that support in the context of everyday family life.

Iliana Reyes, Ph.D. (UC Berkeley), is a research scientist at the *Departamento de Investigaciones Educativas* at the Center for Research and Advanced Studies (CINVESTAV), in Mexico City, and affiliated faculty in early childhood at the University of Arizona. Her research focuses on transnational communities and socialisation practices with young children.

Johanna Ringarp is Senior Lecturer in History of Education at the Department of Education at Stockholm University, Sweden. Her research specialties include educational history and policy, teacher professionalism and post-Second World War German history.

Jonathan Rix is Professor of Participation and Learning Support at The Open University, UK. His latest book *Must Inclusion be Special? Rethinking Educational Support Within a Community of Provision* examines the discord between special and inclusive education and why this discord can only be resolved when wider inequalities within mainstream education are confronted.

Sharn Rocco is a teacher, teacher educator and founder of Mindful Works. She designs and facilitates mindfulness-based personal and professional development for educators.

Martin Rothland is Professor of Educational Science at University of Münster, Germany. His interests include research on teachers, teacher education and the teaching profession.

Lisa Ruzzi is an elementary school guidance counsellor in Pennsylvania, USA, helping teachers to create a welcoming classroom for all their students and families.

Kimberly Safford is Senior Lecturer in Education at The Open University, UK, with a specialism in literacy. She works in teacher development programmes in India and Sub-Saharan Africa. She recently carried out field work in Ghana for research on the opportunities and challenges of English as the medium of instruction in primary schools.

Michele Schweisfurth is Professor of Comparative and International Education at the University of Glasgow, Scotland. She is interested in tensions between global frameworks (such as children's rights and 'best practice' in teaching and learning) and local and cultural imperatives.

Marlene Sewell worked with Indigenous students in the Northern Territory prior to heading overseas, where she taught in an American international School in Guangzhou, and a start-up school in Mumbai before heading to the Middle East, Oman, to direct a start-up school. Back in Australia she worked as a classroom teacher at an Indigenous school.

Kym M. Simoncini is Assistant Professor of Early Childhood and Primary Education at the University of Canberra, Australia. Prior to her university role she was a primary school teacher in England and Queensland.

Margaret Sims is Professor of Early Childhood, University of New England, New South Wales, Australia. She has practised as a clinical psychologist and a community worker and maintains extensive engagement in the children's services/integrated early childhood services profession.

Graciela Slesaransky is Founding Dean of the School of Education at Arcadia University, USA. She received the 2017 Champion of Social Justice award from the Parent Education and Advocacy Leadership (PEAL) Center for her work in creating welcoming, inclusive and safe schools and organisations for gender non-binary and transgender children, youth and adults.

Geri Smyth is Professor Emeritus, School of Education, University of Strathclyde, Scotland. Her research focuses on social justice in education, specifically on bilingualism and plurilingualism amongst teachers and pupils.

Jeanne Stanley is Executive Director of Watershed Counselling Services, USA. She is a psychologist and national trainer for school districts and academic institutions regarding policies and best practices for supporting gender expansive and transgender students and staff.

Kris Stutchbury is Senior Lecturer in Teacher Education at The Open University, UK, a Science teacher, and the Academic Director of TESSA.

Juliet Thondhlana lectures in Education and Applied Linguistics at Nottingham University, England. She has studied migrants' social and economic integration and the role of language in facilitating integration and resettlement in the education sector and labour market.

Patricia Wambugu is Senior Lecturer in Teacher Education and Director of Quality Assurance at Egerton University, Kenya.

Freda Wolfenden is Professor of Education and International Development at The Open University, UK. Her research and teaching interests focus on issues of pedagogy, new technologies and open practices and their nexus in teacher education in Sub-Saharan Africa and South Asia.

Dominic Wyse is Professor of Early Childhood and Primary Education at University College London, Institute of Education, England. His research focuses on young children's writing, reading and creativity.

Andrea S. Young is Professor at Ecole Supérieure du Professorat et de l'Education at the University of Strasbourg (UNISTRA), France.

Introduction

'Close-up' and 'wide angle' lenses on primary education

Kimberly Safford

Welcome to this Reader in comparative and international primary education studies.

The twenty-five chapters in *Learning and Teaching Around the World* present diverse experiences, practices and developments in global education. In this book you will hear the voices of teachers and student teachers, school and community leaders, teacher educators, policy makers and NGOs, researchers, parents and, of course, children. The perspectives here are like camera lenses. The foci of chapters range from 'close-up' to 'wide angle', from the experiences of one child to the systemic structures that sustain, and in some cases disempower, quality education. The 'close-up' lens identifies local problems and solutions. The 'wide angle' view highlights shared global experiences and goals.

The five parts of this book reflect key issues in primary school education: (1) appropriate provision and enabling pedagogies; (2) languages of and for learning; (3) patterns of inclusion and exclusion; (4) teacher education and preparedness; and (5) the impact of educational change and reform at local, national and global levels.

The scope of this Reader

Education is a rich site for comparative study because, as the comparativist Harold Noah noted, it is the 'touchstone' of any society (Noah 1986: 553–554): a standard by which a society is judged, where we find its core values embedded, and where such values may be examined and challenged. One of the authors in this book, Mark Bray, has written elsewhere about the different actors and the wide and varied purposes of comparative education studies, for instance:

- parents commonly compare schools and systems of education in search of the institutions which will serve their children's needs most effectively;
- practitioners, including school principals and teachers, make comparisons in order to improve the operation of their institutions;
- policy makers in individual countries examine education systems elsewhere in order to identify ways to achieve social, political and other objectives in their own settings;

- international agencies compare patterns in different countries in order to improve the advice they give to national governments and others;
- academics undertake comparisons in order to improve understanding of both the forces which shape education systems and processes in different settings, and of the impact of education systems and processes on social and other development.

(Bray 2007: 15–16)

Each chapter of *Learning and Teaching Around the World* relates to one or more of the above examples. We would add an additional explicit purpose of comparative studies which is evident in this book and which all of the above actors undertake: to improve knowledge, understanding and practice of effective pedagogies for children's learning.

Chapters in this book focus largely on contemporary events and are 'locational', looking at education in specific contexts. Chapter 25 by Nicola Ansell is unique in taking a 'temporal' approach, comparing education over time and place. A few chapters make direct cross-national comparisons, for instance, comparing the language-in-education policies of Ghana and India in Chapter 6, comparing Sweden and Germany's responses to their international assessment performance in Chapter 21, and comparing education policies for creativity in the European Union states in Chapter 22. But comparative education is much more than a comparison of two or more different countries and, in general, most comparative education studies are located in a single country. Although this might seem to contradict the term 'comparative', 'single unit' studies can contribute to the wider field of knowledge about education. A virtue of this book is that it collects a number of single country studies in one place where you, the reader, are invited to make the comparisons.

So, for example, as you read about the schooling of a Mayan child in Mexico in Chapter 9, you may compare her experiences to those of the young Muslim learners in English primary schools in Chapter 12; the issues raised in these two chapters are seen again from a different perspective in Chapter 8, where teachers in Alsace, France give their views about linguistic minority pupils. The systemic barriers to inclusive education in South Africa described in Chapter 14 can be contextualised in the discussion of ongoing exclusion within universal education in Chapter 15; these 'wide angle' lenses can be refocused to understand the 'close up' individual actions in Chapter 13 that enable the inclusion of a gender nonconforming child in a USA primary school. The focus of Chapter 2 is education for refugees, but its attention to pedagogy makes its findings relevant to many more learning and teaching contexts around the world. Chapter 3 is about the value of multigrade pedagogies in Africa, but its implications for primary schooling and the Education for All agenda are globally relevant.

The research studies in *Learning and Teaching Around the World* tend toward qualitative approaches and smallness of scale. Whilst we recognise the interest of comparative international analyses of educational achievement using large data sets (such as PISA, TIMSS and PIRLS) we would question what these studies can tell us about the experiences of individual learners or groups of learners. In collecting chapters, we have highlighted the exploration of local, national and global problems that create barriers to learning and inclusion across international settings today. The comparative focus is largely pragmatic, particularly in relation to pedagogy and teacher education. Two methodologies can be seen across and within the chapters of this book: a local problem-solving approach focused on activity and practice, and an international orientation that draws on wider theory and knowledge. The effect on readers, we hope, is to look outwards and then look back at one's own education system and experience over time and place.

Education for All 1948–2016

Learning and Teaching Around the World is published at a time of urgent international action plans for educational quality and equity. Free and compulsory primary (or elementary) education has been a cornerstone of international agreements since the end of World War II. It is a goal that continues to challenge states, schools and teachers.

International goals for primary education 1948–1989

Everyone has the right to education. Education shall be free, at least in the elementary and fundamental stages. Elementary education shall be compulsory.
   1948 United Nations Universal Declaration of Human Rights Article 26.1

The child is entitled to receive education, which shall be free and compulsory, at least in the elementary stages.
   1959 United Nations Declaration of the Rights of the Child, Principle 7

Primary education shall be compulsory and available free to all.
   1966 United Nations International Covenant on Economic,
   Social and Cultural Rights, Article 13

[States should] make primary education compulsory and available free to all.
   1989 United Nations Convention of the Rights of the Child, Article 28

The Education For All movement was launched in 1990. The conference was convened in Jomtien, Thailand by UNESCO, UNICEF, the United Nations Development Programme, and the World Bank. It brought together delegations from 155 countries, 33 inter-governmental organisations, and 125 nongovernmental organisations (NGOs) and institutes. The most high-profile goal of the conference was to achieve universal primary education by 2000 through increasing school enrolments. But in the target year 2000, the follow-up World Education Forum in Dakar, Senegal acknowledged that, whilst much progress had been made, this goal had not been achieved. The WEF reiterated the aim of the 1948 Universal Declaration of Human Rights for free, universal and compulsory primary education:

> For the millions of children who live in poverty, who suffer multiple disadvantages, there must be an unequivocal commitment that education be free of tuition and other fees, and that everything possible be done to reduce or eliminate costs such as those for learning materials, uniforms, school meals and transport.
>
> (World Education Forum, 2000: 15)

The Education For All agenda was subsequently linked to the United Nations' eight Millennium Development Goals, the second of which was to '. . . *ensure that, by 2015, children everywhere, boys and girls alike, will be able to complete a full course of primary schooling*' (United Nations 2000), but this goal was also not met by its target date.

In 2016 the Millennium Development Goals were replaced by 17 Sustainable Development Goals (SDGs) and the 2030 Agenda for Sustainable Development. SDG 4 is about education and is accompanied by the Education 2030 Agenda. The numerical target to enrol children in school has been superseded by much more complex goals, including: the provision of quality education with effective and relevant learning outcomes, and safe, non-violent, inclusive and effective learning environments for all. The field of comparative and international education studies has developed in relation to these complex goals, with researchers, practitioners, international agencies and policy makers asking questions such as: What does quality education look like? In a quality learning environment, what are teachers and children doing? How do education systems and processes impact on children's learning? How is real inclusion achieved? What kind of training, qualifications and in-service professional development should teachers have?

The chapters in *Learning and Teaching Around the World* are only a small, recent selection from the long history and varied research strands of comparative and international education studies. As you read about experiences and systems of education in this book, we hope you will be able to make better sense of your own experiences and systems of education; in some cases you may be able to take ideas that you read about here and apply them to your own context. Of course, we also recognise the value of reading comparatively to acquire knowledge for its own sake. According to one of the grandfathers of this field, George Bereday: 'The foremost justification for Comparative Education is intellectual. [People] study foreign education systems simply because they want to know, because [they] must forever stir in the quest of enlightenment' (1964: 5). We hope *Learning and Teaching Around the World* enables you to gain knowledge and insights about the field of education.

At the end of each chapter there are questions and further reading. Whether you are a teacher or learning to teach, whether you work in or plan to enter the education sector anywhere in the world, we hope the chapters and questions stimulate your thinking about children's learning in this era of global change and migration.

The authors in this book represent the breadth, experience and diversity of comparative education studies, and we thank them for their contributions to *Learning and Teaching Around the World*.

Sustainable Development Goal 4 and Education 2030 Targets

Goal 4

Ensure inclusive and equitable quality education and promote lifelong learning opportunities for all

Targets

- 4.1: By 2030, ensure that all girls and boys complete free, equitable and quality primary and secondary education leading to relevant and effective learning outcomes.
- 4.2: By 2030, ensure that all girls and boys have access to quality early childhood development, care and pre-primary education so that they are ready for primary education.
- 4.3: By 2030, ensure equal access for all women and men to affordable and quality technical, vocational and tertiary education, including university.
- 4.4: By 2030, substantially increase the number of youth and adults who have relevant skills, including technical and vocational skills, for employment, decent jobs and entrepreneurship.
- 4.5: By 2030, eliminate gender disparities in education and ensure equal access to all levels of education and vocational training for the vulnerable, including persons with disabilities, indigenous peoples and children in vulnerable situations.
- 4.6: By 2030, ensure that all youth and a substantial proportion of adults, both men and women, achieve literacy and numeracy.
- 4.7: By 2030, ensure that all learners acquire the knowledge and skills needed to promote sustainable development, including, among others, through education for sustainable development and sustainable lifestyles, human rights, gender equality, promotion of a culture of peace and nonviolence, global citizenship and appreciation of cultural diversity and of culture's contribution to sustainable development.

Targets around means of implementation

- 4.a: Build and upgrade education facilities that are child, disability and gender sensitive and provide safe, non-violent, inclusive and effective learning environments for all.
- 4.b: By 2020, substantially expand globally the number of scholarships available to developing countries, in particular least developed countries, small-island developing states and African countries, for enrolment in higher education, including vocational training and information and communications technology, technical, engineering and scientific programmes, in developed countries and other developing countries.
- 4.c: By 2030, substantially increase the supply of qualified teachers, including through international cooperation for teacher training in developing countries, especially least developed countries and small-island developing states.

Education 2030 Framework for Action
http://unesdoc.unesco.org/images/0024/002456/245656E.pdf

Where chapters are abridged from original sources, full text citations are provided.

All the children in this book are anonymised or given pseudonyms.

References

Bereday, G. (1964) *Comparative Method in Education*. New York: Holt, Rinehart & Winston.

Bray, M. (2007) Actors and Purposes in Comparative Education. In Bray, M., Adamson, B. and M. Mason (Eds) *Comparative Education Research Approaches and Methods*. New York: Springer.

Noah, H.J. (1986) The Use and Abuse of Comparative Education. In Altbach, P. and Kelly, G. (Eds) *New Approaches to Comparative Education*. Chicago, IL: University of Chicago Press.

United Nations (2000) Millennium Development Goals. New York: United Nations.

World Education Forum (2000) The Dakar framework for action – education for all: Meeting our collective commitments. Paris: UNESCO.

Part 1
Pedagogy and provision

1 Primary education

Why and how to compare?

Kimberly Safford

Introduction

This chapter offers a brief overview of some of the history, methodologies and current direction of travel in comparative and international education studies. The aim is to provide readers with some background and context to appreciate the different approaches taken by researchers in this book and elsewhere, and to suggest starting points for further study.

Comparative and international education has grown in scope since the 1948 Universal Declaration of Human Rights[1] and in response to global agendas for educational equity and quality. It is a field of study concerned with understanding systems, groups and individuals, with education as the location of enquiry. As Nicola Ansell points out in her chapter of this book, the education of children from the nineteenth century onwards was radically different from earlier forms of learning and teaching, as nation states began to fund and supervise systems of formal schooling for large numbers of children. State systems were the focus of early comparative education studies. The 'grandfather' of the field Marc-Antoine Jullien de Paris (1775–1848) lived in an era of enlightenment and revolution, and his thinking reflects some of the ideals of his time. In 1816 he outlined a plan for surveying all the governments of Europe about their systems of education in the belief that education 'like all other arts and sciences, is composed of facts and observations':

> It thus seems necessary to produce for this science, as has been done for the other branches of knowledge, collections of facts and observations arranged in analytical tables, so that these facts and observations can be compared and certain principles and definite rules deduced from them.
>
> (In Palmer 1993: 171)

Jullien envisaged comparative education as a modern 'scientific' discipline, where causes and effects could be identified to reveal universal truths about education. Comparative and international studies today continue to be based on 'facts and observations', what can be seen and what can be measured, on large or small scales, although truths may be only cautiously or partially claimed. Very broadly speaking, two comparative orientations have evolved: one that prioritises the collection of quantifiable data and the search for causality, and another that values an interpretive, qualitative exploration of human experience.

Studying education

In 1900, the historian and educator Michael Sadler said that international studies of education were valuable because they would enable us to better understand and appreciate our 'home' systems. Examining 'foreign' education should, in his words, cause us to 'prize, as we have never prized before, the good things which we have at home' and make us realise what needs 'prompt and searching change' domestically (Sadler 1900/1964: 310–312). The purpose of looking outward to other systems of education is, in this view, to generate benefits for ourselves. Sadler specifically commented that such comparisons should take place 'in a right spirit', with 'sympathy and thoroughness'.

In 1933 Issac Kandel proposed a set of questions for comparative studies to investigate the causes of problems in education systems worldwide. Kandel's 'problems of education' continue to appear in the field of comparative studies and can be seen across the chapters of *Learning and Teaching Around the World*:

- What is the place of private education and of private schools?
- What is the scope of post-elementary or secondary education?
- What should be the curriculum in each type of school?
- How are teachers prepared and what is their status?
- How can standards be maintained? What should be the place of examinations?
- Who shall formulate curricula and courses of study?
- What is the meaning of equality of educational opportunity?

(Kandel 1933: xviii)

The early comparativists looked for similarities and differences in national systems that educated children. But they were aware that systems do not exist in isolation. Kandel argued that education can only be understood in its historical, cultural, political, social and economic contexts. He warned against using decontextualised statistical measures (such as children's attainment, enrolment or attendance) to set educational standards and purposes. Kandel believed that comparisons must appreciate the 'intangible, impalpable, spiritual and cultural forces' which influence education and famously declared that 'factors and forces' outside the school were more significant than what went on inside it (1933: xix).

Developing this line of thought, Edmund King in 1958 wrote *Other Schools and Ours*, comparing schooling and culture in Denmark, England, France, the United States, Japan, India and the Soviet Union. *Other Schools and Ours* examined the moral assumptions of education systems, as well as their achievements and challenges. King believed that comparative education is, essentially, the complex study of human behavior. His investigations included the hopes and expectations of children, teachers and school leaders, and the ways in which children and adults interpret and respond to education systems – all of these factors, he believed, should be valid and important to education policy making.

Today there is a very wide range of rationales for comparative and international studies of primary schooling: to describe children's education in its social, cultural, economic and historical contexts; to understand, interpret or explain the forces which shape learning and teaching; to evaluate and disseminate achievements or failures of school systems and practices, and make suggestions for improvement; to design or reform teaching; to innovate by comparing and evaluating new methods, resources and technologies; to apply global perspectives to local problems, since many countries face common challenges; to improve inclusion by comparing the experiences and outcomes of children with social, economic, physical or linguistic disadvantages to children without such disadvantages; to identify ways of providing basic education in disasters and refugee crises; to highlight the ideologies of primary school curricula and practices; to promote understanding of other cultures, customs and traditions.

Methods and purposes

Alongside the comparativists taking historical, social and cultural approaches to exploring education systems, others developed quantitative and systematic methods, for example, collating large data sets from a large number of countries to identify causal relationships between policy, educational inputs and children's educational outcomes. In 1969 Harold Noah and Max Eckstein wrote *Towards a Science of Comparative Education*, where they argued that the larger the number of nations included in data collection, the more reliable would be the conclusions, and that rigorous methods should shape comparative studies, using 'hypothesis formulation and testing . . . controlled investigation through careful selection of cases . . . precise specification of variables and . . . qualification of the indicators by which they may be decided' so that researchers could 'seek quantitatively expressed explanations of the relationships between variables' (Noah and Eckstein 1969: 789). According to Noah and Eckstein, comparative education has four broad purposes:

- to describe educational systems, processes, or outcomes.
- to develop educational institutions and practices.
- to analyse the relationships between education and society.
- to produce statements about education that are valid in more than one country.

These purposes are salient today in national policy making decisions, for instance, when a country makes changes to its education system based on international comparisons of children's academic attainment, as discussed by Martin Rothland and Johanna Ringaarp in this book. Comparativists now have access to educational data from national and local governments, international organisations such as UNESCO and OECD, and international agencies such as the World Bank. However, increasing the number of countries in a comparative study increases the level of abstraction (Landman

2003: 25); large data sets may lack attention to small but significant internal variations, and they reveal little about the experiences of children and teachers.

Studies that are small in scale or examine individual cases seek a different type of understanding, exploring the personal factors which constitute education systems and how education shapes individuals and groups. Theisen and Adams's classification criteria for questions and purposes of comparative education studies (see Figure 1.1) give space for the exploration of human experience by referring to the 'behaviour' of 'actors', 'roles' and 'relationships'.

The potential complexities of comparative and international education can be seen in 'Bray's Cube' of geographical locations, demographic groups and aspects of society or education (see Figure 1.2). This 'multi-level analyses' model shows the interconnectedness of factors that influence children's education. In Figure 1.2, the black cube represents a comparative study of the curriculum in two or more states or provinces in a single country: a meaningful study would need to take account of the relationships between the curriculum, where it is used, and the children and adults who use it. Spinning the cube in other directions, a comparative study could, for instance, collect information on the attainment of 7-year-olds in schools where new methods of teaching mathematics are implemented.

Criteria for Classification of Comparative Research		
Research Type	*Typical Questions*	*Purpose of Research*
ANALYTICAL	What are the explanations for relationships between components? Why do actors or systems behave in the way they do?	Description of roles. Specification of cause-and-effect relations or explanation of relations and consequences.
DESCRIPTIVE	What is the current status of the phenomena? What are the relationships between variables?	Description of roles. Specification of cause-and-effect relations or explanation of relations and consequences.
EVALUATE	Is program A better or more cost effective than program B? Is the program or policy appropriate for a particular context?	Judgement of the merit value, or worth of any given program or technique. Interpretations useful for decision-making.
EXPLORATORY	What issues pertaining to roles, relationships and processes exist which are worthy of examination by other modes of research? What models, paradigms, or methods might be useful in designing future research?	Generating new hypotheses or questions. Exploration of relationships and functions with potential for in-depth research.

Figure 1.1 Classification of comparative research
Source: Theisen and Adams, 1990: 281.

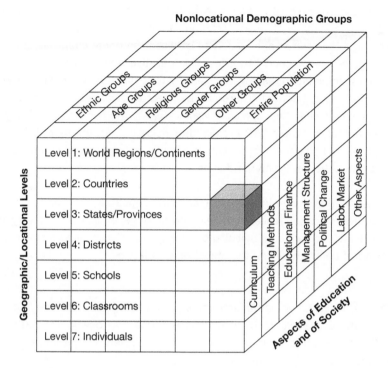

Figure 1.2 Bray's Cube
Source: Bray and Thomas 1995: 475.

Comparative and international education is a multi-disciplinary field, drawing on multiple knowledge domains and methods. It is a network of study with meeting-points in anthropology, ethnography, linguistics, geography, history, political science, philosophy of education, history of education, sociology, psychology, child development, pedagogy, economics and statistics. Keith Watson argues that comparative education 'cannot lay claim to any single conceptual or methodological tool that sets it apart from other areas of education or from the applied social sciences' (2003: 31). David Phillips however points out that what distinguishes comparativists and their research methods from other educationalists is 'the obvious fact that they are concerned essentially with other cultures and countries' (2006: 304). But today's global movement of children is increasingly generating research about 'others' not in 'foreign' locations but in the domestic culture of the researcher, as the chapters by Geri Smyth and Alison Davies in this book illustrate, and the concern with 'others' can be problematic.

Problematising comparative and international education

The narratives and purposes of comparative and international education have been largely formulated by white, mainly male educators and academics in Global North institutions. Takayama et al. (2017) offer a cogent critique of the field, arguing that comparativists have given little attention to the politics of their own concepts about difference, the inequality of power relations in the way comparative knowledge is constituted, and the structural inequalities between the home countries of researchers and the 'targeted' researched countries. Comparative and international education is dominated by scholarship in the English-speaking Global North, and the field's knowledge base is, visibly, highly unequal. There can be great imbalances of power between the researcher and the researched, and *Learning and Teaching Around the World* may arguably perpetuate what Sharon Stein (2017) calls 'thin inclusion'. According to Takayama et al. the homogeneity of the field represents a significant challenge to authentic under-standings of education in its myriad forms:

> If we assume that the methodological, epistemological, and ontological premises of comparative education research are globally homogeneous, we lose a very important possibility: to use epistemological and ontological differences as a starting point for new ways of conceptualizing the object of knowledge.
>
> (2017: S7)

Martin Carnoy in *Education as Cultural Imperialism* (1974) took the starting point that education in the Global South (Africa, Latin America and developing nations in Asia and the Middle East) has been dominated and poorly served by European and North American educational structures, expectations and development aid. Carnoy argued that education systems 'colonise' people's minds, not only in locations such as Africa but, for example, the minds of girls in highly developed countries to accept subservient status, and that schools colonise the minds of children to accept assessments of their inferiority or superiority.

Crossley and Tikly (2004) and others have sought to integrate postcolonial per-spectives into comparative and international studies to create a less Eurocentric, more comprehensive account of the impact of colonialism and globalisation on education. The Canadian scholar Vandra Masemann has attended to the ways in which children make meaning of education in different cultural contexts, for instance, exploring the 'hidden curriculum' in a West African girls boarding school (1974), and calling for comparativists to be attuned to cultural differences and different 'ways of knowing' (1990). Lê Thành Khôi (1976, 1986) in Vietnam and Gu Mingyuan (2006) in China have separately discussed the distinctive cultural and historical roots of education in their countries, and the unique educational ethos of indigenous cultures. Tikly (2001a, 2001b in Watson) has described how economic globalisation has stifled local and indigenous solutions to education problems. The chapter by Kathy Mills and colleagues in this book offers an example of indigenous knowledge being used for children's literacy learning in a primary school. In the ongoing work of 'decolonising knowledge', comparative and international education should prompt reflection on 'what we know as well as what we do not know, how we come to know as well as how we come not to know, and how we relate with one another in producing comparative knowledge on a planetary scale' (Takayama et al. 2017: S19).

Comparing problems, power and pedagogies

Educators and researchers around the world continue to expand conceptual frameworks for comparative and international education. Nóvoa and Yariv-Mashal (2003) argue that the focus of such studies should be only on problems, not on comparing 'facts' or 'realities':

> By definition, the facts (events, countries, systems, etc.) are incomparable. It is possible to highlight differences and similarities, but it is hard to go further. Only problems can constitute the basis for complex comparisons: problems that are anchored in the present, but that possess a history and anticipate different possible futures . . .
>
> (Nóvoa and Yariv-Mashal 2003: 437–438)

Sobe and Kowalczyk (2014) characterise their approach to comparison as 'exploding' Bray's cube (in Figure 1.2) to emphasise the significance of local and global contexts and the power and knowledge inherent in these contexts:

> It seems intuitive or common sense to say that the daily practices of schooling around the globe take place within some context. Questions about the salience of educational contexts cut deeply across debates in the field on the global-local nexus . . . Context cannot be taken-for-granted nor treated as uncontestable . . . Context is also heavily · and irrevocably · linked to power/knowledge concerns.
>
> (Sobe and Kowalczyk 2014: 9)

Sobe and Kowalczyk argue that power and knowledge are, together, the 'starting and ending' points of any educational context, and awareness of this is therefore essential in any comparative study.

Another starting and ending point of primary schooling anywhere in the world is, of course, pedagogy: 'the observable act of teaching together with its attendant discourse of educational theories, values, evidence and justifications' (Alexander 2009: 5). Robin Alexander has argued persuasively for a focus on the theory and practice of teaching, which he calls a 'startlingly prominent' neglected theme of comparative and international education studies. He proposed a conceptual framework for a 'comparative pedagogy' that recursively crosses the boundary between micro and macro, the child and the system.

> Thus, pedagogy does not begin and end in the classroom. It is comprehended only once one locates practice within the concentric circles of local and national, and of classroom, school, system and state, and only if one steers constantly back and forth between these, exploring the way that what teachers and students do in classrooms reflects the values of the wider society.
>
> (Alexander 1990: 925)

A recurrent theme in this book is the global spread of 'learner-centred education' and responses to it in different cultural, economic and political contexts. Chapters in this book by Sarah Dryden-Peterson, Freda Wolfenden, Michele Schweisfurth, and Kris Stuchbury and colleagues explore this important territory. Alexander (2000) has characterised 'child-centred' learning as a largely Anglo-American concept that is culturally inappropriate in many countries. Anthropological studies (see Lancy 2015) show that worldwide there is a very wide range of assumptions about childhood and learning. 'Learner-centredness' is not just about teachers acquiring new skills – it may demand changes to deeply held cultural frameworks and beliefs on the part of teachers, children and parents. A cross-cultural review of psychology literature (Sternberg 2007) concluded that children's talents are better recognised and activated, and teaching and assessment are more effective, when cultural contexts are acknowledged in education. Local studies in Namibia (O'Sullivan 2004), Tanzania (Vavrus 2009), Shanghai (Mok 2006), India (Sarangapani 2015), the Maldives (di Biase 2015) and Cambodia, Egypt, Jordan, Kyrgyzstan and Malawi (Ginsburg 2010) illustrate that 'learner-centred' education in local practice may be productively reconceptualised as 'learning-centred' and include distinct elements of 'traditional' formal, didactic transmission teaching.

It is appropriate to conclude this chapter with thoughts about pedagogy, keeping in mind the focus of this book: learning and teaching in primary schools. Jullien de Paris, Sandler and Kandel viewed education through the lens of the nation state, and such perspectives continue to inform our understanding. But comparative and international education studies today are just as likely to focus on an individual child in Mexico (Chapter 9 by Patricia Azuara and Iliana Reyes), or the parents of a child in the United States (Chapter 13 by Graciela Slesaransky and colleagues) or a new teacher in Ghana (Chapter 23 by Alison Buckler). In such cases, researchers, children and adults are not distant from each other. They often share concerns, cultures and also, importantly, languages. Together, they are contributing to comparative knowledge of primary school education on a global scale. Such studies may go some way towards 'decolonising knowledge', and comparativists who explore the classroom experiences of children and teachers are, implicitly or explicitly, interrogating education systems.

Questions

1. Have you undertaken a comparative study of education, informally or formally, as a parent, teacher, school leader or policy maker? What prompted your comparative study?
2. If you have not undertaken a comparative education study, what kinds of questions or problems do you have that might form the basis of such an enquiry? Would you look outside your own country for comparative information?
3. If you have undertaken some comparative study of education, formal or informal, desk-based or in practice, were you more interested in quantifiable 'countable' data or qualitative 'experiential' data? What seemed to be the most reliable information to answer your question or solve your problem? Did your comparison result in any actions or changes?

Further reading

Bickmore, K., Hayhoe, R., Manion, C., Mundy, K. and Read, R. (2017) *Comparative and International Education: Issues for Teachers*, 2nd ed. Ontario, Canada: Canadian Scholars Press.

Guthrie, G. (2017) The failure of progressive paradigm reversal. *Compare: A Journal of Comparative and International Education*, 47 (1), 62–76.

Ninnes, P. and Burnett, G. (2004) Postcolonial Theory in and for Comparative Education. In Ninnes, P. and Mehta, S. (Eds) *Re-imagining Comparative Education: Postfoundational Ideas and Applications for Critical Times*. New York: Routledge Falmer.

Note

1 Article 26: 1. Everyone has the right to education. Education shall be free, at least in the elementary and fundamental stages. Elementary education shall be compulsory . . . 2. Education shall be directed to the full development of the human personality and to the strengthening of respect for human rights and fundamental freedoms. It shall promote understanding, tolerance and friendship among all nations, racial or religious groups, and shall further the activities of the United Nations for the maintenance of peace. 3. Parents have a prior right to choose the kind of education that shall be given to their children.

References

Alexander, R. (1990) Towards a Comparative Pedagogy. In Cowan, R. and Kazamias, A. (Eds) *International Handbook of Comparative Education* (pp. 923–941). London: Springer.

Alexander, R. (2000) *Culture and Pedagogy: International Comparisons in Primary Education*. Oxford: Blackwell.

Alexander, R. (2009) Towards a comparative pedagogy. Accessed 27 Nov 2017 from www.robin alexander.org.uk/wp-content/uploads/2012/05/IHCE-chapter-59-Alexander.pdf.

Bray, M. and Thomas, R. (1995) Levels of Comparison in Educational Studies: Different Insights from Different Literatures and the Value of Multilevel Analyses. *Harvard Educational Review*, 65 (3), 472–491.

Carnoy, M. (1974) *Education as Cultural Imperialism*. New York: Addison-Wesley Longman.

Crossley, M. and Tikly, L. (2004) Postcolonial perspectives and comparative and international research in education: A critical introduction. *Comparative Education*, 40 (2), Special issue (28), 148–156.

Di Biase, R. (2015) Learning from a small state's experience: Acknowledging the importance of context in implementing learner-centred pedagogy. *The International Education Journal: Comparative Perspectives*, 14 (1), 1–20.

Ginsburg, M. (2010) Improving educational quality through active-learning pedagogies: A comparison of five case studies. *Educational Research*, 1 (3), 62–74.

Gu, M. (2006) An analysis of the impact of traditional Chinese culture on Chinese education. *Frontiers of Education in China*, 1 (2), 169–190.

Kandel, I. (1933) *Comparative Education*. Boston: Houghton Mifflin.

King, E. (1958/1979) *Other Schools and Ours: Comparative Studies for Today*. London: Holt, Rinehart and Winston.

Lancy, D. (2015) *The Anthropology of Childhood: Cherubs, Chattel, Changelings*, 2nd ed. Cambridge: Cambridge University Press.

Landman, T. (2003) *Issues and Methods in Comparative Politics: An Introduction*. London: Routledge.

Lê Thành Khôi (1976) Literacy training and revolution: The Vietnamese experience Prospects – Quarterly Review of Education, 6 (1) Issue 17 "A Turning Point in Literacy" UNESCO. Accessed 22 Nov 2017 from http://collections.infocollections.org/ukedu/en/d/Jh1840e/5.8.html

Lê Thành Khôi (1986) Toward a General Theory of Education. *Comparative Education Review*, 30 (1), 12–29.

Masemann, V. (1974) The 'hidden curriculum' of a West African girls' boarding school. *Canadian Journal of African Studies/Revue Canadienne des Études Africaines*, 8 (3), 479–494.

Masemann, V. (1990) Ways of knowing: Implications for comparative education. *Comparative Education Review*, 34 (4), 465–473.

Mok, I. (2006) Shedding light on the East Asian learner paradox: Reconstructing student‐centredness in a Shanghai classroom. *Asia Pacific Journal of Teacher Education*, 26 (2), 131–142.

Noah, H. and Eckstein, M. (1969) *Toward a Science of Comparative Education*. London: Macmillan.

Nóvoa, A. and Yariv‐Mashal, T. (2003) Comparative research in education: A mode of governance or a historical journey? *Comparative Education*, 39 (4), 423–438.

O'Sullivan, M. (2004) The reconceptualisation of learner‐centred approaches: A Namibian case study. *International Journal of Educational Development*, 24 (6), 585–602.

Palmer, R. (1993) *From Jacobin to Liberal: Marc-Antoine Jullien, 1775–1848*. Princeton NJ: University Press.

Phillips, D. (2006) Comparative education: Method. *Research in Comparative and International Education*, 1 (4), 304–319.

Sadler, M. (1900, reprinted Bereday 1964) Sir Michael Sadler's 'Study of foreign systems of education'. *Comparative Education Review*, 7 (3), 307–314.

Sarangapani, P. (2015) Viewing CCE through an 'Indigenous' Lens. *Compare*, 45 (4), 647–650.

Sobe, N. and Kowalczyk, J. (2014) Exploding the cube: Revisioning 'context' in the field of comparative education. *Current Issues in Comparative Education*, 16 (1), 6–12.

Stein, S. (2017) The Persistent Challenges of Addressing Epistemic Dominance in Higher Education: Considering the Case of Curriculum Internationalization. In Takayama, K., Sriprakash, A. and Connell, R. Toward a Postcolonial Comparative and International Education (pp. S25–S50). *Comparative Education Review*, 61 (S1).

Sternberg, R. (2007) Culture, instruction, and assessment. *Comparative Education*, 43 (1), 5–22.

Takayama, K., Sriprakash, A. and Connell, R. (2017) Toward a Postcolonial Comparative and International Education. *Comparative Education Review*, 61 (S1), S1–S24.

Theisen, G. and Adams, D. (1990) Comparative Education Research. In Thomas, R.M. (Ed.) *International Comparative Education* (pp. 277–300). Oxford: Pergamon.

Tikly, L. (2001a) Globalisation and education in a postcolonial world: Towards a conceptual framework. *Comparative Education*, 37 (2), 151–171.

Tikly, L. (2001b) Post Colonialism and Comparative Education Research, Part 3: Practical Issues and New Approaches. In Watson, K. (Ed.) *Doing Comparative Education Research: Issues and problems*. Oxford: Symposium.

Vavrus, F. (2009) The cultural politics of constructivist pedagogies: Teacher education reform in the United Republic of Tanzania. *International Journal of Educational Development*, 29, 303–311.

Watson, K. (2003) Multidisciplinarity and Diversity in Comparative and International Education. In Crossley, M. and Watson, K. (Eds) *Comparative and International Research in Education: Globalisation, Context and Difference* (pp. 12–22). New York: Routledge Falmer.

2 Refugee children's experiences of education in countries of first asylum

Sarah Dryden-Peterson

Introduction

This chapter, abridged from a longer analysis (Dryden-Peterson 2015), is a unique examination of the education of refugee children in "countries of first asylum" – the countries in which they live after fleeing from their countries of origin, before they are resettled permanently.

We include this chapter in *Learning and Teaching Around the World* because the number of refugee children who have fled across international borders due to conflict and persecution is at the highest level in recorded history, and the pre-resettlement educational experiences of refugee children are, as the author notes, a largely unexplored "black box". The concept of the "black box" is that we do not see the experiences and processes which impact on what we can see, in terms of a student's visible learning or behaviours. If you are teaching or supporting refugee learners, what do you know about their pre-resettlement experiences of schooling, and how might this information inform your support?

The vast majority of refugees – 84 percent at the time of writing – live in exile in low-income countries that neighbour their countries of origin. Fewer than one percent of refugees globally access resettlement in a more distant country. For the majority of refugee children, irregular schooling in countries of first asylum may be their only educational experience for many years. Refugee children who access resettlement in, for instance, Sweden, Scotland or Australia, will arrive with previous educational experiences in their countries of first asylum; these experiences may be several years of schooling in a refugee camp school, in an urban school with large populations of refugees and nationals, or in an informal school run by refugee communities themselves.

Forty percent of refugees globally live in refugee camps, and more than half of refugees now live in cities. Current UNHCR policy focuses on "integration of refugee learners within national systems" (UNHCR, 2012: 8). The adoption of this approach reflects the protracted nature of conflict globally, and also the belief that education within a national system of teacher training and student certification of learning will be of higher quality.

The author identifies three empirical themes that are common to the educational experiences of refugee children in countries of first asylum: language barriers, teacher-centred pedagogy and discrimination in school settings. A strength of the analysis is its synthesis of a range of data to evaluate the global picture, drawing on: United Nations High Commissioner for Refugees (UNHCR) information, key informant interviews in 14 countries of first asylum and ethnographic fieldwork and interviews in Uganda, Kenya, Malaysia and Egypt.

Access to education for refugees

Recent UNHCR data suggest that, in 2014, 50 percent of refugees had access to primary school. This access rate compares to 93 percent of all children globally (UNESCO, 2015: 6). At the secondary level, 25 percent of refugees had access to education in 2014 whereas 62 percent did globally (UNESCO, 2015: 10). Within these global rates, analysis of UNHCR enrolment data indicates wide variation in access to education across countries of first asylum. For example, at the primary level, only 37 percent of refugee children access education in Lebanon.

Low enrolments persist in countries with protracted populations, such as in Pakistan where Afghans represent the largest protracted population globally (UNHCR, 2015a), and where only 43 percent of children access primary education. In some countries of first asylum, access rates are higher, such as in Bangladesh, Egypt, Iran, South Sudan, and Yemen, where more than 80 percent of refugees access primary education. Secondary rates of access for refugees are lower than primary access rates across countries of first asylum. In most countries of first asylum, secondary education is open to very few refugees. In Kenya and Pakistan, for example, which represent two of the largest and most protracted refugee populations in the world, only 4 percent and 5 percent of refugees respectively access secondary school.

Informal schools, initiated by refugee communities, are important sites of access to education. This is particularly true in countries of first asylum where refugee rights are limited. In Uganda, for example, refugees did not have the legal right to reside in urban areas until 2006. Ethnographic fieldwork in Kampala documents that, prior to that time, the only education available to refugee children in urban areas was in refugee-initiated and supported schools that operated outside of any formal assistance from UNHCR or NGOs. Malaysia and Bangladesh do not guarantee the right to education for refugees, and these governments do not permit refugees to access national schools, therefore informal schooling is often the only possibility. The establishment of informal schools can also reflect the kind of education refugee parents seek for their children. In many countries of first asylum, Muslim refugee communities organise Koranic schools to complement formal education, and more formal madrassas also operate in many refugee settings, providing instruction in Arabic, mathematics and history and sometimes other subjects (UNHCR, 2013; Gerstner, 2009: 185). Community-initiated schools may substitute for available formal education, as observed in Dadaab refugee camp in Kenya, where refugee parents chose to create their own primary schools where they could ensure smaller class sizes and control over curriculum (see also UNHCR and CARE, 2009).

Variation in access rates reflects multiple ways in which education is disrupted for refugee children. Ethnographic data from Uganda, Kenya, Malaysia and Egypt indicate the salience of acute conflict, which makes routes to school dangerous, destroys school infrastructure and renders education systems non-functional; legal restrictions whereby a country of first asylum restricts refugee children from entering national schools and/or UNHCR from providing education; and ongoing migration to escape renewed conflicts or to pursue livelihood opportunities. In Kuala Lumpur, the capital of Malaysia, for example, refugee children described being hesitant to go to school. Despite the 73 community-based schools registered with UNHCR, refugee children faced the dangers of exposure to the authorities given a lack of legal status and the distances they needed to walk to get to school. In interviews, parents described the risks of arrest by police and abuse by citizens. They said that at moments when tensions between refugees and the authorities were particularly high, refugee families elected to keep their children home from school.

The experiences of Amaziah, a refugee living in Uganda, illustrate the effects of school disruptions for refugee children. As a researcher, I interviewed Amaziah and his family three times between 2002 and 2005 and observed classes in his school in each of these years. Amaziah did not begin his education at the appropriate age, as militias occupied schools in his home area of eastern Democratic Republic of Congo (DRC). When his family fled to Uganda, they decided to live in Kampala, the country's capital, at a time when it was not legal for refugees to do so. However, they had lived in a city in DRC, and his father, an artisan, could pursue his livelihood in Kampala. The family's longer-term vision was resettlement to the United States, but they were only eligible for resettlement if they established residence in a refugee camp. The dual goals of pursuing a current livelihood and future resettlement were at odds. Amaziah thus moved continuously between the city and the refugee camp. Each time the family received word that UNHCR was conducting a population census in the camp, they boarded up their house in Kampala and travelled back to the camp to take up residence there. One year, this back and forth movement resulted in Amaziah missing his final exams and needing to repeat the entire year of school.

Educational experiences of refugee children

From analysis of classroom observation data and interview data from teachers and refugee children, three themes emerge of the educational experiences of refugees in countries of first asylum: language barriers; teacher-centred pedagogy; and dis-crimination in school settings. Below, I explore the global patterns for each of these themes, providing select country-specific examples. While only brief examples are provided here, they were chosen to be representative of the overall ethnographic dataset and corroborated by interviews in the 14 countries hosting the largest number of refugees globally.

Language barriers

Refugee children spend a disproportionate amount of time learning languages while often falling behind in age-appropriate academic content. Most refugee children transition to a new language of instruction in a country of first asylum. For example, refugees from Somalia transition from Somali to English in exile in Kenya and Uganda; refugees from DRC transition from French to English in Uganda and Rwanda; and refugees from Sudan transition from Arabic to French in Chad. Interviews and observations make clear that a common strategy for language learning in this context of language transition is to place refugees in classes with younger children.

For example, Annette, whom I interviewed in a refugee camp in southwest Uganda three times between 2002 and 2005, had been in high school in DRC before she fled to Uganda. Coming from a French language education system in DRC, Annette was placed in the equivalent of second grade in Uganda, which was an English language education system. Classroom observations revealed that this practice was the norm; about one third of the children in Annette's primary school class were severely overage, their long teenage bodies folded up to sit on the floor with seven- and eight-year-olds.

On-going migration and shifting policies also contribute to the ways in which language learning shapes the educational trajectories of refugee children pre-resettlement. Henri, whom my research team interviewed in Burundi in 2013 when he was a university student, exemplifies a typical pathway through language. Throughout his childhood, Henri lived as a refugee in exile in Tanzania. In primary school, he followed the Tanzanian curriculum in English and Swahili; he began secondary school following the Burundian curriculum officially in French and Kirundi, but since there were only Tanzanian teachers, the languages used remained mostly English and Kiswahili; and then, when his refugee camp was closed, he relocated to a new refugee camp to complete secondary school following the Congolese curriculum in French.

Upon arrival in a resettlement country, refugee children like Annette and Henri may have fallen years behind in content mastery not related to their abilities but due to continual shifting of language of instruction and the resulting lack of exposure to subject-matter content.

Teacher-centred pedagogy

Refugee education in countries of first asylum is characterised by a teaching style that is teacher-centred, with lectures a central feature and heavy reliance on students memorising and repeating limited answers to closed factual questions. This pedagogical style persists in refugee education, and more broadly across low- and middle-income countries (Tao, 2013; Vavrus and Bartlett, 2013), despite policies that place a high value on child-centered, participatory teaching methods (Global Education Cluster, 2010; INEE, 2010).

Classroom observations in schools serving Somali and Sudanese refugees in Nairobi and Kakuma refugee camp in Kenya demonstrate the centrality of lecture as a pedagogical method. Our research team found that lectures were central in 46 of 53 classroom observations conducted in 2013. These lectures were characterised primarily by teachers' didactic presentations. Children's participation was limited to factual questions posed by the teacher that required children to repeat only what the teacher had just said. For example, in an informal school in Nairobi, a teacher asked his almost exclusively Sudanese students: "What do we call [it] when you grow flowers only?", to which the class chorused back, "floriculture," mentioned orally and written on the board only moments before. In a classroom in a Kenyan public school serving mostly Somali students, the teacher asked "who can tell me? We have two forms of trade, which ones are they?" The only accepted answers were "domestic" and "international," again cited in the lecture and written on the board earlier in the same lesson. In only 17 of the 53 lessons we observed did children ask any questions at all, and in only 6 was more than one question posed during the entire lesson. These questions, like the ones posed by teachers, were primarily factual or definitional in nature.

Classroom observations across the dataset indicate that in their pre-resettlement education, refugee children often have no experience with child-centred activities or with expectations for working in groups, asking questions, or engaging in exploration. In resettlement countries, teachers may assume that silence, failure to ask questions, and difficulty in self-directed exploration means refugee children have few contributions to make in class. Instead, refugee children may be following what they understand from their pre-resettlement education to be proper classroom conduct.

Discrimination in school settings

Refugee children often experience discrimination in their pre-resettlement education. Assumed in much of the literature is that refugee children experience the process of cultural adaptation and marginalisation vis-à-vis schools and teachers for the first time when they arrive in a resettlement country. For most refugees, however, these experiences are not usually new: by definition, they fled their homes due to persecution, and most also previously entered a new education system in a country of first asylum. Ethnographic observations and interviews with children reveal frequent experiences of discrimination, primarily in the content of the curriculum and in treatment by peers and teachers.

The instructional content to which refugee children are exposed in countries of first asylum can be at best difficult to relate with and at worst highly politicised and discriminatory. For example, ongoing violence in Kenya attributed to Al-Shabaab, a militant group based in Somalia, has fostered a hostile environment for Somali refugee children in Kenyan schools, where the discourse has at times been reduced to, "refugees equal terrorists." At the end of one class in Nairobi, observed in 2013, the Kenyan teacher said to the mostly refugee children: "Do we fight?" "No!" the children exclaimed in response. "Do we call each other refugee?" he said "No!" they chanted again. "Refugee" was a bad word.

Similarly, in Egypt, refugee parents described bullying among children in school settings, which increased in intensity in relation to the overall climate of fear for Syrians in Egypt. After the overthrow of Egypt's short-lived Muslim Brotherhood government by a military coup, the Egyptian media adopted a stronger public position against the opposition in Syria related to the opposition's perceived links with the Syrian Muslim Brotherhood. Refugee children felt the impact of this change in public perception in schools. Syrian parents, in 2014, described how their children were faced with aggressive questions about "why they quit Syria, why they were in Egypt . . . why [they] did not go back to their own country." These pre-resettlement experiences of discrimination in school settings have the potential to make refugee children and their parents wary of schools and teachers in resettlement countries. These previous experiences may also compound additional discrimination refugee children face in resettlement schools, including expectations of how discrimination is addressed – or not addressed – by teachers and parents.

Educational trajectories of refugee children

This chapter begins to build conceptual and empirical understandings of educational experiences of refugee children in countries of first asylum, before they are resettled to countries such as the U.S.A., Canada, Australia, the UK, and others. Conceptually, the analysis emphasises the relevance of conflict conditions to the structures of refugee education and the types of educational experiences refugee children have pre-resettlement. It also highlights that, rather than starting anew upon arrival in a resettlement country, most contemporary refugee children have experienced education in countries of first asylum, which are in most cases low-income countries.

Refugees must leave behind many aspects of their lives: material goods, social and family networks, and usually any clear sense of what the future holds for them and for their children. Many refugees express the idea that education is the one thing that cannot be left behind (Dryden-Peterson, 2011; Winthrop and Kirk, 2011). Yet pre-resettlement educational experiences of refugee children remain largely opaque to post-resettlement researchers and teachers. Whether or not these experiences are made visible or understood, they do remain part of the educational trajectories of refugee children. Refugee children do not leave them behind.

Three themes emerge as common to global trajectories of refugee children's education: language barriers; teacher-centred pedagogy; and discrimination in school settings. Equipped with knowledge of these general experiences, teachers in resettlement schools stand to be better able, for example: to identify educational needs based on prior exposure to academic content and language as opposed to innate capacities for learning; to explicitly teach skills for the kind of participation expected in classrooms; and to openly discuss issues of discrimination in schools toward the development of trusting relationships. Bringing students' personal histories – educational and otherwise – into the classroom is, of course, not a new line of thinking. It speaks to a "funds of knowledge" approach in which teachers are also learners about the cultural and cognitive resources of their students' families and can incorporate these assets into the classroom (Moll et al., 1992).

These three themes do not encompass the totality of refugee children's pre-resettlement educational experience and do not take the place of understanding the unique experiences of each child. The themes do, however, help to define the kinds of questions to ask about pre-resettlement education. Awareness of these themes can help to support the work of teachers as they continue to open the "black box" of global educational experiences of refugee children.

Questions

1. The author identifies three barriers to learning for refugee children in their countries of first asylum: the language of instruction and assessment, teacher-centred pedagogy and discrimination in school settings. What practical steps can classroom teachers take to begin to address each of these barriers?
2. How might addressing these barriers make a positive impact on the experiences of all learners, and on the experiences of teachers themselves?
3. Do you think the "black box" concept can apply to our understanding of the learning behaviours of children who are not refugees? Give an example of this.

Afterword from the editors: Learner-centred education

This chapter specifically identifies the problem of "teacher-centred" pedagogy in the educational experiences of refugee children in countries of first asylum.

In the global agendas to promote quality education for all, there is increasing focus on pedagogy: the visible act of teaching and the discourses (ideas, theories and debates) which inform and make sense of teaching (see Alexander, 2009). National and global education policies often refer to learner-centred and child-centred pedagogy but offer little exemplification of what this should look like in practice.

We note two frameworks that provide practical starting points to observe and evaluate the educational experiences of children and the practices of teachers. These frameworks have been developed from empirical research in classrooms around the world.

Michelle Schweisfurth (2013:146) has proposed a set of minimum standards for learner-centred education:

1. Lessons are engaging to pupils, motivating them to learn (bearing in mind that different approaches might work in different contexts).
2. Atmosphere and conduct reflect mutual respect between teachers and pupils. Conduct such as punishment and the nature of relationships do not violate rights (bearing in mind that relationships might still be relatively formal and distant).
3. Learning challenges build on learners' existing knowledge (bearing in mind that this existing knowledge might be seen collectively rather than individualistically).
4. Dialogue (not only transmission) is used in teaching and learning (bearing in mind that the tone of dialogue and who it is between may vary).
5. Curriculum is relevant to learners' lives and perceived future needs, in a language accessible to them (mother tongue except where practically impossible) (bearing in mind that there will be tensions between global, national and local understandings of relevance).

6. Curriculum is based on skills and attitude outcomes as well as content. These should include critical and creative thinking skills (bearing in mind that culture-based communication conventions are likely to make the "flavour" of this very different in different places).
7. Assessment follows up these principles by testing skills and by allowing for individual differences. It is not purely content-driven or based only on rote learning (bearing in mind that the demand for common examinations is unlikely to be overcome).

Drawing on Alexander (2009), Schweisfurth (2013), Wagner et al. (2012), and Wiggins and McTighe (2005), Mary Mendenhall and colleagues (2015: 100) used a framework of 'core elements' of learner-centred education to observe teaching and learning in refugee schools in Kenya:

*   Meaningful and active pupil engagement
*   Inclusive and respectful learning environment
*   Differentiated instruction
*   Constructive classroom discourse
*   Varied comprehension checks and assessments
*   Conceptual learning and critical thinking
*   Relevant curriculum and language(s) of instruction.

We recognise that no classroom will evidence all these descriptors all the time. Also, what constitutes "meaningful and active" engagement and "constructive" discourse will differ from classroom to classroom. Nevertheless, frameworks such as these begin to concretise the concept of learner-centred education. We appreciate the further development and application of such frameworks that focus on the day to day interactions of teachers and children and offer practical indicators of quality education for all.

Further Reading

Dryden-Peterson, S. (2015) Refugee Education in Countries of First Asylum: Breaking Open the Black Box of Pre-Resettlement Experiences. *Theory and Research in Education* (December 21). [Available at http://nrs.harvard.edu/urn-3:HUL.InstRepos:2398948.]
Mendenhall, M., Dryden-Peterson, S., Bartlett, L., Ndirangu, C., Imonje, R., Gakunga, D., Gichuhi, L., Nyagah, G., Okoth, U. and Tangelder. M. (2015) Quality education for refugees in Kenya: Pedagogy in urban Nairobi and Kakuma refugee camp settings. *Journal on Education in Emergencies*, 1 (1), 92–130.
Schweisfurth, M. (2015) Learner-centred pedagogy: Towards a post-2015 agenda for teaching and learning. *International Journal of Educational Development*, 40 (1), 259–266.

The full text of this chapter is: Dryden-Peterson, S. (2015) Refugee Education in Countries of First Asylum: Breaking Open the Black Box of Pre-Resettlement Experiences. *Theory and Research in Education* (December 21).

References

Alexander, R. (2009) *Towards Dialogic Teaching: Rethinking Classroom Talk*, 4th ed. York: Dialogos.
Dryden-Peterson, S. (2011) *Refugee Education: A Global Review*. Geneva: UNHCR.

Gerstner, E. (2009) Hope for the Future: Issues of Educational Certification in Dadaab, Kenya. In Kirk, J. (Ed.) *Certification Counts: Recognizing the Learning Attainments of Displaced and Refugee Students* (pp. 183–191). Paris: UNESCO-IIEP.

Global Education Cluster. (2010) *The Joint Education Needs Assessment Toolkit.* Geneva: Education Cluster Unit.

INEE. (2010) *Minimum Standards for Education: Preparedness, Response, Recovery.* New York: INEE.

Mendenhall, M., Dryden-Peterson, S., Bartlett, L., Ndirangu, C., Imonje, R., Gakunga, D., Gichuhi, L., Nyagah, G., Okoth, U. and Tangelder. M. (2015) Quality education for refugees in Kenya: Pedagogy in urban Nairobi and Kakuma refugee camp settings. *Journal on Education in Emergencies,* 1 (1), 92–130.

Moll, L.C., Amanti, C., Neff, D., et al. (1992) Fund of knowledge for teaching: Using a qualitative approach to connect homes and classrooms. *Theory into Practice,* 31, 132–141.

Schweisfurth, M. (2013) *Learner-Centred Education in International Perspective: Whose Pedagogy for Whose Development?* New York: Routledge.

Tao, S. (2013) Why are teachers absent? Utilising the Capability Approach and Critical Realism to explain teacher performance in Tanzania. *International Journal of Educational Development,* 33, 2–14.

UNESCO. (2015) *EFA Global Monitoring Report: Education for All 2000–2015: Achievements and Challenges.* Paris: UNESCO.

UNHCR. (2012) *Education Strategy 2012–2016.* Geneva: UNHCR.

UNHCR. (2013) *Finding our Way: Education Strategy for Refugees in Chad 2013–2016.* N'Djamena: UNHCR.

UNHCR. (2014a) *Facts and Figures about Refugees.* [Available at www.unhcr.org.uk/about-us/keyfacts-and-figures.html.]

UNHCR. (2014b) *UNHCR Policy on Alternatives to Camps.* Geneva: UNHCR.

UNHCR. (2015a) *2015 UNHCR country operations profile – Pakistan.* [Available at www.unhcr.org/cgibin/texis/vtx/page?page=49e487016&submit=GO.]

UNHCR. (2015b) *UNHCR Refugee Resettlement Trends 2015.* Geneva: UNHCR.

UNHCR and CARE. (2009) *Filling the Gap? Informal Schools in Dadaab Refugee Camps: A Joint Study of UNHCR and CARE International Kenya.* Dadaab Refugee Camp, Kenya: UNHCR and CARE.

UNRWA. (2011) *UNRWA Education Reform Strategy, 2011–2015.* Amman: UNRWA.

Vavrus, F. and Bartlett, L. (2013) *Teaching in Tension: International Pedagogies, National Policies, and Teachers' Practices in Tanzania.* Rotterdam: Sense Publishers.

Wagner, D., Murphy, K. and Haley de Korne, H. (2012) *Learning First: A Research Agenda for Improving Learning in Low-Income Countries.* Washington DC: The Brookings Institution.

Wiggins, G. and McTighe, J. (2005) *Understanding by Design.* Alexandria, VA: Association for Supervision and Curriculum Development.

Winthrop, R. and Kirk, J. (2011) Learning for a Bright Future: Schooling, Conflict, and Children's Well-Being. In Mundy, K. and Dryden-Peterson, S. (Eds) *Educating Children in Conflict Zones: Research, Policy, and Practice for Systemic Change (A Tribute to Jackie Kirk)* (pp. 101–121). New York: Teachers College Press.

3 Multigrade pedagogies

Africa's response to Education for All

Charles Kivunja and Margaret Sims

Introduction

In the 'Scramble for Africa' some 250 years ago, colonial powers transplanted their education systems to their newly acquired territories. These systems positioned 'monograde' teaching as the 'gold standard' of instruction in schools, where one teacher instructs a class of same-age pupils. Learning theories of the time described children's knowledge development as a sequence of age-linked steps. Grouping pupils of several ages and grade levels, to study different curricula in classes taught by a single teacher, was not considered an effective approach to teaching and learning. Today, this type of grouping is known as 'multigrade' or mixed-age teaching. Theories of children's learning have evolved significantly since the African colonial period, yet there is still a widespread perception that monograde teaching is superior to multigrade teaching.

In this chapter, the authors use findings from their research in Uganda and Zambia, together with existing literature, to argue that multigrade pedagogy is the only way African nations can meet the challenges of Education for All children.

Multigrade education around the world

Data on multigrade teaching are not systematically collected in many countries, yet a large number of primary school children continue to learn in multigrade classes in both the poor and rich countries (Kyne 2005; Little 1996, 2001, 2006b; Miller 1990; UNESCO 2007; Veenman 1995). For instance, in her review of data on multigrade teaching throughout the world, including the USA, Europe, Africa, South America and Asia, Little (2001) found that both the percentage of schools and students in multigrade contexts had significantly increased since the mid-1980s. In subsequent work, Little (2006b) found that in 2005, some 30% of children worldwide went to school in multigrade schools.

UNESCO (2007) data also show that multigrade classes are found in many highly developed countries, including USA, UK, Canada, Norway, Australia, Germany, Greece, Russia, Finland, France, and Ireland. In Norway, for example, the country which has the highest Human Development Index (1/189), the figure of all primary schools with multigrade classes was 35% in 2000 (Little 2006a). In England, Little (2006a: 33) found that 'a quarter of all learners were studying in mixed-year classes' in 2000. For the same year she reported that 'in France, 34% of public schools had combined classes'. In the Netherlands, 53% of all primary school teachers were found to be teaching in multigrade classes (CEB-Commissie Evaluatie Basisonderwijs 1994). In the Republic of Ireland, some 40% of primary school classes were found to be multigrade (Department of Education and Science [Ireland] 2004). In Canada, Gayfer (1991) found that 20% of all primary school children were enrolled in multigrade classes.

Literature shows that multigrade schooling has resulted in improved social and cognitive skills, retention rates, attendance and other indicators of educational success in many countries in North America, Europe, Latin America, Asia and the Caribbean (Brown 2010). In choosing multigrade education, schools in these countries have developed ways of improving teaching and learning: for example, new methods utilising structures such as self-directing learning and peer mentoring, cooperative learning and peer coaching that have proven potential to enhance active learning (Kagan 1988). Because of this new knowledge around multigrade teaching and learning, jurisdictions across Western Europe and North America are now offering multigrade education on ideological grounds, rather than because of pragmatics. Consequently, such schools are now evident in both metropolitan and rural areas.

In addition to their use in developed countries, multigrade classes are found in numerous developing countries such as China, India, Vietnam, Bhutan, Nepal, Bangladesh and Sri Lanka, and throughout South America. The work of Juvane (2007) illustrates the positive impact of multigrade teaching on the quality of education for all. Little (2006a: 33) found children in multigrade schools in the Turks and Caicos Islands performed better in reading than those in monograde classes. Likewise, Berry (2010) contends that multigrade teaching can be particularly effective in improving the reading progress of low-achieving children. Colombia, Brazil and Guatemala offer good examples of how multigrade teaching has been developed to positively impact on teaching and learning. The New School programme, called Escuela Nueva (see http://escuelanueva.org), originated in rural Colombia where small and isolated communities might have a one-room school with students at many grade levels. Escuela Nueva is based on multigrade teaching strategies for contexts that may not be well-resourced, and it has been effective and efficient in expanding access to primary education. The program has been so successful it is being tried in some secondary schools.

However, evidence from meta-reviews of research on multigrade teaching is mixed, with some showing enhanced child academic outcomes, and others, no difference or worse outcomes (Little 2004). Beukes (2006) suggests that improved academic outcomes may be associated with 'cognitive stretching' (50) achieved when younger, less able students work with older, more able classmates. Negative outcomes for students may be linked to the increased demands on teachers needing to cater for a wide range of student learning needs (Benveniste and McEwan 2000). Higher levels of teacher stress are likely to reduce the quality of teaching (Mason and Burns 1997).

Pragmatic realities

In many developing countries, small primary and community schools have a well-established tradition. In the majority of such schools, particularly in rural areas, the children are normally grouped for various subjects and there may be several grade levels in one classroom taught by one teacher. Such a context is what is characterised as typical multigrade organisation (Little, 2007: 5). Schools have been established and organised in this way because of the needs of children in remote, isolated and scattered small communities, where the numbers of pupils of the same age and grade are too few to comprise a class of their own on the monograde model.

Most universities and teacher training colleges in Sub-Saharan Africa train teachers for monograde classrooms. Our research in Uganda and Zambia (Kivunja and Wood 2012) found that most of the teachers teaching multigrade classes had received little or no training in applying multigrade strategies. Earlier studies found that although multigrade teaching had been introduced in Zambia in the mid-1980s there had been no ministerial support to provide a central curriculum for multigrade teaching (Lungwangwa 1989; Mukupa et al. 2010); there is a curriculum for monograde primary classrooms only, thus teachers who find themselves teaching multigrade classes have to improvise, and multigrade teaching is perceived as a 'poor relation' to monograde in school organisation (Beukes 2006: 23).

In Sub-Saharan Africa multigrade teaching is very common but accurate data are not publicly or readily available (Juvane 2005). Little referred to this situation as the apparent 'invisibility' of multigrade in Africa (1996). Even in South Africa, which has more reliable data than most Sub-Saharan African countries, Brown (2010: 65) found that the magnitude of multigrade teaching is 'unknown'. But we know from the statistical review of multigrade teaching conducted in South Africa by Schindler (1997) and Wilson's (2002) historical analysis that the prevalence of multigrade teaching in South Africa is far greater than reported in official accounts. Data from the South African Department of Education (2009) support a similar conclusion.

Driven mainly by necessity, particularly in the rural and remote areas, multigrade classes are common in the west, central, eastern and southern parts of the African continent as exemplified, for instance, in Zambia, Kenya, Uganda, Tanzania, Mali and South Africa. In South Africa, for example, a study on rural schooling by the Department of Education (2005) found that nearly 40% of all public schools are in rural areas and multigrade practice was common in all of them. These proportions are consistent with our findings in Uganda and Zambia (Kivunja and Maxwell 2009), which we report here because we believe they represent quite well the realities that most Sub-Saharan countries face in trying to provide universal primary education.

In both Zambia and Uganda, parents indicated a preference for monograde education, and those who can afford to send their children to monograde schools in Lusaka (the Zambian capital) and Kampala (the Ugandan capital) do so. As children migrate to urban areas, fewer children are left in the rural areas and, in most instances, there are too few to warrant monograde classes. As a result, the remaining children are aggregated into a single multigrade class consisting of a great range of grades, ages and abilities.

This situation exacerbates the problem of teacher shortages, because teachers are reluctant to accept appointments in rural and remote areas. Apart from the difficulties of access to these areas, there is little opportunity for professional development and social networking.

When we investigated perceptions of multigrade formation amongst three primary school principals and six primary teachers, we found that their key reason was pragmatic: an issue of numbers of students and lack of teachers. Participants appeared to view this as a poor compromise and this negative perception is likely linked to lack of support for multigrade classes. This lack of understanding of the benefits of multigrade education, and the reification of monograde education, we posit as a significant barrier preventing the achievement of Education For All.

Despite this universal perception of our interviewees that multigrade had been forced upon them by necessity rather than choice, there was a clear understanding that multigrade schooling was filling an important gap in the education of their children. However, interviewees unanimously argued that multigrade teaching involved more work than monograde. For example, a teacher said:

> I think multigrade is very important in Zambia because we do not have enough teachers and schools and other resources. But the problem with it, I think, is that the teachers prepare a lot more work than in monograde. I think the government should pay multigrade teachers twice as much as monograde teachers because they do more work; or it should give them an allowance.
>
> (Teacher M, Basic School A)

An exception to the generally negative perceptions of multigrade education was articulated by a principal whose primary school has both monograde and multigrade classes. He explained that the historical results showed that the children in the multi-grade class were doing very well. The reality illustrated in Table 3.1 shows that children in the multigrade class had actually performed better in examinations than those in monograde classes for three successive years.

Endorsement for multigrade teaching came not only from this one school principal but from a parent as well. One mother said that her daughter who is in a multigrade class was doing better than her son who is in a monograde class. However, in general,

Table 3.1 Comparison of children's results in monograde and multigrade classes at Basic School A

Year	Monograde			Multigrade		
	Number that sat the exam	PASS	% Pass	Number that sat the exam	PASS	% Pass
2007	41	32	78	15	14	93.3
2008	43	30	69.8	18	16	88.9
2009	45	35	77.8	20	19	95

parents claimed that children in multigrade classes were not taught by fully qualified teachers, and they saw this as hugely disadvantageous.

The real problem is that inexperienced teachers have to teach very large classes comprising several grades without adequate resources, so it is likely that teachers in multigrade classes are less effective in their teaching. Teachers themselves identified one of their greatest challenges as having been trained only to teach monograde and yet they were being asked to teach multigrade classes. An additional problem was that they were working with a curriculum designed for monograde classes. Teachers complained that it was unfair that whereas their peers who taught a monograde class were given a prepared curriculum from which to work, those teaching multigrade had to improvise and modify the monograde curriculum by themselves to fit the multigrade class setting.

These findings are not unique to Zambia or Uganda. Rather, they are quite common in Sub-Saharan countries wherever there is a low population density in a large spatial area where only a few children of primary schooling age live. Consequently, schools are very small with some of them being set up as one-teacher schools, thus operating as de-facto multigrade classes. Despite these difficulties on the ground, UNESCO has supported the development of multigrade as a means of accelerating Education For All. By bringing schools closer to communities, more children, especially girls, are encouraged to enrol and stay in school. In such contexts, if the benefits of multigrade education were understood, and teachers resourced appropriately, children's outcomes could be significantly enhanced.

Pedagogical considerations

> ... there are rich intellectual and social benefits of grouping children in mixed-age rather than single-age cohorts ... teachers are more likely to address individual differences in a mixed-age group because the pressure of needing to work at a particular age or stage level disappears.
>
> (Groundwater-Smith et al. 2003: 93)

In many developed countries multi-age groups are formed by choice, when school communities believe that educating children of different age groups together is beneficial. In such groups, teachers tend not to assume that students' learning is based on their age or grade level, and learning opportunities are shaped around individual student needs. Variation in the learning needs of children within a single-age cohort can be significant, so it has been argued that training teachers for multigrade teaching creates opportunity for an improvement in teaching that can benefit all children (Berry 2010; Blum and Diwan 2007). Likewise, research in India has demonstrated that multigrade teaching can be effective if the curriculum is designed specifically to provide for the handling of multigrade, multi-level classrooms with no correlation between age and ability (Padmanabha and Rama 2010).

Research has identified components of successful multigrade instruction. For example, Miller (1991) argued that classroom organisation, classroom management, behaviour management strategies, instructional organisation and curriculum, teaching delivery and grouping and the use of self-directed learning and peer tutoring were the key factors influencing successful multigrade teaching. Many of these depend on the skills of the teacher, and other research has identified this as a key component contributing to successful implementation (see for example Soliman and Ismail 2010).

Work in Columbia, where the *Escuela Nueva* programme emphasised the importance of multigrading, focused on changing teacher practices and resources (Benveniste and McEwan 2000). Teachers received self-study materials in Spanish, science and social studies. In-service training was offered to teachers to move them from traditional instructional techniques (such as lecturing, rote memorisation and hierarchical relationships with students) towards a constructivist approach to teaching and learning focusing on collaborative inquiry. Whilst these factors were found to have a small impact on teachers' practices, a more profound impact arose from teachers' attitudes. The authors argue that whilst teachers continue to perceive multigrade teaching as a poor alternative to monograde teaching they will remain unable to effectively implement the strategies they are taught; teachers need to change their perceptions so that they are positively inclined towards multigrade teaching.

Conclusion

Sub-Saharan Africa will need 2.1 million new teachers by 2030 (UNESCO 2013). This figure does not include the number of teachers who will have to be replaced due to attrition. Sub-Saharan Africa simply won't have the resources to provide the millions of teachers required to provide Education For All, if educational systems try to provide EFA based on the monograde model. Our view is that given the experiences around the world, pragmatic realities in African countries and sound pedagogical considerations, the application of multigrade teaching to effect Education For All is not an option. It is an imperative.

Multigrade education is associated with many problems. Multigrade schools are often in remote rural areas of population decline, or in areas where student numbers in upper grades are too small to comprise a one-grade class. Multigrade schools tend to have only a few teachers, be in areas of widely scattered population, have few students and high teacher absenteeism. As Brown (2010: 71) noted in South Africa:

> Due to teacher shortage and instances of absenteeism, a normal class of between 40 and 50 students often had to be combined to form one multigrade class. Class size is a serious problem that multigrade teachers confront in such instances.

In Uganda and Zambia, as in most Sub-Saharan countries, there is no curriculum designed and provided specifically for the teaching of multigrade. Instead, teachers and learners have to work with the national curriculum that is purpose-built for monograde teaching. Such a curriculum does not have in-built flexibility for combined grades. Moreover, in most countries, there are simply no government policies that recognise multigrade teaching as an on-going practice. This leaves schools without policies, principles or strategies to guide their multigrade practice.

The success of multigrade education in some Latin America countries should help to dismiss the negative stereotypes associated with multigrade pedagogy. The lack of adequate planning and government support for multigrade in Sub-Saharan Africa should not be used to characterise multigrade pedagogy as a poor cousin to monograde. Our governments need to recognise the potential value of multigrade teaching in contributing to the attainment of Education For All. Proper training of teachers in multigrade education and appropriate resourcing make a big difference in the efficacy of multigrade teaching.

Teaching a multigrade class is not just a matter of managing such a class. Multigrade education is a specialised pedagogy with a demanding conceptual framework and teaching skills. As Juvane and Joubert (2010: 6) prudently advise, 'a paradigm change is required if multigrade education is to escape the bonds of the present system. It needs to be allowed the freedom to exist as an authentic pedagogy in its own right.' It is inefficient and inefficacious to ask teachers who were trained only in monograde teaching to teach multigrade. Multigrade teachers should be specially trained and, faced with the reality that their contexts are difficult, multigrade teachers, especially in remote rural areas, should have a pay incentive. To achieve Education For All, education systems need to focus on multigrade education: sharing the teaching and learning strategies that make this pedagogy effective, communicating the value of this pedagogical approach and providing sustainable support (teacher training, curriculum and other resources) to make it as successful as it can possibly be.

Questions

1. How do the arguments of Kivunja and Sims for multigrade pedagogy relate to the minimum standards for learner-centred education presented in the afterword of the Dryden-Peterson chapter?
2. What would 'specialised multigrade pedagogy' look like? In other words, what would teachers and children be doing in the effective multigrade classroom?
3. The authors refer to evidence from multigrade settings of effective self-directed learning, peer mentoring, cooperative learning and peer coaching. Do you have experience of these practices in mixed-age classrooms, as a learner yourself or as an education worker?
4. The authors cite research characterising effective multigrade pedagogy as less hierarchical and relying less on rote learning and memorisation. Why do you think this would be the case? What would the teacher need to do, to make this happen?

Further reading

Ramrathan, L. and Ngubane, T. (2013) Instructional leadership in multi-grade classrooms: What can mono-grade teachers learn from their resilience? *Education as Change,* 17 (Supplement on School Instructional Leadership), 93–105.
UNESCO (2015) Practical Tips for Teaching Multigrade Classes. UNESCO: Paris and Bangkok.

The full text of this chapter is: Kivunja, C. and Sims, M. (2016) Demystifying Misperceptions and Realities About the Efficacy of Monograde and Multigrade Pedagogies: Africa's Response to Globalisation of Education. In Shizha and Diallo (Eds) *Africa in the Age of Globalisation: Perceptions, Misperceptions and Realities* (pp. 187–203). Routledge.

References

Benveniste, L. and McEwan, P. (2000) Constraints to implementing educational innovations: The case of multigrade schools. *International Review of Education*, 46 (1/2), 31–48.

Berry, C. (2010) *Multigrade Teaching – A Discussion Document* (p. 12). London: Institute of Education, University of London.

Beukes, F. (2006) Managing the effects of multi-grade teaching on learner performance in Namibia. (Master of Education), University of Johannesburg, Johannesburg. [Available at http://ujdigispace.uj.ac.za:8080/dspace/bitstream/10210/692/1/MEd-Florida-Beukes.pdf.]

Blum, N. and Diwan, R. (2007) *Small, multigrade schools and increasing access to primary education in India: National context and NGO initiatives.* (Vol. Research Monograph No. 17). Brighton, Sussex: Consortium for Research on Educational Access, Transitions and Equity (CREATE) Pathways to Access.

Brown, B. (2010) *Multigrade Teaching: A Review of Issues, Trends and Practices, Implications for Teacher Education in South Africa*. Johannesburg: Centre for Education Policy Development.

CEB-Commissie Evaluatie Basisonderwijs. (1994) *Inhoud en opbrengsten van het basisonderwijs [Contents and Results of Primary Education]*. Leiden, The Netherlands: Distributie Centrum DOP.

Department of Education, South Africa. (2005) *Report of the Ministerial Committee on Rural Education: A new vision for rural schooling*. Pretoria: Department of Education.

Department of Education, South Africa. (2009) *Pilot project on the training of 100 teachers and 30 officials in multigrade teaching in the Eastern Cape. Institutional Management Development and Governance*. Zwelitsha: Eastern Cape Department of Education.

Department of Education and Science (Ireland) (2004) *Tuarascáil Statisticiúl [Statistical Report], 2002–2003*. Dublin: Government Publications.

Gayfer, M. (Ed.) (1991) *The Multigrade Classroom: Myth and Reality*. Toronto: Canadian Education Association.

Groundwater-Smith, S., Ewing, R. and Le Cornu, R. (2003) *Teaching: Challenges and Dilemmas*. Southbank, Vic: Nelson Australia.

Juvane, V. (2005) Redefining the Role of Multi-Grade Teaching. Paper presented at the Ministerial Seminar on Education for Rural People in Africa: Policy Lessons, Options and Priorities Addis Ababa, Ethiopia, 7–9 September 2005.

Juvane, V. (2007). Multi-grade Teaching: Can it support achievement of quality universal primary education? *Commonwealth Education Partnerships 2007*, Cambridge, Commonwealth Secretariat/Nexus Strategic Partnerships, 236–239.

Juvane, V. and Joubert, J. (2010) South African Multigrade Education Conference. Paper presented at the Post Conference Report, Lemoenskloof Conference Centre: Paarl, South Africa.

Kagan, S. (1988) *Cooperative Learning: Resources for Teachers*. University of California: Riverside Books.

King, S. and Young, P. (1996) Opening the door on best practice: Contrasting teaching styles in the multigrade classroom. *Education in Rural Australia*, 6 (1), 29–36.

Kivunja, C. and Maxwell, T. (2009) Multigrade capacity building in Uganda and Zambia. Seminar Paper, University of New England, Armidale: School of Education.

Kivunja, C. and Wood, D. (2012) Multigrade pedagogy and practice: Accelerating Millennium Development Goals for Sub-Saharan Africa. *International Journal of Learning*, 18 (11), 17–32.

Kyne, C. (2005) The grouping practices of teachers in small two-teacher primary schools in the Republic of Ireland. *Journal of Research in Rural Education*, 20 (17), 1–20.

Little, A. (1996) Globalisation and educational research: Whose context counts? *International Journal of Educational Development*, 16 (4), 427–438.

Little, A. (2001) Multigrade teaching: Towards an international research and policy agenda. *International Journal of Educational Development*, 21 (6), 481–497.

Little, A. (2004) Learning and Teaching in Multigrade Settings. Paper prepared for the UNESCO 2005 EFA Monitoring Report (p. 23). Geneva: UNESCO.

Little, A. (2006a) All together now. Multigrade education: Several grades, one room. *IOE Life*, Winter (4), 32–33.

Little, A. (Ed.) (2006b) *Educational for All and Multigrade Teaching: Challenges and Opportunities*. Dordrecht: Springer.

Little, A. (Ed.) (2007) *Education for All and Multigrade Teaching: Challenges and Opportunities*. Dordrecht: Springer.

Lungwangwa, G. (1989) Multigrade schools in Zambian Primary Education: A report on the pilot schools in Mkushi district. SIDA Educational Division Documents, (Vol. 47). Stockholm: SIDA.

Mason, D. and Burns, R. (1997) Reassessing the effects of combination classes. *Educational Research and Evaluation*, 89 (1), 36–45.

Miller, B. (1990) A review of the qualitative research on multigrade instruction. *Research in Rural Education*, 7 (1), 1–8.

Miller, B. (1991) A review of the qualitative research on multigrade instruction. *Research in Rural Education*, 7 (2), 3–12.

Mukupa, B., Ndhlovu, D. and Sichula, A. (2010) *Assessment of Multigrade Teaching in Sparsely Populated Communities: A Case Study of Selected Schools in Serenje*. Lusaka: School of Education, University of Zambia.

Padmanabha, R. and Rama, A. (2010) *Re-designing the Elementary School – Multilevel Perspectives from River*. India: Rishi Valley Institute for Educational Resources.

Pridmore, P. (2007) *Adapting the Primary School Curriculum for Multigrade Classes in Developing Countries: A Five-step Plan and Agenda for Change*. London: Institute of Education, University of London.

Schindler, J. (1997) Education in South Africa. A statistical overview. *Education Africa Forum* (1st ed.). Pinegowrie: Education Africa.

Soliman, M. and Ismail, A. (2010) Integrating multi-grade collaborative learning pedagogy into design studios. *Journal of Education and Sociology*, March, 40–50.

UNESCO (2007) *Education for All by 2015: Will we make it? Global Monitoring Report 2008*. Paris: UNESCO.

UNESCO (2013) A Teacher for Every Child: Projecting Global Teacher Needs from 2015 to 2030. *UNESCO Institute for Statistics*, 27.

Veenman, S. (1995) Cognitive and noncognitive effects of multigrade and multiage classes: A best evidence synthesis. *Review of Educational Research*, 65 (4), 319–381.

Wilson, S. (2002) Farm school conditions and their historical context. Transforming Farm Schools. Issue Paper 3. [Available at www.erp.org.za/htm/issue3–2.htm.]

4 Thinking about a community of provision

Jonathan Rix

Introduction

In primary schools around the world, children are taught subject lessons in classrooms. This is considered 'normal' practice and experience, which should include all children. But, as you will read in other sections of this book, inclusion is far from universal.

This chapter explores how the class and the subject can act as barriers to participation. The author argues that if teachers and other education practitioners wish to overcome these barriers, there is a need to reimagine the class and how it operates. This change needs to happen holistically, building upon an understanding of the class as situated within a 'community of provision'. Using this framework, the chapter offers questions to consider moments of learning within the traditional confines of class and subject, in order to allow for more collaborative and inclusive practice.

We include this chapter in *Learning and Teaching Around the World* for its creative use of metaphor to develop a fresh and radical conceptualisation of how true and universal inclusion may be achieved in practice.

The boundaries which disguise our experience

There are two overarching structures that bring together the dominant aspects of current educational support: The Subject and The Class. These two structures create the primary internal boundaries within schools, dividing pupils and teachers and situating their knowledge and position within the whole. They define the curriculum, the pedagogy, the assessment and the space within which teaching and learning emerge; it is in relation to them that the identity of the learner and teacher is primarily framed; through them the opportunities for change will either emerge or submerge.

It has long been suggested that subjects create a fundamental barrier to transforming the education system.[1] They are the backbone of the status quo, because only through them are we allowed to know and/or change that status quo. Not only do they divide up knowledge but they also create a cellular view of the world. This makes it harder to explore the complexity and interrelationship of reality. The manner in which subjects are taught (and assessed) encourages people to believe there are singular correct answers and that solutions are right or wrong. Subjects therefore encourage a folk belief that with appropriate expertise we can know everything about something.

Subject areas are both underpinned by and maintain the notion of technical rationality; the belief that to become a professional one must acquire generalised, systematic, theoretical or scientific knowledge. Superior status comes to those who have owner-ship of that knowledge and even greater status to those who research and deepen that knowledge (Schön 1983). To advance within subjects you must pass through the levels. You must work towards a pre-ordained standard for your status within the field to be recognised. Teachers are situated towards the edges of these subject fields; they are unlikely to be regarded as among the 'elite'. At the same time, they sit between the learners and the field, trying to serve as a link. This places teachers on the boundary. Here they are positioned as the expert on both the subject and the learners (and their support), even though their understanding of both can only ever be partial.

The teacher, subject and learner are also placed within another boundary or series of boundaries within school; the class. The class serves as an internal boundary in many ways. It is serves to delineate the realm of the class teacher, organising the daily time-table and physical places within the school. It can separate according to age, ability and subject area. It is where long-term relationships between pupils and between pupils and teachers are situated, and it carries with it an identity and expectation. The class is where virtually all formal education begins and where the voice of the learner can be heard.

The class is traditionally a hierarchical space, both for pupils and staff. It is frequently a site of alienation and marginalisation. The class teacher's primary challenge is one of control. Without control, teachers cannot guide the learning situation or undertake the functions required of them in meeting institutional goals. Consequently, the class' character is fundamentally dominated by the identity, knowledge and behaviours of the class teacher. The nature of the student response within the traditional system is dependent upon the nature of the space which is thereby made available to them. They become confrontational or a source of amusement, unintelligent or attentive, bored or full of enthusiasm dependent upon their relationship with this solitary figure.

The closed nature of these boundaried worlds is problematic if we are looking for a shift in practice. However, the overlapping boundaries of the subject and class also provide us with a visible point at which learning is situated. They reveal our tendency to see challenges as emerging from individuals within those boundaries. Just as many people conceive of problematic learners as having a deficit (a special educational need) in the context of what and where they can learn, many focus upon the individual teacher's subject knowledge and their skill as supporter of learning.

If we step back from the defined socially created structures of education, however, we get a different picture. If we look beyond the subject and the class, beyond quali-fications and the curriculum, beyond the formal roles of teachers and pupils, we can see that teaching and learning is merely a moment of social interplay. Teaching and learning occur within a complex dynamic social and physical environment where the boundaries of who we are and our knowledge is always in a state of flux, depending

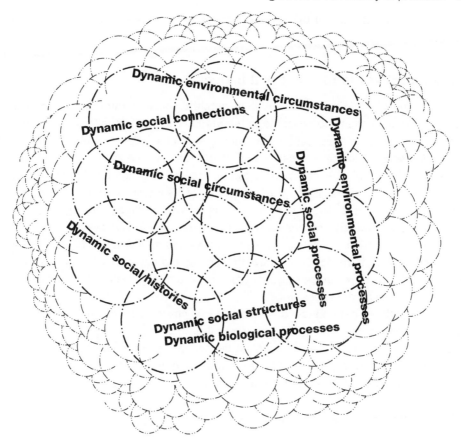

Figure 4.1 Moments of learning within an expansive model of interdependence

upon the context we are within. Figure 4.1 attempts to represent this complex, permeable, interrelationship between all the possible factors that can be influencing a given moment or are being influenced by that moment. It suggests an expansive model of interdependence. Things are linked and frequently in ways which are hard to discern. Even labelling the components of this complex interplay (such as skills or needs or knowledge) reduces our capacity to represent its fundamental interrelationship.

If we wish to explore and understand a moment of teaching and learning, therefore, we have to look beyond it being a momentary interaction between two individuals or between an individual and a group of individuals. As teachers, we are working in a constantly emerging social and cultural context. We are immersed in numerous histories and experiences of power, within personal and communal politics. We may be physical, biological entities situated within a predictable but infinite and shifting environment, yet we are entirely defined by our social relationships. When we try to define moments of teaching and learning with simple or linear models of thinking we make it far harder to recognise this complexity. It encourages us to over-simplify the causes of difficulties we may face and solutions we might seek. We forget that we are far more than a collection of individuals and that the boundaries which define us are socially created mirages.

Six perspectives to focus your thinking

Accepting the complexity of our situation and the social mirage of our boundaries creates a problem. We need concepts to think with. This was a challenge the author of this chapter faced with colleagues examining special education globally (Rix et al. 2013). We were exploring a linear model of thinking, widely associated with special education (and social sciences more broadly); the notion of the continuum (Rix et al. 2015). Undertaking an extensive systematic review of the literature, we came to recognise the limitations of these old ways of describing provision. We also recognised that to encapsulate the diversity of provision and the complex interweave of relationships within which education and schools are situated we had to devise a different metaphor. Metaphors help us think about our ways of working and being to see how best we can support each other. We proposed adopting the community metaphor, as part of the notion of *a community of provision*.

A community is defined by the interweaving characteristics, resources, groupings and priorities of its members. Its internal and external boundaries can be both porous and restrictive; its shape is context dependent and its relationships tenuous. It carries with it a sense of an ideal, but also a warning of insularity, serving to remind its members that they can both welcome and marginalise others from inside and outside the community.

Our broad definition of a community of provision was:

> *A community of provision is made from the settings and services which work together to provide learning and support for all children and young people within their locality.*

By its nature a community of provision will be full of contradictions and challenges, opportunities and aspirations. It is full of people with different theoretical positions, who never think about theory or don't feel sure what they think. It is full of excellent practice and less than excellent practice, people who like being there and people who do not; it can include all kinds of schools and support services, funding mechanisms and exam systems; its current reality varies from country to country, region to region, school to school, class to class, from child to child, and yet it will have overarching similarities at numerous levels of the system.

In an attempt to provide a frame for considering this complex reality, we drew upon an empirical study of all the literature associated with the continuum as applied to special needs education. Across 65 papers we identified 194 concepts and 29 different types of continua, which could be situated under six headings. This provided us with an empirical base for the six perspectives associated with a community of provision:

1. **Community space**: concerned with where support takes place
2. **Community staffing**: concerned with who is providing the support

3. **Community of students**: concerned with who is being supported
4. **Community support**: concerned with the quantity and type of support
5. **Community strategies**: concerned with the quality of support
6. **Community systems**: concerned with issues of governance.

Each perspective must be seen in relation to each other and all educational issues will be affected by all of the perspectives. These are the means by which provision is described but they are also the means by which it is delivered. They do not apply solely to a singular grouping or separate contained aspect of provision; the entirety needs to be understood through them.

Thinking about moments of learning within a class

Because certainty is a mirage, the best we can achieve is an open approach to any moment of learning. We can seek contradictions between our practice and our aims, questioning how we might create greater involvement for more of our learners. Using the six perspectives will help us to think about each situation. They can help us to prepare or reflect, prior to an activity, in the moment or subsequent to it. So here are some of the questions we might ask when we our work is constrained within the traditional structures of the class and the subject.

What is this **community space**? Could it allow for individual, small group and large group work as well as online virtual-world work. Can there be privacy and public sharing? Does the space allow us to work in different places within and beyond the school? Are we used to working with other people because we share an interest or like each other, because we can support them or they can support us, because we can learn from each other or want to achieve the same goal? Is it a chance to learn how to get on with each other or that life throws up random combinations? Are we able to receive very specific support or very regular support, or to practice something, perhaps in private or without distraction?

Who is the **community of students?** Do they reflect the local geographical area or a wider community relationship? Are they a particular age range or 'category' of child? Could they include pupils from a different year or space? Do they spend a sizeable part of the day working with a broad range of linked peers? What do I know of their interests and skills, their homes and values, their beliefs and sense of self? Do I feel responsible for them all? Are we building links with each other?

What is the **community staffing?** Do I call upon a cross-section of the local community? Do I involve other teachers, support staff, outside professionals, members of the wider school community and beyond? Are we open to critical reflection? Do we share responsibilities and work with each other and the children in different circumstances? Could we experience alternative staffing arrangements or create opportunities for new collaborative partnerships, perhaps working with teachers or support staff across classes? Do we collaborate in planning and assessing learning? Do we create time for each other? What do I know of our interests and skills, our homes and values, our beliefs and sense of self?

What is the **community support?** Do we think about support in relation to all those associated with the class? Could we provide additional support to staff? Are there people who can build links between the different professions and groupings involved? Do we have simple agreements with our partners? Is support provided to individuals and groups of children? Do we consider this support within the whole class context? Do we seek ways to meet diverse access needs collectively or separate people off? Do we hold ourselves accountable? Do we encourage people to voice their needs and how they can be support others? Do we demonstrate our trust in each other by letting people be responsible?

What are our **community strategies?** Are they underpinned by a wide range of pedagogical approaches? Do our approaches reflect the views and experiences of all involved professionals? Do we deliver the strategies as people wish us to? Are we honest about our use of strategies? Are there strategies that are contradictory? Are we assessing collective learning and does our assessment include the views of diverse individuals in the community space? If we are seeking to be inclusive are we using open-ended activities and multiple literacies, alongside multimodal learning and assessment? Are we supporting self-direction, valid purposes and useful outcomes within the curriculum? Do we plan for the social aspects of learning? Do our strategies include professional training and sharing knowledge across boundaries? Do we recognise that we can always find a way to teach any subject or concept to any pupils? Do we make use of our knowledge about the children and our colleagues in organising our day and our work?

What are the effects of our **community systems?** Could this moment make use of our funding, administrative and political processes, policies and plans? How could institutional leadership support me to work in the way I wish? How can/might I/we tie into our internal and external networks? How might we organise for collaboration, sharing of resources and co-ordinated activity? How might our networks support us to learn from each other? Are there mechanisms to share our knowledge and experiences? Could we make more use of people/opportunities/resources from beyond the school? Are there other activities within this community space that can tie in with what I/we are doing?

Towards this end

Many schools recognise the limitations of the class. In many places the class is already a far more fluid institution than in the past. Similarly, in many communities there is a recognition that the curriculum has to be more responsive to the learners and less constrained by top-down presumptions about what needs to be learned. However, evidence suggests that when these more flexible notions emerge, not all staff take best advantage of them. Practices, it would seem, remain deeply entrenched. At the heart of this resistance are attitudes, at all levels of the education system. If we wish to create effective change that enhances participation, then the desire for this needs to be reflected across the wider educational community. To this end, the community of provision offers a metaphor and framework for thinking which can facilitate our conversations and collective imaginings about both the smaller and the wider moments out of which education emerges.

Questions

1. Consider a moment of difficulty and a moment of delight in a teaching and learning situation you have experienced, as a learner yourself or as a teacher, education worker or parent. Using the six perspectives of the Community of Provision, consider how those moments were interdependent with their context.
2. If you are a teacher, or if you work or volunteer in the education sector, in what ways do you feel traditional ideas about the classroom and the subject constrain your practice and your thinking?

Further reading

Hart, S. (1996) *Beyond Special Needs: Enhancing Children's Learning Through Innovative Thinking.* London, Paul Chapman.

Benjamin, S., Nind, M., Hall, K., Collins, J. and Sheehy, K. (2003) Moments of inclusion and exclusion: Pupils negotiating classroom contexts. *British Journal of Sociology of Education*, 24 (5), 547–558.

Notes

1 Bourdieu and Gros suggested this, for example, in their evaluation of the French education system (Bourdieu, 1990).

References

Bourdieu, P. (1990) Principles for reflecting on the curriculum. *Curriculum Journal*, 1 (3), 307–314.

Rix, J., Sheehy, K., Fletcher-Campbell, F., Crisp, M. and Harper, A. (2013) Exploring provision for children identified with special educational needs: An international review of policy and practice. *European Journal of Special Needs Education*, 28 (4), 375–391.

Rix, J., Sheehy, K., Fletcher-Campbell, F., Crisp, M. and Harper, A. (2015) Moving from a continuum to a community – reconceptualising the provision of support. *Review of Educational Research*, 85 (3), 319–352.

Schön, D. (1983) *The Reflective Practitioner: How Professionals Think in Action*. London: Maurice Temple Smith.

5 Shadow education and its implications for social justice

Mark Bray and Ora Kwo

Introduction

In the introductory section of *Learning and Teaching Around the World* we offered a brief overview of the history of global agreements on children's education, from the Universal Declaration on Human Rights to United Nations Sustainable Development Goal Four. Since 1948, the aim has been for children's education to be free, compulsory and a right, and quality has also become a focus in global education agendas. Much progress has been made. However, as quantitative enrolments have increased, and more children attend mainstream schools, the 'shadow' of private supplementary tutoring has likewise expanded. In this chapter, the authors illustrate the impact of shadow education on the Education for All movement.

The increasing significance of shadow education

The scale of private supplementary tutoring is much greater than in previous periods of history. During the last quarter of the twentieth century, shadow education emerged as a major feature in parts of East Asia (Harnisch 1994; Bray 1999; Zeng 1999); and since that time the shadow has spread globally on a significant scale (Bray 2009; Lee et al. 2009; Mori and Baker 2010). The expansion of shadow education has penetrated poor as well as middle-income and rich communities. The scale of shadow education in a spread of countries is shown in Table 5.1. While shadow education is especially evident at the senior secondary level, in many countries it is increasingly prominent at the primary level.

Private tutoring is not just for pupils who are lagging behind their peers. It is more common among students who are already performing well. The principal subjects are those which are crucial to progress in the education system, typically mathematics and national languages. Some students receive tutoring throughout the year, while others mainly receive it immediately before major examinations.

Comparative survey also shows diversity in the types of tutoring. At one end of the spectrum is one-to-one tutoring received by students at home or elsewhere. At the

Table 5.1 Cross-national indicators of supplementary private tutoring

Country	Patterns
Bangladesh	According to a government-conducted household survey, in 2008 68.4% of secondary students and 37.9% of primary students were receiving tutoring (Nath 2011: 3).
Canada	In 2007, about one third of Canadian parents reported that they had hired tutors for their children. The number of businesses providing tutoring services had expanded between 200% and 500% in major Canadian cities during the previous three decades (Davies and Guppy 2010: 111–112).
China	A survey of 1,773 junior middle school students in Jinan found in 2010 that 29.3% were receiving supplementary tutoring in English and 28.8% in mathematics (Zhang 2011: 124).
Egypt	A 2009 report indicated that 81% of households with children in secondary schools had paid for tutoring. At the primary level, 50% had done so (Sobhy 2012: 49).
England	A 2008 random telephone survey of 1,500 parents found that 12% of primary school pupils and 8% of secondary school pupils were receiving tutoring (Peters et al. 2009: 2).
Georgia	A 2010 survey of 1,200 students found that 15% in primary grades and 57% in the final secondary grade received private tutoring (Machabeli et al. 2011: 14).
Germany	A 2010 report indicated that 1.1 million pupils, representing 14.8% of the student population, received regular tutoring (Klemm and Klemm 2010: 7).
Ghana	A 2008 survey of 1,020 households found that 48% were paying for private tutoring in primary education (Antonowicz et al. 2010: 21).
India	A 2011 survey indicated that 61.0% of Grade 1 students in rural government schools in Tripura State received private tutoring, and the proportion rose to 75.0% in Grade 6. In West Bengal, respective proportions were 55.6% and 77.5% (Pratham 2012: 215, 235).
Pakistan	A 2011 survey showed that tutoring was especially prominent in cities. In Lahore, 60.5% of students in Grades 1–10 received tutoring, and in Karachi the figure was 47.8% (SAFED 2012: 395). Proportions increased at higher grades but were prominent even in Grade 1. In Karachi, 35.5% of Grade 1 children in government schools received tutoring; and in Lahore the proportion was 35.7%.
Romania	A survey of 1,500 children aged 6–19 in 2010 found that 17% were receiving tutoring (Daedalus Millward Brown 2010).
South Korea	In 2008, 60.5% of pupils in general high school were estimated to be receiving tutoring. In middle school the proportion was 72.5%; and in primary school it was 87.9% (Kim 2010: 302).
Tunisia	A 2008 survey of 250 households (quoted by Akkari 2010: 51) found that 73.2% paid for tutoring among whom 90.2% described it as a strain on the family budget. The phenomenon existed from the first year of elementary school.
Vietnam	Data from 9,189 households in 2006 indicated that 32.0% of primary students were receiving tutoring. In lower and upper secondary, respective proportions were 46.0% and 63.0% (Dang 2011).

other end are classes in lecture theatres with overflow rooms served by video screens, as exemplified by 'star tutors' in Hong Kong (Kwo and Bray 2011). In between is tutoring in small groups or in medium-sized classes. In addition, technology is permitting tutoring through the internet within and across national boundaries (Ventura and Jang 2010).

Further variations arise in the identities of tutors. Some tutoring is provided by university students and secondary students as a way to earn extra pocket money. Other tutoring is provided by self-employed people working full-time or part-time, and there is considerable expansion of tutoring through companies, some of which operate national or international franchises (Davies and Aurini 2006; Burch 2009). In some countries, many full-time teachers also provide private supplementary tutoring. This can benefit the wider society and the students, where there is extra use of teachers' talents and students gain further attention from teachers who already know them well. However, it can also raise concerns about corruption. Dawson (2009) has highlighted the 'tricks of the teacher' in Cambodia, noting that some teachers deliberately reduce their effort during regular classes in order to promote demand for the extra lessons. Similar problems have been noted elsewhere in Asia and in parts of Africa, Europe and the Middle East (Foondun 2002; Akkari 2010; Gök 2010; Farah 2011; Johnson 2011; Sobhy 2012).

Shadow education and social inequalities

Higher-income households can more easily afford both superior quality and greater amounts of private tutoring. Middle-income and low-income families have found themselves forced to invest in private tutoring alongside public provision that is supposedly egalitarian, despite the constraints on their budgets. For example, 2008 data in South Korea indicated that while 91.8% of households in the highest income groups invested in tutoring, the figure was still as much as 34.3% in the lowest income group and 55.3% in the next lowest (Kim 2010: 303–304). Similar patterns emerged from Smyth's (2009: 9) data in Ireland: while 58% of students from higher professional households had received private tutoring, the proportions were still as high as 32% among students from semi-skilled households and 28% from unskilled households.

An example from India illustrates this point. The Pratichi Trust surveyed education in West Bengal in 2001/02 and 2008/09. The second report observed increased dependence on private tutoring for pupils in both primary schools and Sishu Siksha Kendras (SSKs), which are community-based alternatives to primary schools. Sen (2009: 13) observed that:

> The proportion of children relying on private tuition has gone up quite a bit (64% from 57% for the students of standard primary schools, and 58% from 24% for SSK children). Underlying this rise is not only some increase in incomes and the affordability of having private tuition, but also an intensification of the general conviction among the parents that private tuition is 'unavoidable' if it can be at all afforded (78% of the parents now believe it is indeed 'unavoidable' – up from 62%).

Comparable observations have been made in Africa. In Madagascar, for example, Andriamahavonjy and Ravelo (2009: 38) described tutoring as 'almost obligatory for all students'. And in Egypt, Sobhy (2012: 47) observed that:

> Almost from a child's first year in school, poor families ... are pressured and intimidated by poorly paid teachers to enrol their children in private tutoring in order to pass from one year to the next. Middle and upper middle class families are equally pressured to enrol their children in tutoring to secure an acceptable level of education.

Tutoring consumed one fifth of the incomes of poor households in Egypt, in a country where schooling is supposedly free.

Quantitative expansion and qualitative decline

In many settings, the expansion of schooling has been achieved at the expense of quality. Schools have introduced double or even triple shifts; untrained teachers and poorly trained teachers have been recruited; and facilities have been stretched even more thinly than before (UNESCO 2004; Acedo et al. 2012). These patterns have been especially obvious in the less developed countries of Africa and Asia. For example, data from the Southern and Eastern Africa Consortium for Monitoring Educational Quality (SACMEQ) have shown sharp declines in achievement scores in Mozambique due to 'massive increases in Grade 6 enrolments without corresponding increases in human and material resources' (Makuwa 2010: 3). Six other countries in the region showed mixed performance, which highlighted 'the EFA challenge for all countries to strike a balance between increases in enrolment and improvements in quality of education for all' (Makuwa 2010: 3).

Expansion of schooling has led families around the world to consider the quality of education provided by public schools as inadequate. Some families have migrated to the private sector (see e.g. Oketch et al. 2010; Noronha and Srivastava 2012), while others have remained in the public sector but supplemented this with private tutoring. In Cambodia, for example, the double-shift school day lasts only four hours, and even diligent teachers assert that it is impossible to cover the full curriculum (Dawson 2010: 20). Similar constraints are evident in Vietnam, where regulations prohibit teachers from providing private tutoring to pupils in full-day schools but permit it for students in double-shift schools (Ko and Xing, 2009: 23).

Impact on mainstream schooling

Teachers who are also tutors may reduce their efforts in regular classes and reserve their energies for private tutoring. Aslam and Mansoor (2012: 3) have commented on the problems in Pakistan where government teachers are "virtually un-sackable" and the culture of extra tutoring has become entrenched. And in Turkey, Gök (2010: 132) highlighted the case of a teacher who told a student: 'You didn't attend my private course so I'm not talking to you anymore'. Again with reference to West Bengal, India, Sen (2009: 14–15) observed that the tutoring classes covered content that could and should have been taught in the regular lessons.

Shadow education may damage regular schools by taking away talent altogether. The tutoring industry has many amateurs, but it also has many strong professionals. In some countries the tutoring sector is perceived to be innovative in use of technology and pedagogical approaches. When the market attracts talented tutors and adminis-trators to the shadow sector, it leaves the regular system more impoverished than it otherwise would be.

Tutoring has helped many children to overcome learning obstacles and has reinforced content which was touched upon in regular classes but not fully comprehended (e.g. Marhic 2009: 67–73; Walls 2009: 209–216). Yet a corollary can be that children are exhausted from excessive regimes of full-time schooling plus academic tutoring, and have inadequate time for sports, hobbies and relaxation. This has a psychological toll, and can lead to inefficient use of school time. In South Korea, Kim (2007: 7–8) noted that many of the young people who attend tutorial centres until late in the evening have inadequate energy for daytime schooling. Since they are paying for the tutorial classes, the students value them more; and since they are nevertheless required to go to school, they sleep during many daytime lessons.

State budgets and shadow education

Schooling is a heavy financial burden for governments, which commonly allocate 15–20% of their budgets to education and in some cases, devote 25% or more (UNESCO 2007: 142; UNESCO Institute for Statistics 2011: 29). Privatisation is one way to spread the load (see Belfield and Levin 2002: 30; Kitaev 2007: 93). Most obviously, privatisation occurs when increasing proportions of children attend private rather than public schools. But in the case of shadow education, the prevalence of private supplementary tutoring allows the state to provide just the minimum since families will pay for 'extras'. Sobhy (2012: 47) states that this has been a deliberate strategy by the Egyptian govern-ment, and no doubt other governments have also seen shadow education from this perspective.

The rise of the neoliberal approach to education has made it acceptable for education to be treated as a marketable service (Belfield and Levin 2002; Zajda 2006; Ball and Youdell 2008). In this context, governments can espouse fee-free education even though considerable payments are being made to the tutoring industry. Ministries of Education prefer not to know too much about the shadow education sector; if confronted, they may say that shadow education is beyond their remit and in any case parents have the right to pay for extra services if they wish.

Much of the concern about privatisation of education systems has focused on schools that are operated privately and attract children as an alternative to public institutions. Less focus has been devoted to shadow education, which in many nations is a fee-paying supplement in officially fee-free systems. When operating positively, supplementary tutoring can help students to overcome obstacles to learning and can stretch talented pupils. It can synergise well with regular lessons, and may contribute to both economic and social development. However, shadow education can also undermine mainstream schooling, leading to inefficiencies and to exclusion of some social groups. As Sen (2009: 14–15) remarked in the context of West Bengal, India, tutoring "divides the student population into haves and have-nots", and "effectively negates the basic right of all children to receive elementary education".

Questions

1. What are your experiences of private supplementary tutoring in your country, as a learner, a parent or an education worker?
2. How does private tutoring impact on the quality of education in your country?
3. In your experiences, does shadow education contribute to educational inequality or help to promote equality?

Further reading

Liu, J. and Bray, M. (2017) Understanding Shadow Education from the Perspective of Economics of Education. In Johnes, G., Johnes, J., Agasisti, T. and López-Torres, L. (Eds) *Handbook of Contemporary Education Economics*. Cheltenham, UK: Edward Elgar Publishing.

Bray, M. (2017) Schooling and its supplements: Changing global patterns and implications for comparative education. *Comparative Education Review*, 62 (3), 469–491.

UNESCO (2015) Education for all 2000–2015: Achievements and challenges. EFA global monitoring report 2015. Paris: UNESCO. [Available at http://unesdoc.unesco.org/images/0023/002322/232205e. pdf.]

The full text of this chapter is: Bray, M. and Kwo, O. (2013) Behind the façade of fee-free education: Shadow education and its implications for social justice. *Oxford Review of Education*, 39 (4), 480–497.

References

Acedo, C., Adams, D. and Popa, S. (Eds) (2012) *Quality and Qualities: Tensions in Education Reforms*. Rotterdam: Sense.

Akkari, A. (2010) Privatizing Education in the Maghreb: A Path for a Two-Tiered Education System. In Mazawi, A.E. and Sultana, R.G. (Eds) *Education and the Arab 'World': Political Projects, Struggles, and Geometries of Power* (pp. 43–58). London: Routledge.

Andriamahavonjy, F. and Ravelo, A. (2009) *Enquête nationale d'évaluation du secteur education primaire publique à Madagascar*. Antananarivo: Transparency International.

Antonowicz, L., Lesné, F., Stassen, S. and Wood, J. (2010) *Africa Education Watch: Good Governance Lessons for Primary Education*. Berlin: Transparency International.

Aslam, M. and Mansoor, S. (2012) *The Private Tuition Industry in Pakistan: An Alarming Trend*. Policy Brief. Islamabad: South Asia Forum for Education Development.

Ball, S.J. and Youdell, D. (2008) *Hidden Privatisation in Public Education*. Brussels: Education International.

Belfield, C.R. and Levin, H.M. (2002) *Education Privatization: Causes, Consequences and Planning Implications*. Paris: UNESCO International Institute for Educational Planning.

Bray, M. (1999) *The Shadow Education System: Private Tutoring and its Implications for Planners*. Paris: UNESCO International Institute for Educational Planning.

Bray, M. (2009) *Confronting the Shadow Education System: What Government Policies for What Private Tutoring?* Paris: UNESCO International Institute for Educational Planning.

Bray, M. (2011) *The Challenge of Shadow Education: Private Tutoring and its Implications for Policy Makers in the European Union*. Brussels: European Commission.

Burch, P. (2009) *Hidden Markets: The New Education Privatization*. New York: Routledge.

Daedalus Millward Brown (2010) Piata Meditatiilor, estimate la peste 300 milione euro anual. Study commissioned by Fundatia Dinu Patriciu, Bucharest. [Available at www.fundatia dinupatriciu.ro/ro/media_room/stiri/249, accessed 13 June 2012.]

Dang, H.A. (2011) *Private tutoring in Vietnam: A review of current issues and its major correlates*. Unpublished manuscript. Washington DC: The World Bank.

Davies, S. and Aurini, J. (2006) The franchising of private tutoring: A view from Canada. *Phi Delta Kappan*, 88 (2), 123–128.

Davies, S. and Guppy, N. (2010) *The Schooled Society: An Introduction to the Sociology of Education*. Toronto: Oxford University Press.

Dawson, W. (2009) The Tricks of the Teacher: Shadow Education and Corruption in Cambodia. In Heyneman, S.P. (Ed.) *Buying Your Way into Heaven: Education and Corruption in International Perspective* (pp. 51–74). Rotterdam: Sense Publishers.

Dawson, W. (2010) Private tutoring and mass schooling in East Asia: Reflections of inequality in Japan, South Korea, and Cambodia. *Asia Pacific Education Review*, 11 (1), 14–24.

Farah, S. (2011) *Private Tutoring Trends in the UAE*. Policy Brief No. 26. Dubai: Dubai School of Government.

Foondun, A.R. (2002) The issue of private tuition: An analysis of the practice in Mauritius and selected south-east Asian countries. *International Review of Education*, 48 (6), 485–515.

Gök, F. (2010) Marketing Hope: Private Institutions Preparing Students for the University Entrance Examination in Turkey. In Amos, K. (Ed.) *International Educational Governance* (pp. 123–134). London: Emerald.

Harnisch, D.L. (1994) Supplemental education in Japan: Juku schooling and its implication. *Journal of Curriculum Studies*, 26 (3), 323–334.

Johnson, E.M. (2011) Blaming the Context not the Culprit: Limitations on Student Control of Teacher Corruption in Post-Soviet Kyrgyzstan. In Silova, I. (Ed.) *Globalization on the Margins: Education and Postsocialist Transformations in Central Asia* (pp. 233–258). Charlotte: Information Age.

Kim, M. (2007) School choice and private supplementary education in South Korea. Paper IIEP/SEM 279/7. Paris, UNESCO International Institute for Educational Planning.

Kim, K.K. (2010) Educational Equality. In Lee, C.J., Kim, S.Y. and Adams, D. (Eds), *Sixty Years of Korean Education* (pp. 285–325). Seoul: Seoul National University Press.

Kitaev, I. (2007) Education for All and Private Education in Developing and Transitional Countries. In Srivastava, P. and Walford, G. (Eds) *Private Schooling in Less Economically Developed Countries: Asian and African Perspectives* (pp. 89–109). Oxford: Symposium Books.

Klemm, K. and Klemm, A. (2010) *Ausgaben fur Nachhilfe: teurer und unfairer Ausgleich fur fehlende individuelle Föderung*. Gutersloh, Bertelsmann Stiftung.

Ko, I. and Xing, J. (2009) *Extra Classes and Subjective Well-being: Empirical Evidence from Vietnamese Children*. Young Lives Working Paper No. 49. Department of International Development: University of Oxford.

Kwo, O. and Bray, M. (2011) Facing the shadow education system in Hong Kong, *IIAS Newsletter*. University of Leiden: International Institute for Asian Studies, 56, 20.

Lee, C.J., Park, H.J. and Lee, H. (2009) Shadow Education Systems. In Sykes, G., Schneider, B. and Plank, D.N. (Eds) *Handbook of Education Policy Research* (pp. 901–919). New York: Routledge, for the American Educational Research Association.

Levin, L. (2009) *Human Rights: Questions and Answers*, 5th ed. Paris: UNESCO.

Machabeli, G., Bregvadze, T. and Apkhazava, R. (2011) *Examining Private Tutoring Phenomenon in Georgia*. Tbilisi: International Institute for Education Policy, Planning & Management.

Makuwa, D. (2010) The SACMEQ III project: Mixed results in achievement. *IIEP Newsletter XXVIII*, (3), 3.

Marhic, P. (2009) L'enseignement individuel: Une alternative à l'échec scolaire. Paris: L'Harmattan.

Mori, I. and Baker, D. (2010) The origin of universal shadow education: What the supplemental education phenomenon tells us about the postmodern institution of education. *Asia Pacific Education Review*, 11 (1), 36–48.

Nath, S. (2011) Shadow education in Bangladesh. Presentation at a seminar organised by UNESCO in conjunction with the National Academy of Educational Management (NAEM), Dhaka, 11 August.

Noronha, C. and P. Srivastava (2012) The Right to Education Act in India: Focuses on Early Implementation Issues and the Private Sector. Ottawa: Collaborative Research and Dissemination (CORD), University of Ottawa.

Oketch, M., Mutisya, M., Ngware, M. and Ezeh, A.C. (2010) Why are there proportionately more poor pupils enrolled in non-state schools in urban Kenya in spite of FPE policy? *International Journal of Educational Development*, 30 (1), 23–32.

Peters, M., Carpenter, H., Edwards, G. and Coleman, N. (2009) *Private Tuition: Survey of Parents and Carers*. Research Brief DCSF-RBX-09–01. London: Department for Children, Schools and Families.

Pratham (2012) *Annual Status of Education Report 2011*. Mumbai: Pratham.

Sen, A. (2009) Introduction: Primary schooling in West Bengal. In Rana, K. (Coordinator), *The Pratichi Education Report II: Primary Education in West Bengal – Changes and Challenges*. New Delhi: Pratichi Trust.

Smyth, E. (2009) Buying your way into college? Private tuition and the transition to higher education in Ireland. *Oxford Review of Education*, 35 (1), 1–22.

Sobhy, H. (2012) The de-facto privatization of secondary education in Egypt: A study of private tutoring in technical and general schools. *Compare: A Journal of Comparative and International Education*, 42 (1), 47–67.

SAFED [South Asia Forum for Education Development] (2012) *Annual status of education report 2011*. Islamabad: SAFED.

UNESCO (2004): *Education for all – The quality imperative: EFA global monitoring report 2005*. Paris: UNESCO.

UNESCO (2007) *Education for all by 2015 – Will we make it? EFA global monitoring report 2008*. Paris: UNESCO.

UNESCO Institute for Statistics (2011) *Financing education in sub-Saharan Africa: Challenges of expansion, equity and quality*. Montreal: UNESCO Institute for Statistics.

Ventura, A. and Jang, S. (2010) Private tutoring through the internet: Globalization and offshoring. *Asia Pacific Education Review*, 11 (1), 59–68.

Walls, F. (2009) *Mathematical Subjects: Children Talk About Their Mathematical Lives*. Dordrecht: Springer.

Zajda, J. (2006) Introduction. In Zajda, J. (Ed.) *Decentralisation and Privatisation in Education: The Role of the State* (pp. 3–27). Dordrecht: Springer.

Zeng, K. (1999) *Dragon Gate: Competitive Examinations and Their Consequences*. London: Cassell.

Zhang, Y. (2011) The determinants of national college entrance exam performance in China – with an analysis of private tutoring. PhD dissertation, Columbia University.

Part 2
Languages and learning

6 Primary school medium of instruction policies in Ghana and India

Elizabeth J. Erling and Lina Adinolfi

Introduction

Multilingualism in low- and middle-income countries (LMICs) poses ongoing challenges for education policy makers and teachers. These countries need to ensure that all children receive high quality schooling, and children's first or home languages are recognised as the most effective way of achieving this (Cummins 2000; Kosonen 2005; Alidou et al. 2006; Pinnock 2009; Trudell and Young 2016; UNESCO 2016). But a lack of human and material resources makes it difficult to provide education in every child's first language. At the same time, the association of English with national and individual economic and social opportunities (Erling and Seargeant 2013; Erling 2017) has led to increasing demands to introduce English as a subject at early levels of primary schooling or for English to be the medium of instruction for the whole curriculum from the start of primary schooling.

This chapter briefly compares medium of instruction policies in Ghana and India, two distinctive postcolonial countries with similarities to many LMICs (see Erling et al. 2016; 2017). Both Ghana and India are extremely diverse ethno-linguistically, with high levels of societal and individual multilingualism. The language-in-education policies of Ghana and India aim to provide inclusive, equitable, quality schooling. The authors outline four challenges to the achievement of this aim. Language-in-education policies significantly impact on children's experiences of schooling and on their opportunities for achievement, particularly in the world's poorest countries. The medium of instruction also can also impact significantly on children's learning experiences, as this chapter and others in Part 2 illustrate.

Two countries and educational contexts

Ghana and India are committed to achieving universal primary schooling and improving the outcomes of their national education systems in order to bolster economic growth, national stability, equity and social justice. Both countries have witnessed progress at all levels of education since the start of the millennium, particularly in terms of school enrolment. Yet pupil retention and progression remain problematic. Data from

2010–2015 reveal that, while 64.6% of the population in Ghana complete primary school, only 54.3% complete lower secondary school, and 20.5% upper secondary school (UNESCO UIS stats 2017). The figures from India are no more encouraging: data from 2010–2015 reveal that only 51.4% of the population complete primary school, with the percentage falling to 37.5% for lower secondary school and 26.8% for upper secondary school (UNESCO UIS stats 2017).

Evidence from both countries indicates that a large proportion of children attending primary school are underachieving. In Ghana, where English is the medium of instruction from Grade 4, pupils' levels of proficiency in English are not high enough for many of them to learn through it (MoE Ghana 2016; Darvas and Balwanz 2013; UNESCO 2014). Low pupil achievement is also a chronic issue in India, where Hindi or another state language is the medium of instruction throughout primary schooling. The Annual Status of Education Report (ASER) has been tracking the ability of children to read in the language of schooling and undertake basic arithmetic since 2005. Recent findings indicate that half of all children enrolled in primary Class 5 cannot read at the level expected of Class 2 (ASER 2016). Research undertaken in both countries suggests that medium of instruction in schools is a contributing factor to low levels of retention and progression (Smits et al. 2008) and low levels of performance across the curriculum (e.g. Alidou et al. 2006; Pinnock 2009).

Linguistic landscapes and languages of instruction

At the time of writing, Ghana has a population of just under 30 million people. English is the official language, and the number of Ghanaian languages is commonly cited as 79 (Opoku-Amankwa et al. 2015). Eleven of these languages are 'government-sponsored' for use in primary schooling. The medium of instruction policy for primary school has fluctuated over many years, from requiring English-only to recommending children's home language (secondary and tertiary education have always been in English). The current policy stipulates that one of the 11 government-sponsored Ghanaian languages is the medium of instruction for children in primary Grades 1–3, with English taught as a subject. In Grades 4–6 English becomes the medium of instruction and a Ghanaian language is taught as a subject. This policy aims to enable primary school pupils to be functionally literate and numerate in their home language, and to have reading fluency in their home language and in English, when they complete basic schooling. In reality, many primary schools use English from the start of Grade 1, because the majority of curriculum subject textbooks, and assessments, are in English. Furthermore, in highly multilingual schools English may be the main language that is shared by teachers and children.

India has a population of 1.2 billion people. Four hundred and forty-eight different languages have been identified, with many additional variants of these (Simons and Fenning, 2017). India's official language is Hindi, with English representing an 'associate' language. A further 20 languages are formally recognised across 29 states. India has a long-held 'three language formula' (NCERT 2005; NCERT 2006). Each state has one or more official languages. Based on the majority language spoken in a particular geographic area, one of these languages is used as the medium of instruction in government schools at primary and secondary levels. The intention is that this language corresponds to children's home language. According to the formula, an additional Indian language and English are taught as curriculum subjects. The trilingual formula aims to ensure that every child enters secondary education with competence in at least three languages. The recommendation is to introduce English towards the end of primary school, but there is growing parental pressure to introduce it earlier. Many government primary schools introduce English as a subject in Class 3 and, increasingly, at entry level in Class 1. Elite private primary and secondary schools, and the entire higher education sector, use English as the medium of instruction. A recent development in India is the growth of low-cost private primary schools, where English is often the medium of instruction.

Both Ghana's and India's language-in-education policies aim to provide primary education in children's home languages in order to best support their learning. Yet each policy faces challenges in implementation which have the potential to limit pupil learning.

Challenge 1: The medium of instruction is not the language children use

In Ghana, the home language of many pupils is not one of the 11 Ghanaian languages approved for primary Grades 1–3, and there are no teaching resources available in those other languages (Ansah and Agyeman 2015; Opoku-Amankwa et al. 2015). This is particularly the case in rural areas, but the mismatch also occurs in urban areas where government census records do not reflect the actual languages of communities. Schools often face a choice between teaching through one of two languages, both of which are unfamiliar to pupils: a Ghanaian language or English. Such schools often opt to teach through English from the start, as this is the language pupils will eventually use in upper primary level. Likewise, in India, Hindi or an official state language is the medium of instruction throughout primary and secondary government schooling. However, the state language may not correspond to one of the many languages or varieties used by pupils at home and in their communities (Mohanty 2010; Singh and Bangay 2014; Woodhead et al. 2013; c.f. Mackenzie and Walker 2013).

Challenge 2: Finding a language in common

In Ghana and India, schools take in children from a wide range of ethnic and linguistic backgrounds. This is particularly the case in urban areas (D'Souza 2006; Mfum-Mensah 2005; Jhingran 2009) where classrooms can contain pupils from around the country. Children may know several languages, but they may not share a language with many other pupils or the teacher. Such situations pose additional challenges to teachers who are unlikely to be proficient in all the languages of children. In both countries, teachers are deployed to areas where they may not speak the local languages. Even when teachers know the home languages or varieties used by their pupils, the 'unofficial' status of these languages may make teachers reluctant to use them to help children's learning, and using a local or minority language to support some children may be perceived as privileging one ethnic group or community over another.

Challenge 3: Assessment and gatekeeping practices

In Ghana, English is the language of assessment at the end of upper primary school and teachers understandably feel obliged to prepare their pupils for this (Yiboe 2011). Passing this exam is required to enter secondary school. In India, government school exams are taken through the state language. However, higher education is in English and pupils require sufficient knowledge of English to make the transition to study at this level. In both countries, English is considered necessary for access to a range of employment, particularly in the public sector, even though it may in fact be used rarely in the workplace (Hayes 2016). Such perceptions increase the demand for English as the language of instruction, instead of local and home languages through which pupils might be better able to understand, learn, express themselves, and demonstrate what they know.

Challenge 4: Teachers' language competence

In Ghana some language groups are under-represented in the teaching workforce and it is not possible to appoint sufficient numbers of teachers who are competent in the local languages designated for primary schooling. Where English is the default language, there are a large number of teachers – particularly in rural areas – who do not have sufficient proficiency in English to teach through it (Ankohmah et al. 2012). Recent data from India indicate that the number of children studying in English nationally has doubled over the last five years to approximately 29 million (Nagarajan 2015), yet primary teachers often have very low levels of proficiency in English.

Languages, learning and teaching

The language of instruction in highly multilingual LMICs such as Ghana and India raises issues for the quality of education and the inclusion of children, particularly the most marginalised. A mismatch between home language and school language contributes to pupils' low attendance and educational underachievement. Limited competence in the medium of instruction is a barrier to pupils' learning the curriculum. Furthermore, when teachers use a language of instruction in which they are not proficient or comfortable, or a language that children are not familiar with, teaching and learning are less dynamic. Teachers in this situation are more likely to rely on a limited range of methods such as a lecture, closed questions and 'safe talk': 'safe talk' allows some pupil participation without any risk of loss of face for the teacher or the pupils and maintains an appearance of 'doing the lesson', while limited teaching and learning is actually taking place (see Chick 1996; Williams 2014).

The increasing demand for English from the early years of schooling is problematic. Teachers who are not confident in English, and teach in English, rely more on drilling and memorisation (Ankohmah et al. 2012; Opoku-Amankwa 2009). Teachers who have low levels of English proficiency are less skilled in using the language to mediate textbooks and encourage pupils to talk in an exploratory, open-ended way for learning. This can limit pupils' attainment in English and in other subject areas, impacting negatively on their progression through schooling to higher education. Children from economically deprived backgrounds are more likely to be disadvantaged in this way (Darvas and Balwanz 2013; UNESCO 2016). Research has established that when teachers use their first languages they use a wider range of teaching methods (Alidou et al. 2006; Ankohmah et al. 2012), their teaching is more animated, with the effect that pupils are more motivated and understand more. Teachers whose training makes use of their first languages are more likely to have the technical and pedagogical vocabulary needed to teach curriculum subjects and the confidence in their own language ability to teach productively (Heugh et al. 2007).

Around the world, and particularly in multilingual LMICs, policy-makers could draw on evidence of classroom teaching and learning to develop language-in-education practices that better utilise the language resources of teachers and children. One emerging recommendation is for more holistic policies that promote what can be called 'sustainable additive multilingualism', where children's home or heritage languages are used flexibly throughout the education system and additional languages are learned without detracting from the development of the home language. This recognises that language is a valuable resource, and that teachers may not have fluency in all children's languages. Implicit in sustainable additive multilingualism is the recognition that home languages can be mobilised in the teaching of additional languages such as English. 'Sustainable' refers to the capacity of languages to endure through their use in schooling, and to language-in-education policies as dynamic and future-oriented.

In India and Ghana, as in many other LMICs, the medium of instruction is just one of many factors that contribute to low levels of retention, progress and attainment in state primary schooling. Other factors contribute to the challenges of providing mass-scale quality education: poorly resourced schools, large class sizes, and inadequate pre- and in-service teacher training. In both countries, many children must leave school to contribute to the family income, and many parents are unable to support their children with their studies (particularly children who are first generation learners). Attending to the language problem will not be sufficient without addressing these and other fundamental elements of education systems, including high-stakes exams which encourage memorisation rather than deeper forms of learning, and deeply entrenched transmission teaching models.

Questions

1. What is the language-in-education policy in your country? Where is this documented?
2. Does the policy differ between primary, secondary and higher education, or between state education and the private education sector?
3. In your experience, how far is the policy actually implemented in schools? What challenges, if any, does it face?
4. In your experience, how does the policy influence children's experiences and achievements?

Further reading

Erling, E.J., Adinolfi, L. and Hultgren, A.K. (2017) *Multilingual Classrooms: Opportunities and Challenges for English Medium Instruction in Low and Middle Income Contexts*. London: Education Development Trust.

Benson, C. and Kosonen, K. (Eds) (2013) *Language Issues in Comparative Education: Inclusive Teaching and Learning in Non-Dominant Languages and Cultures*. Rotterdam: Sense.

UNESCO (2016) *If you don't understand, how can you learn?* Global Education Monitoring Report. Policy Paper 24.

References

Alidou, A., Brock-Utne, B., Diallo, U.S., Heugh, L. and Wolff, E. (2006) *Optimising Learning and Education in Africa – the Language Factor: A Stock-taking Research on Mother Tongue and Bilingual Education in Sub-Saharan Africa*. Libreville: ADEA.

Ankohmah, Y., Afitska, O., Clegg, J., Kiliku, P., Mtana, N., Osei-Amankwah, L., Rubagumya, C. and Tarimo, E. (2012) EdQual: Language and Literacy Project Overview Report. [Available at www.edqual.org/publications/rpcstrategiesandreports/browse%3Ftheme=language literacy.html, accessed 4th July, 2017].

Ansah, M.A. and Agyeman, N.A. (2015) Ghana Language-in-Education Policy: The survival of two South Guan minority dialects. *Per Linguam*, 31 (1), 89–104.

ASER (2016) Annual Status of Education Report (Rural) 2016. New Delhi: ASER. [Available at http://img.asercentre.org/docs/Publications/ASER%20Reports/ASER%202016/aser_2016.pdf, accessed 5 July 2017].

Chick, J.K. (1996) Safe-talk: Collusion in Apartheid Education. In Coleman, H. (Ed.) *Society and the Language Classroom*. Cambridge: Cambridge University Press.

Cummins, J. (2000) *Language, Power, and Pedagogy: Bilingual Children in the Crossfire*. Clevedon: Multilingual Matters.

D'Souza, J. (2006). Language, education and the rights of the child. *World Englishes*, 25 (1), 55–166.

Darvas, P. and Balwanz, D. (2013) Basic Education Beyond the Millennium Development Goals in Ghana: How equity in service delivery affects educational and learning outcomes. World Bank Report.

Erling, E.J. and Seargeant, P. (2013) *English and Development: Policy, Globalization and Pedagogy*. Bristol: Multilingual Matters.

Erling, E.J. (2017) Language planning, English language education and development aid in Bangladesh. *Current Issues in Language Planning*, 18 (4), 388–406.

Erling, E.J., Adinolfi, L., Hultgren, A.K., Buckler, A. and Mukorera, M. (2016) Medium of instruction policies in Ghanaian and Indian primary schools: An overview of key issues and recommendations. *Comparative Education*, 52 (3), 294–310.

Erling, E.J. et al. (2017) Multilingual classrooms: Opportunities and challenges for English medium instruction in low and middle income countries. [Available at www.educationdevelopment trust.com/~/media/EDT/Reports/Research/2017/r-english-medium-instruction-in-low-and-middle-incomecontexts.pdf.]

Hayes, D. (2016) *Social Attitudes to English in Bihar*. London: British Council. [Available at www.teachingenglish.org.uk/article/social-attitudes-towards-english-language-bihar.]

Heugh, K., Benson, C., Bogale, B. and Yohannes, M.A.G. (2007) Final report study on medium of instruction in primary schools in Ethiopia. Commissioned by the Ministry of Education.

Jhingran, D. (2009) Hundreds of Home Languages in the Country and Many in Most Classrooms – Coping with Diversity in Primary Education in India. In Mohanty, A.K., Panda, M., Phillipson, R. and Skutnabb-Kangas, T. (Eds) *Multilingual Education for Social Justice: Globalising the Local*. New Delhi: Orient Black Swan.

Kosonen, K. (2005) *Education in Local Languages: Policy and Practice in Southeast Asia. First Languages First: Community-based Literacy Programmes for Minority Language Contexts in Asia*. Bangkok: UNESCO Bangkok.

MacKenzie, P. and Walker, J. (2013) *Mother-tongue Education: Policy Lessons for Quality and Inclusion*. South Africa: Global Campaign for Education Policy Brief.

Mfum-Mensah, O. (2005) The impact of colonial and postcolonial Ghanaian language policies on vernacular use in schools in two northern Ghanaian communities. *Comparative Education*, 41 (1), 77–85.

Ministry of Education (MoE) Ghana (2016) Ghana 2016 National Education Assessment Report of Findings. Education Service. National Education Assessment Unit. [Available at http://pdf.usaid.gov/pdf_docs/PA00MHMR.pdf, accessed 26th June 2017].

Mohanty, A.K. (2010) Languages, inequality and marginalization: Implications of the double divide in Indian multilingualism. *International Journal of the Sociology of Language*, 205, 131–154.

Nagarajan, R. (2015) Number of children studying in English doubles in 5 years. [Available at http://timesofindia.indiatimes.com/india/Number-of-children-studying-in-English-doubles-in-5-years/articleshow/49131447.cms, accessed 26th June 2017].

NCERT (National Council for Educational Research and Training) (2005) National Curriculum Framework. New Delhi. Document 1. [Available at www.ncert.nic.in/new_ncert/ncert/rightside/links/pdf/focus_group/english.pdf, accessed 26th June 2017].

NCERT (National Council for Educational Research and Training) (2006) National Curriculum Framework Position Paper. New Delhi: National Focus Group on Teaching of English.

Opoku-Amankwa, K. (2009) English-only language-in-education policy in multilingual classrooms in Ghana. *Language, Culture and Curriculum*, 22 (2), 121–135.

Opoku-Amankwa, K., Edu-Buandoh, D.F. and Brew-Hammond, A. (2015) Publishing for mother tongue-based bilingual education in Ghana: Politics and consequences. *Language and Education*, 29 (1), 1–14.

Pinnock, H. (2009) Language and education: The missing link. How the language used in school threatens the achievement of Education for all. CfBT Education Trust.

Simons, G.F. and Fennig, C.D. (Eds) (2017) *Ethnologue: Languages of the World*, 20th ed. Dallas, TX: SIL International. Online version: www.ethnologue.com.

Singh, R. and Bangay, C. (2014) Low fee private schooling in India – More questions than answers? Observations from the Young Lives longitudinal research in Andhra Pradesh. *International Journal of Educational Development*, 39, 142–150.

Smits, J., Huisman, J. and Kruijff, K. (2008) Home language and education in the developing world. Paris: UNESCO. [Available at http://unesdoc.unesco.org/images/0017/001787/178702e.pdf.]

Trudell, B. and Young, C. (Eds) (2016). *Good Answers to Tough Questions in Mother Tongue-Based Multilingual Education*. Dallas, TX: SIL International.

UNESCO (2014) Ghana: Education for All 2015 National Review. [Available at http://unesdoc.unesco.org/images/0016/001611/161121e.pdf, accessed 26th June 2017].

UNESCO (2016) If you don't understand, how can you learn? Global Education Monitoring Report. Policy Paper 24.

UNESCO UIS Stats (2017) Data to transform lives. [Available at http://uis.unesco.org/, accessed 1st July 2017].

Williams, E. (2014) English in African politics of education: Capital or capital illusion? *International Journal of the Sociology of Language*, 225, 131–145.

Woodhead, M., Frost, M. and James, Z. (2013) Does growth in private schooling contribute to Education for All? Evidence from a longitudinal, two cohort study in Andhra Pradesh, India. *International Journal of Educational Development*, 33 (1), 65–73.

Yiboe, K.T. (2011) Ideological Perspectives of Language of Instruction in the Ghanaian Primary Schools, Centrepoint Humanities Edition, 14 (1), 168–183.

7 English language as an inclusion tool

The case of Syrian refugees in UK primary schools

Juliet Thondhlana and Roda Madziva

Introduction

The rapid increase in complex refugee flows into the European Union states has led to what has come to be known as the worst refugee crisis of the current generation. While some EU states, particularly the UK, were initially reluctant to engage with the transnational project of coordinating access and settlement, the wrenching images of a Syrian toddler, Aylan Al-Kurdi, lying dead on a Turkish beach, emerged as evidence of a crisis that demanded a coordinated response (Postles 2015). Consequently, there was a shift in political and public debate away from borders and security, and towards refugee support which saw the British government in 2015 committing to resettle up to 20,000 Syrian refugees within a five year period (Gower and Cromarty 2016).

Unlike other refugees, Syrian refugees enter the UK with a special five years' Humanitarian Protection status, which grants them direct access to services such as education and employment. However, this group faces a range of challenges when it comes to adapting to their new environment, with language emerging as the major obstacle to children's inclusion in schools (Madziva and Thondhlana 2017). Using the lived experiences of Syrian refugee primary school children, their families, school teachers and other key informants, this chapter explores the critical role of language as an inclusion tool in schools.

Data for this chapter are part of a larger study exploring the integration and resettlement of Syrian refugees in the United Kingdom. The research took place in a large northern city in England and involved four primary schools, 57 participants through interviews, observations, focus group discussions, and school reports. The sample comprised Syrian families (16 adults and 20 children aged 5 to 12) and 21 key informants, including school teachers, local government authorities, representatives from faith organisations and migrant support organisations. The broad selection aimed to capture views of the different stakeholders involved in supporting Syrian refugees.

We include this chapter in *Learning and Teaching Around the World* for its use of the concept of linguistic capabilities as an analytical tool to examine the inclusion processes for participants such as the ones in this study. The linguistic capabilities concept has been used to address barriers to the wellbeing of marginalised communities (Robeyns 2006; Thondhlana and Madziva 2017). Capabilities are the opportunities available to individuals that enable them to accomplish certain functions (e.g. Sen 1999), and language is a critical capability for realising all other capabilities (Tikly 2016). For refugees in particular, language is critical for accessing education, the labour market, goods and services.

Arrival

In the statement below, Nasim describes her first day of school in the United Kingdom:

> When we first came to school, so the other students . . . started asking us things like 'What's your name?' . . . We know you are from Syria, and that you can't speak English . . . you have gone through many problems so we want to help you . . .
>
> (Nasim)

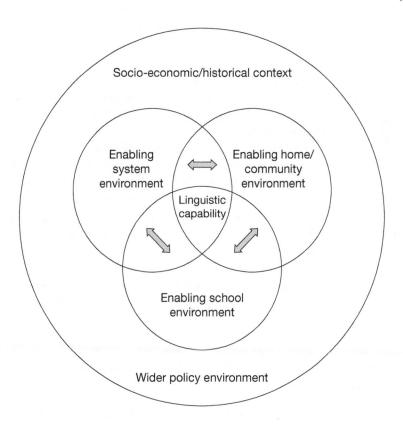

Figure 7.1 Tikly's Linguistic Capability Model
Source: 2016: 420.

Research has shown that mobility of people internationally and the consequent diversity of national populations have impacted education systems in complex ways (e.g. Taylor and Sidhu 2012). Research has noted the critical role of schools in facilitating the social inclusion of refugee children and young people in the school and broader community (Madziva and Thondhlana 2017; Arnot and Pinson 2005). Drawing on the 'linguistic capabilities' model of Tikly (2016, see Figure 7.1), we suggest that English is a powerful tool for the inclusion and integration of refugee and asylum seeker children in mainstream schools, as well as in the intersecting environments of the community and the wider education system.

Syrian refugee children and English language learning

In the UK, English language provision for migrants and refugees in school settings is generally referred to as English as an Additional Language or EAL, and its main purpose is to facilitate children's access to the school curriculum. Children may also learn English outside school in classes described as English for Speakers of Other Languages or ESOL (Mallows 2014). The two main language learning strategies used in EAL and ESOL programmes are a 'total immersion' approach, which requires the exclusive use of the target language, and a 'partial immersion' approach in which the mother tongue, the target language and any other language may be used to support the development of the target language. Resources may include the use of bilingual classroom assistants who use strategies such as translation, peer support and codeswitching between the target and the home language(s) to increase 'the inclusion, participation, and understandings of pupils in the learning processes' (Arthur and Martin 2006: 197). Effective language learning can be enabled by the interaction of school, community and parents (e.g. Baquedano-López et al. 2013).

Syrian refugee children were involved in two types of programmes at the time of fieldwork. The first programme was the school system, which was the primary means of English language learning for the children involved in the study. The four schools of our fieldwork used mainly a total immersion approach, with bilingual approaches employed in an ad hoc manner. The second programme for Syrian children was a bilingual provision offered by a local ethnic minority community in collaboration with the Syrian refugee community.

Interviews with the caseworkers who supported Syrian children with school admissions revealed that school staff reacted in different ways to enrolling Syrian children, depending on their previous experiences of working with refugee children. As one female caseworker related to us:

> I've had schools ask me, 'How do we educate these children? What do we do with these children?' because most of them had not been in school for a while and all had no English at all . . .

The challenges that Syrian children faced were confirmed by one 9-year-old boy, Abrahim. He described learning English as a necessary step to form relationships with other children.

I like school, but when I first started it was hard because I only had two Arabic friends from Syria, now I can speak more English so I have a few English friends. . . .

We used Tikly's (2016) linguistic capability model (see Figure 7.1) to explore the school, home/community and system environments that enabled English language learning for the participants.

The school as an enabling environment

In two primary schools (out of 4) teachers told us that the arrival of Syrian children was treated with sensitivity, taking into account the children's traumatic experiences in their home and transit countries and even their journeys within the UK. Teachers initially employed strategies for gaining children's trust before placing them in the mainstream classroom. An account of this is captured by a father whose children attended one of the schools:

> When my children (8 and 6 years old) started school teachers did not mix them with other children. They worked with a helping teacher who encouraged them to like school, by offering toys, games and play activities. Within a week they started to wake up early in the morning as they looked forward to going to school. Because they attended school for only half a day then, they would cry when we went to pick them up because they wanted to stay in school for longer. The teachers could see that they were now ready to be together with other children.

At the point of inclusion in the mainstream classroom, teachers kept a close eye on how the Syrian children were settling in, given their lack of English language. As one male primary school teacher explained:

> When they come into the class, it's all about visually being able to see what mood they're in, or how they act, and then as a teacher you act on that instantly. So if you can see that they're quite comfortable you go along with that, or they look confused, or you can see any signs of discomfort, that's when, personally, I look to put her with comforting students, or I'll comfort her with the TA [Teaching Assistant], so they'll work one-on-one.

Teachers had to go beyond physical inclusion to ensure that children quickly developed the linguistic capabilities to enable them to understand the curriculum, communicate with others and engage in learning activities. Depending on children's needs, a common strategy involved full-placement in mainstream classes and occasional withdrawal for targeted English language activities. We also noted that depending on resources, some schools were able to make use of bilingual teachers and teaching assistants as a way of supporting the newcomers.

As one 8-year-old girl, Salim related to us:

> I have someone who come to talk to me in Arabic . . . she teaches me how to say Arabic words in English . . .

However, we noted that after a period of bilingual learning, some children preferred moving on to total immersion to expedite their language learning. As one 9-year-old boy, Issam put it:

> If I learn in English all the time with others I will learn more words and can speak better English . . . I now have many friends who speak English, so I learn quickly if I stay with them all the time . . .

The Syrian children who participated in our research were diverse. Our sample included children with physical, cognitive and emotional needs. The uniqueness of some children's learning needs meant that teachers had to try different approaches. One example is the case of Fahid, a 10-year-old boy with complex eyesight problems, where teachers initially had to teach him in one-to-one sessions while they worked with other professionals to develop effective strategies to include him in the mainstream class. We were able to access Fahid's school report, which demonstrated that the techniques that the teachers had adopted were proving to be effective in the teaching of reading:

> [Fahid] can now read CVC [Consonant Vowel Consonant] words largely by sight (enlarged to 40+) and is able to work out the pronunciation of more complex words using quite sophisticated blending and segmenting skills.[1]

Our sample included two deaf siblings. Teachers had to develop specialised methods and techniques of teaching English to them, as one of the teachers related to us:

> We're using a [commercial] scheme . . . which has got a lot of visual material. So using pictures, using videos, getting them to go around and video each other, teaching them sign language for the words that we're doing. And very quickly, they have started to try to communicate . . . now you can see them out there trying to play with others because they now have a bit of language . . . Before, they would make an effort to communicate, but without language other children would just stare at them . . .

Closely related to this is the issue of the capability of teachers to implement appropriate language supportive pedagogy for teaching of English as an Additional Language (EAL). To this end one school offered specialised EAL training for teachers:

> Staff have been given a number of different training sessions . . . to support them in how to adapt their teaching to make it suitable for EAL students.
>
> (Syrian Pupil School Report 1)

The training included methods of identifying language needs of learners and differ-entiating language needs from other types of individual special needs, and developing appropriate classroom activities to support children using EAL as well as managing cultural and linguistic diversity in the classroom.

Within the scope of our fieldwork, it was too early to arrive at a precise judgement of the extent to which Syrian children were developing their English language capabilities and the extent to which they were fully included in schools. However, reports from one school show that these children are generally making good progress:

> [Yadar] is making excellent progress. He is able to make himself understood about most things and his natural exuberance means he is very sociable and thereby hearing a great deal of new language, which he is soaking up.
>
> (Syrian Pupil School Report 2)

Home and community as enabling environments

Syrian refugee parents initially struggled to support their children with homework due to their lack of English language proficiency. To manage this gap, some schools supported Syrian refugee children with their homework in school, with others setting homework that did not require parental support. As noted by one male teacher:

> In terms of homework we do have little tasks that we set her to take home and because of parents' language problem, every task has to be achievable.

The community played a striking role in supporting the children's education and language learning. For example, in one family a neighbour would regularly help check homework and English learning progress. The same neighbour helped the school and the family to communicate. This voluntary support improved the home-school partnership as noted by the parent:

> Our [English] neighbour visits to help our son with homework and to check how good his English is progressing ... If there is anything we do not understand about the school we talk to her and the school also talks to her if they have any concerns ...

In the case of the deaf siblings we referred to earlier, we noted a reciprocal relation-ship where the parent and the teacher took turns to visit each other to discuss chil-dren's progress. This enabled the mother and the teacher to work together for the children's education, particularly English language learning. As the teacher explained:

> Through these visits, I now know a lot about children's lives because the children themselves can't tell us anything about themselves ... initially, mum was anxious about a lot of things, so I got the opportunity to explain things to her ...

We observed how the community supported English learning for Syrian children. For example, in the 2016 summer holidays, a number of community agencies worked together to provide a summer English language learning classes for Syrian children. A community engagement pastor from a local church explained:

> There are worries across stakeholders about the Syrian children picking up English in school, and then over the six weeks holiday they won't have interaction with school, so their English could regress a little bit. So we are putting on afternoon sessions for them across August. So they will be working with volunteers . . .

Sustaining the enabling systems

English as an inclusion tool enables refugee children to learn and participate in mainstream classes in a way that reduces their exclusion from the cultures and curricula of local schools. In so doing, the education system accommodates their unique circumstances and capabilities in a way that enriches learning for all. Our data show that a combination of a positive political environment, sensitive school reception and a sympathetic host community all work to shape the inclusion of Syrian children in schools. Cooperation amongst various agencies is critical to refugee integration in communities in general and the integration of refugee children in schools in particular.

Our study has shown some of the ways a small number of UK primary schools have responded to the arrival of Syrian children, and the strategies and resources used to gain children's trust, include them in the mainstream classroom and develop their English language skills. Schools evidenced partnerships with parents, particularly in relation to the challenges of Syrian refugee parents' lack of English language proficiency. Parents interviewed were unable to support their children's learning fully, and the community played an important role in sustaining home-school partnership and children's language learning. Teachers used a range of strategies and approaches. They demonstrated readiness to address complex situations. Two schools were able to provide appropriate professional development in EAL pedagogy in order to improve teachers' capabilities.

We observed, however, that school and community initiatives at the time of our fieldwork were often hampered or made unstable by financial constraints imposed by government cost-cutting and austerity policies. The sustainability of wider enabling systems is key to the sustainability of systems at the school and community/home levels. Governments need to make consistent financial provision for schools to undertake staff development for supporting asylum seeker and refugee children. There is also a need for a formal, structured and coordinated multi-agency language provision as a step towards developing a more universal framework for supporting refugees and asylum seekers. Given the worldwide rise in refugee movement, it is important for governments to update and transform language-in-education policies relating to education of the refugee child, recognising that inclusion in school is a key aspect of inclusion in society.

Questions

1. What do you understand by 'linguistic capabilities'? Can you apply this concept to different contexts that you know of?

2. The authors briefly refer to EAL and to ESOL, and to total immersion and partial immersion strategies for language learning. Do you have experience of any of these methods, as a learner or as an education or community worker?

3. Thinking about the needs of learners such as the Syrian refugee children in this chapter, what should be the criteria for selecting an English language learning strategy in a school?

Further reading

Madziva, R. and Thondhlana, J. (2017) Provision of quality education in the context of Syrian refugee children in the UK: Opportunities and challenges. *Compare: A Journal of Comparative and International Education*, 47 (6), 942–961.

Thondhlana, J. and Madziva, R. (2017) English Language as an Integration Tool: The case of Syrian Refugees to the UK. In Erling, E. (Ed.) *English across the Fracture Lines: The Contribution and Relevance of English to Security, Safety and Stability in the World*. British Council.

Notes

1 Blending is the reading skill of combining letter sounds such as 'i', 'n' and 'g' to read the second syllable of the word 'loving'. Segmenting is the skill of separating individual letter sounds in order to spell, for instance, the letter string 'ing'.

References

Arnot, M. and Pinson, H. (2005) *The Education of Asylum-seeker and Refugee Children: A Study of LEA and School Values, Policies and Practices*. Cambridge: University of Cambridge.

Arthur, J. and Martin, P. (2006) Accomplishing lessons in postcolonial classrooms: Comparative perspectives from Botswana and Brunei Darussalam. *Comparative Education*, 42, 177–202.

Baquedano-López, P., Alexander, R.A. and Hernandez, S.J. (2013) Equity issues in parental and community involvement in schools: What teacher educators need to know. *Review of Research in Education*, 37 (1), 149–182.

Education Queensland (2005) Inclusive education statement. [Available at http://education.qld.gov.au/Studentservices/learning/docs/inclusedstatement2005.pdf, accessed June 16 2009].

Gower, M. and Cromarty, H. (2016) Syrian Refugees and the UK. Briefing Paper no. 06805. London: House of Commons Library.

Madziva, R. and Thondhlana, J. (2017) Provision of quality education in the context of Syrian refugee children in the UK: Opportunities and challenges. *Compare: A Journal of Comparative and International Education*, 47 (6), 942–961.

Mallows, D. (Ed.) (2014) *Language issues in migration and integration: Perspectives from teachers and learners*. London: British Council. [Available at https://esol.britishcouncil.org/sites/default/files/Language_issues_migration_integration_perspectives_teachers_learners.pdf.]

Postles, H. (2015) Aylan Kurdi: How a single image transformed the debate on immigration. [Available at www.sheffield.ac.uk/news/nr/aylan-kurdi-social-media-report-1.533951, accessed 20 October 2017].

Robeyns, I. (2006) The capability approach in practice. *Journal of Political Philosophy*, 14 (3), 351–376.

Sen, A. (1999) *Commodities and Capabilities*. Oxford: Oxford University Press.

Taylor, S. and Sidhu, R.K. (2012) Supporting refugee students in schools: What constitutes inclusive education? *International Journal of Inclusive Education*, 16 (1), 39–56.

Thondhlana, J. and Madziva, R. (2017) English Language as an Integration Tool: The Case of Syrian Refugees to the UK. In Erling, E. (Ed.) *English across the Fracture Lines: The Contribution and Relevance of English to Security, Safety and Stability in the World*. British Council.

Tikly, L. (2016) Language-in-education policy in low-income, postcolonial contexts: Towards a social justice approach. *Comparative Education*, 52/3, 408–425.

8 Unpacking teachers' language ideologies in schools in Alsace, France

Andrea S. Young

Introduction

In France, most teachers receive scant training in how to support plurilingual children in their learning of and through the language of instruction. In the absence of relevant, in-depth knowledge about language, this chapter examines the extent to which teachers are practising language policies based on beliefs rooted in ideologies unsupported by research findings.

This chapter presents findings from interviews with 46 primary headteachers (PHT), nursery headteachers (NHT) and lower secondary school headteachers (LSHT) in the Strasbourg area. The interviews were carried out by student teachers in the schools, who asked the headteachers two questions:

1. Are there any rules at school concerning the use of the pupils' languages? Why?
2. Do you think it would be useful to encourage plurilingualism in schools? Why?

The answers reveal evidence of linguistic hierarchies, separate spaces for different languages, a profusion of bilingual myths and a persistent monolingual habitus at school. We include this chapter in *Learning and Teaching Around the World* to emphasise the importance of teachers' language ideologies and how these influence their classroom practices, and the potential impact on children's learning.

Republican principles and language ideologies in the French education system

Education in France is national, state funded, compulsory, secular, and based on the republican values of liberté, égalité, fraternité. As civil servants owing allegiance to the state, French teachers are frequently reminded of their duty to uphold these values. Unfortunately, the principle of equality for all pupils can be interpreted as a duty to disregard difference, including recognising that a pupil may speak a language other than French. Thus, equality is equated with uniformity and equal opportunities amalgamated with identical treatment.

This reluctance to acknowledge diversity within unity may also be responsible for the dearth of systematically recorded information relating to the number of plurilingual children attending schools in France and the variety of languages they speak at home. It is not common practice for teachers to enquire about home languages, as such information is associated with the private sphere, considered to be of a personal nature and therefore not the business of the school.

Pupils who are officially recorded and identified as having specific linguistic needs are new arrivals. However, these statistics do not accurately reflect the numbers of plurilingual children attending schools in France as, technically, new arrivals must have arrived in France within the last 12 months and young children (aged 3–5) attending école maternelle (nursery school) are not considered as new arrivals regardless of their arrival date and their competences in French. Their young age and assumed consequent ability to naturally acquire language in situ serve as justification for their systematic integration directly into mainstream classrooms with no specific language support provision and their consequent exclusion from the new arrivals statistics.

One headteacher (NHT30 Q1) explained during an interview that, in her nursery school, teachers reminded children speaking Turkish together in the classroom to speak French so that everyone might understand and the other children would not feel excluded from the discussion, which would be incompatible with the notions of exchange, sharing, and above all of living peacefully together. This teacher also explained how, at the beginning of the school year, Turkish-speaking children were deliberately assigned to classes to create a certain Turkish/French balance and thus avoid difficulties arising from cultural, religious, and linguistic differences. The opportunity to allow otherness into the classroom in a bid to foster acceptance of difference amongst dominant language speakers was not mentioned. Instead, it is practiced policy to banish Turkish from the classroom and to separate Turkish-speaking children in order to avoid issues of difference. It is hard to see how a policy of avoiding differences, rather than explaining them, could help the children to learn to live together peacefully. Plurilingualism is clearly seen as a problem rather than as a resource or a right (Ruiz 1984) by this teacher.

Another headteacher likened the speaking of other languages in the classroom to 'anarchy' (PHT10 Q1). The fear of failing to integrate/assimilate pupils into an imagined homogeneous linguistic and cultural unity at school and of allowing a disastrous tower of Babel situation to arise in the classroom is strongly expressed in this statement. Integration, a recurrent term in the data, is often viewed as a one-way street, the burden of responsibility to integrate, to learn French, being placed firmly on the foreign pupil's shoulders:

> The pupils are invited to speak French with the other children for reasons of equality and also to facilitate their integration within the class.
>
> (PHT35 Q1)

The idea of simultaneously developing both languages and multiple identities is viewed as inconceivable and/or incompatible with the school's role in upholding French monolingual republican ideals.

The monolingual habitus: schools as monolingual spaces of the nation state

Article 2 of the French Constitution reads: 'La langue de la République est le Français' (the language of the Republic is French). This declared language policy symbolises the unification of the nation state through the use of a single language, which all citizens are required to share.

Whilst home languages may be paid lip service on the periphery, in reports and pedagogical guides, within the more widely read national curriculum texts, there is an absence of explicit or declared policy and learners who are not new arrivals but who may use a language at home other than French are simply not mentioned. The fact that children born and raised in France might speak languages other than French at home has been referred to as ignored bilingualism (Hélot 2007), and the refusal to officially acknowledge the existence and needs of these children within mainstream documents could be regarded as a covert policy of neglect.[1]

Many examples of concern for the development of the national language, often coupled with the belief that a child's home language has no role to play in their learning, were identified in the discourse of the interviewed headteachers such as: 'at school, we are there to speak French and that's all' (LSHT9 Q1). Another headteacher (PHT5 Q1) spoke of how Turkish speakers were requested not to speak Turkish amongst themselves at school so that they would not turn culturally inwards, especially if they found speaking French difficult. The idea that children should forfeit their home language and culture in order to learn successfully is perplexing from both a linguistic and an educational perspective. We learn by building on what we already know. If no links are made between prior learning and current learning, it is difficult to see how this can be effective.

As well as focusing almost exclusively on the learning of French, many headteachers interviewed in our sample also spoke of mastery (perfect or correct) of the language of instruction, for example, 'we should not forget the main objective of school: attaining mastery of the French language' (PHT26 Q1), 'speaks French perfectly' (PHT15 Q1), 'perfect mastery of a language' (LSHT12 Q2), 'the pupils master the French language correctly' (PHT13 Q2). This idealised, normative, error-free vision of language reveals a lack of awareness as to how languages are acquired and used and uncovers traces of a monolingual ideology, which permeate many teachers' discourse. In the monolingual mindset, there is no room for more than one, unique, standardised, perfect language.

Furthermore, from this monolingual perspective, difficulties in acquiring the language of instruction are often attributed to the other languages in the plurilingual pupil's linguistic repertoire which must therefore be eradicated in order for the national language to take root and develop. A headteacher (LSHT11 Q2) stated that she did 'not think that it would be useful to encourage plurilingualism in the school' because it seemed to her that 'the school should focus on French in the interests of efficient learning'. This idea that the use of and knowledge about several languages might in some way contaminate the national language is in direct opposition to European declared language policy (Council of Europe 2001, p. 4) which promotes communicative competence where 'all knowledge and experience of language' interact and contribute to learning.

Illegitimate languages and separate, disconnected spaces

Another theme which emerged from the headteachers' discourse was that of legitimate and illegitimate languages, and the strong belief that languages should be kept separate in both time and space, as can be observed in the following extract:

> Yes there are rules in the school concerning the use of other languages, for example, speaking dialect is not authorised in class. Furthermore, German is only used during the introduction to the German language hours, that is, two hours per week.
>
> (PHT43 Q1)

By *dialect* this headteacher is referring to Alsatian, a regional variety of German which is still spoken in some families, especially in rural areas near the German and Swiss borders (see Huck et al. 2005). In spite of its linguistic proximity to German (the foreign language taught in most primary schools in Alsace), Alsatian is prohibited in class, leaving room only for standard *Hochdeutsch* during the timetabled hours. Alsatian is not viewed as a legitimate language by the headteacher and as such has no place at school. This teacher's lack of awareness about the interrelated nature of linguistic varieties and standardised norms is depriving the pupils who speak Alsatian of valuable plurilingual competences which could support their learning of the standard variety.

Another headteacher (PHT26 Q1), this time referring to heritage languages taught on school premises but usually outside school hours, reiterates the idea of confining different languages to specific timeslots in the curriculum: 'Yes, rules are necessary concerning the use of these languages: these languages are only used during time-tabled hours (so not during playtime). No more than two hours of classes per week.' Many teachers spoke of the pupils' freedom to use the language of their choice in the playground, some referred to the impossibility of *policing* a playground policy and hardly any endorsed the idea of allowing home languages to be used in the class-room:

> . . . no rules for the playground. However, it's a completely different matter in the classroom. I wouldn't say that it is forbidden since my teachers each have their own pedagogy, but it is a rule that I tell them to respect. Teaching is done exclusively in French, so the language spoken in the classroom is French full stop.
>
> (PHT10 Q1)

Twenty-four out of the 46 headteachers (52.2%) in our sample mentioned explicit or implicit rules which discourage or even forbid children from using their home languages in the classroom and sometimes even in the playground. For such a high proportion of teachers to practise policies which outlaw the use of home languages at school, we can hypothesise that teachers are not only language-unaware, but are also misinformed about language and learning, adhering to beliefs deeply rooted in monolingual ideologies.

Conclusion

Children for whom the language of instruction is not the language of the home are particularly dependent on their teachers for learning support. Overt support (the *what* and the *how*) may take the form of language support tools and strategies implemented by the teacher to help the child initially to understand and ultimately to acquire the language of instruction. However, covert support may also take the form of supportive, language-aware attitudes on the part of education professionals. Whether teachers are aware or unaware, informed, uninformed, or misinformed about plurilingual learning, the beliefs they hold, rooted in the ideologies they construct, will inevitably influence the language policies which they adopt at school and consequently impact on children's learning.

Although many teachers are encountering plurilingual children at school in the Strasbourg area, our data indicate that teachers appear to be unaware of both nationally and European-endorsed language policies in relation to the plurilingual competences and educational needs of these children and often show very limited knowledge about language and language learning. The absence of a declared language policy referring explicitly to plurilingual pupils who are not new arrivals is leaving ordinary class teachers in limbo. The vacuum is being filled by perceived policy and the practice of inefficient and discriminatory language policies. This is of particular concern in nursery schools where very young, extremely vulnerable children are required to adapt to a different social, linguistic, and cultural context very quickly.

Our data reveal that, faced with the immediate urgency of educating plurilingual children, teachers are practising policies within schools based on personal beliefs. These policies are, unfortunately, all too often based on monolingual myths, rooted in popular language ideologies inherited from former times when France's major concern was the construction of a nation state around one common exclusive language.

France needs a coherent and relevant language education policy for the multilingual classroom, together with a critical language awareness component in teacher education and continuing professional teacher development. It is our belief that teacher language awareness is the key to greater understanding and more appropriate support for plurilingual learners. Teachers need to recognise and respond appropriately to the specific needs of plurilingual students and in so doing may have to challenge the monolingual habitus. Teacher educators need to explain *how* to do this, but also *why* this is important. A deeper understanding of complex concepts such as multiple identities, plurilingualism, and translanguaging (García 2012) is required in order to teach children in and prepare them for our multicultural, multilingual world. If our teachers do not understand these phenomena, how can we hope to educate the future citizens of an increasingly globalised world and guarantee equity and inclusion?

Questions

1. Does your country have an education policy about the languages of children?
2. How is your national language positioned in the primary school, in terms of its status compared to other languages or dialects?
3. Is your national language the only language used for learning in the primary school?

Further reading

Cummins, J., Hu, S., Markus, P. and Kritina Montero, M. (2015) Identity texts and academic achievement: Connecting the dots in multilingual school contexts. *TESOL Quarterly*, 49, 555–581.

European Parliament. (2009) *Educating the children of migrants* (Report No. 2008(2328(INI)). Committee on Culture and Education. Luxembourg: Publications Office of the European Union. [Available at www.europarl.europa.eu/sides/getDoc.do?pubRef=·//EP//TEXT+TA+P6· TA· 2009–0202+0+DOC+XML+V0//EN].

Gkaintartzi, A. and Tsokalidou, R. (2011) She is a very good child but she doesn't speak: The invisibility of children's bilingualism and teacher ideology. *Journal of Pragmatics*, 43 (2), 588–601.

Thomauske, N. (2011) The relevance of multilingualism for teachers and immigrant parents in early childhood education and care in Germany and in France. *Intercultural Education*, 22 (4), 327–336.

The full text version of this chapter is: Andrea S. Young (2014) Unpacking teachers' language ideologies: Attitudes, beliefs, and practiced language policies in schools in Alsace, France. *Language Awareness*, 23 (1–2), 157–171.

Notes

1   The French Ministry of Education (MEN) has published a new early years curriculum which explicitly mentions children who speak languages other than French at home and which encourages teachers to view these languages as resources for the whole class. This is a significant policy change (MEN 2015).

References

Castellotti, V. and Moore, D. (2002) Social representations of languages and teaching. Language policy division. Strasbourg: Council of Europe. [Available at www.coe.int/t/dg4/linguistic/source/castellottimooreen.pdf].

Council of Europe. (2001) Common European framework of reference for languages. Cambridge: Cambridge University Press.

García, O. (2012) Theorizing Translanguaging for Educators. In Celic, C. and Seltzer, K. (Eds) *Translanguaging: A CUNY-NYSIEB guide for educators* (pp. 1–6). New York: CUNY-NYSIEB. [Available at www.nysieb.ws.gc.cuny.edu/files/2012/06/FINAL-Translanguaging-Guide-With-Cover-1.pdf].

Hélot, C. (2007) *Du bilinguisme en famille au plurilinguisme a l'école* [From Bilingualism in the Family to Plurilingualism at School]. Paris: l'Harmattan.

Hélot, C. and Young, A. (2005) The notion of diversity in language education: Policy and practice at primary level in France. *Journal of Language, Culture and Curriculum*, 18 (3), 242–257.

Huck, D., Bothorel-Witz, A. and Geiger-Jaillet, A. (2005) Rapport sur la situation linguistique en Alsace (France) [Report on the linguistic situation in Alsace (France)]. LANGUAGE BRIDGES, a sub-theme working group of the Interreg IIIC project 'Change on Borders', Strasbourg: Departement de dialectologie, Universit‚e de Strasbourg. [Available at http://ala.u-strasbg.fr/documents/Publication%20-%20L%27Alsace%20et%20ses%20langues.pdf].

MEN (2015) Programme d'enseignement de l'école maternelle. In BO spécial du 26 mars 2015, Ministère de l'Education nationale, Paris.

Ruiz, R. (1984) Orientations in language planning. *NABE: The Journal for the National Association for Bilingual Education*, 8 (2), 15–34.

Tsokalidou, R. (2005) Raising bilingual awareness in Greek primary schools. *International Journal of Bilingual Education and Bilingualism*, 8 (1), 1–14.

9 Negotiating worlds

A young Mayan child developing literacy at home and at school in Mexico

Patricia Azuara and Iliana Reyes

Introduction

In Mexico almost 10 million people speak an indigenous language. There are 62 indigenous languages and of these Yucatec Maya is the second in number of speakers (after Nahuatl). This chapter is a case study of a Mayan child, Yadira Yah Cab, growing up between two cultures (Mayan and Mexican) and languages (Spanish and Yucatec Maya).

The research took a participant-observer approach. One of the authors did field work over a period of two years in a Yucatecan village, observing and interviewing Yadira and members of her family and school community, and collecting examples of Yadira's emergent literacy. 'Literacy events' in the research framework were defined as instances where written language was central to the participants' interactions, with consideration of the cultural uses and meanings of these interactions. The literacy events were analysed in terms of the function of written language for the different participants, which the authors refer to as 'domains'.

This chapter in *Learning and Teaching Around the World* looks closely at the experiences of a child who is making sense of learning. We include this research for its focus on the individual learner, and to draw attention to the considerable gap children may experience between home and school.

Yadira's community and home

Chak k'iin is a small rural Mayan community in the state of Yucatán that is characterised by economic marginalisation but rich cultural and linguistic traditions. Most families in town practice sustainable farming and supplement their income with other forms of production, such as raising livestock and bees, and weaving hammocks. Still, most families live in extreme poverty by Mexican standards and rely heavily on government material and economic subsidies.

Children such as Yadira are exposed to both Maya and Spanish from an early age. Although Maya is the heritage language spoken among family members, Spanish predominates in children's schooling experiences. Parents and adults identify Spanish as the language of opportunity and social mobility, but still consider Maya a significant part of their cultural capital.

Yadira was seven years old when we met her and still an emergent literate. She lived with her younger sister and both parents in a modest, one-bedroom house. Felix, Yadira's father, practices traditional farming, growing crops mainly for family consump-tion. Victoria, Yadira's mother, spends most of the day in her house doing her chores and weaving hammocks which she sells to supplement the family's income. Felix and Victoria both were born and raised in Chak k'iin. Their parents were monolingual Maya speakers who did not receive formal education. Felix left school after the sixth grade. Victoria completed middle school and, at age fourteen, worked as a nanny and housekeeper in the state capitol. They both feel insecure about their literacy skills in Spanish and stated that they cannot read or write in Maya.

Yadira, even though young, has numerous responsibilities at home. She takes care of her sister while her mother runs errands, plus she heats the water for their baths, washes the dishes, and husks the corn. Yet, she still spends most of her leisure time watching cartoons in Spanish on television or playing with her sister and cousins. Together they pretend to be wrestlers, teachers, or shopkeepers, and also like to chase one another or their numerous animals. Yadira is often the leader, and her younger sister and cousins follow her instructions diligently.

Since infancy Yadira and her sister have been acquiring both languages simulta-neously; thus, they can be characterised as *early simultaneous bilinguals* (Hornberger 1989). However, they prefer to use Maya at home.

The Yah Cabs' literacy practices

Literacy tools are limited in the Yah Cab household. Present are a calendar, used mainly for decoration, and the children's old textbooks and notebooks, which are used for play. Reading and writing are not part of the adults' everyday activities.

In the Yah Cab household, twenty-three literacy events were observed, which com-prised seven domains. Written language is used largely in and for school-related activities (Figure 9.1). Every day, Yadira and her sister complete their homework after lunch. Her parents supervise their work very directly. In these interactions the parents take the lead as teachers. Her parents read the directions and give her answers to the problems. Yadira then records the responses as her parents direct her. We also observed Victoria engaging in literacy events not directly related to school but designed to reinforce literacy or mathematical skills (categorised as Educational/Literacy for the Sake of Learning). Using old notebooks, Victoria assigns the girls exercises to practice their handwriting or computation (e.g., writing their names repeatedly or doing addition problems).

But for the children Figure 9.1 shows that written language is an important source of entertainment. Yadira and her sister do not own many toys, but use the materials available in their environment for pretend play, incorporating written language for different functions. For example, Yadira likes to play school. With her sister's and cousins' help, she arranges old pieces of wood to make a table where the 'teacher' sits. They all take turns being the teacher. As the most literate child, Yadira takes the

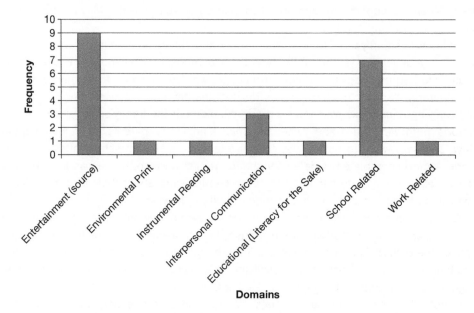

Figure 9.1 The functions of written language in the Yah Cab household

lead, using old notebooks to create attendance lists and assign writing assignments. They also play store, collecting rocks, which become different objects for sale and cutting strips of paper from an old textbook to create money.

Although most of the print present in the home is written in Spanish, in their oral interactions around the text, the family use both Spanish and Yucatec Maya; analysis reveals that only one third of interactions during literacy events are in Spanish only. Both languages are used as resources to construct meaning from print. For example, Yadira might read in Spanish, then ask questions about or comment on the text in Maya. Sometimes, she reads a phrase in Spanish then immediately rephrases it into Maya as a cognitive strategy to monitor her comprehension. We also observed that in their play, the children read and write in Spanish, but almost all of their oral interaction is in Maya. It is evident that Yadira uses her first language as a tool to mediate her literacy learning and as an important linguistic resource in constructing meaning from text.

Yadira's classroom

Yadira does not like attending school and her behaviour is very different there. At home Yadira is outspoken. At school she is shy and very quiet. She often cries when corrected or asked to speak in front of the class. During recess, she usually plays by herself or remains at her desk, completing her work. Throughout her schooling, teachers have identified her as an average student and have not been aware of her actual literacy level. She is able to complete routine tasks assigned in school, such as copying sentences from the board and reading aloud along with her classmates. Thus, her teachers have not noticed that her reading progress is slow: she still struggles to comprehend grade-level texts. Literacy instruction at school is limited to drilling isolated features of written language. Reading is about decoding, and writing about tracing clear letters. Literacy instruction strategies include reading syllables, copying sentences, choral reading, and round-robin reading. Children are expected to read clearly and write neatly. The reading textbooks contain many short texts followed by comprehension questions. Many times the teacher will ask individual children to read different sections of the text aloud then assign the children to answer the comprehension questions independently. The teacher does not afterwards review or discuss the students' answers with them, merely checking whether the assignment was completed.

Even though native language instruction is mandated by law, Spanish is the language of school. Some teachers speak Maya, but they believe children need to acquire the dominant language as quickly as possible to be successful in school. Though many children enter school knowing little if any Spanish, Maya is used by teachers only to communicate with parents and for clarification and directives (see Mijangos-Noh and Romero-Gamboa 2006). Although the state government provides textbooks in the native language, the teachers say they are not proficient enough in Maya to teach it.

Yadira's understandings about print

During leisure time at home Yadira and her sister often engaged in literacy events replicating many school practices. For example, they entertained themselves by writing the same sentence multiple times or copying text from their books. We did not observe them reading stories from their textbooks or drawing as a form of pre-writing. Their literacy practices were constrained by the limited experiences they had with authentic texts.

One literacy event observed at home was letter writing. Yadira receives material donations (e.g., school supplies, shoes) from a religious organisation in the United States. In return, the local coordinators require children to write thank-you notes to the donors. Victoria (Yadira's mother) diligently works with Yadira on this task. Yadira's participation, however, is limited to copying the model written by her mother and then drawing a picture or simply colouring in a picture drawn by her mother.

On one research visit to the home, Yadira surprised us with a welcome-back card (Figure 9.2). In this card she drew a picture of her house with the message: 'te manda es te divojo' (I give you this picture). It was clearly Yadira's idea to create the card, since her mother was visiting a relative when she made it. What was not evident was what prompted Yadira to make this gesture, because writing letters or cards was not a practice commonly observed in her home. We can speculate, though, that Yadira had internalised the value of written messages from her experiences of writing to her donors. Because we had given Yadira coloured markers as a gift, she might have inferred that we valued writing. It is clear though that Yadira realised she could use written language as a medium to express her affection for others.

During one visit Yadira was frustrated and in tears. Victoria explained that the child was learning how to write letters in school, but was very confused. Yadira had never experienced receiving or sending a letter through the post because there was no post office or postal service in her town. Thus, she could not understand how one person

Figure 9.2 Yadira's welcome-back card

could send a letter to someone who lived very far away and have it delivered by a third party. Some days later, however, we observed Yadira pretending to be a letter-carrier and spontaneously creating letters with her sister and two younger cousins. The children were cutting out and pasting figures from an old textbook. Yadira announced her intention to write a letter. She sang in Spanish while writing 'voy a mandar una carta, voy a mandar una carta' ('I will send a letter, I will send a letter'). She then delivered her letter to her cousin. In this literacy event she was assimilating the new knowledge gained in school and accommodating it to her previous experiences. She did not include the different components of a letter as taught in school (i.e., salutation, body, closing, signature) but did distinguish it from other kinds of writing by making an envelope.

This letter reflected the school's literacy practices and language preference. For example, Yadira's written message was clear and neatly written. Specifically, Yadira gave special attention to the mechanics of writing. She carefully wrote one letter in each square of the graph paper. She also followed a pattern commonly used during school literacy instruction, repeating the same sentence structure with different words inserted. She personalised her message by using her cousins' names e.g. 'Quico ama a su mamá; Quico ama a su papá; Quico ama a su primas, . . . tíos' ('Quico loves his mother/ father/cousins/aunts and uncle'). She wrote in Spanish, but most of her oral interaction around her pretend play was in Maya.

In this instance, Yadira reconstructed the action of writing a letter by adapting her experiences and creating new understandings. And, as the following excerpt shows, through the interactions in this event she was also mediating her sister's and cousins' learning (interactions in Maya are in bold font):

Yadira: **Quico je'el a carta'a.** (Translation: Quico, here is your letter) [Yadira hands her cousin the letter she wrote, the message is inside the envelope]

Quico: [Looks at the envelope, confused] **Tun** [tu'ux] **yan** [yaan]? (Translation: Where is it?)

Yadira: *Leelo, leelo.* (Translation: Read it, read it.) [Yadira takes the paper out of the envelope] **Si, jaj . . . je'ela Quico.** (Translation: Here it is, Quico.)

Quico: [Takes the paper from Yadira] **Taache'** [taase']. (Translation: Give it to me.)

Yadira: [Writing on another piece of paper] **In ka'aj in dzíibt u tia'al Carlitos beora'** **. . .** *Cesar ama a sus hermanas.* (Translation: Now I will write to Cesar . . . Cesar loves his sisters.)

Cesar: [He becomes curious about Yadira's writing and looks at her paper] **Ma'a beyo'** . . . *y su hermanos.* (Translation: Is not like this . . . and his brothers.)

Quico: *Una caita* [carta]. (Translation: A letter.) [explaining to Cesar what Yadira is doing]

Yadira: *Esto es para . . . cómo se llama . . . después es para, nadien* [nadie]. (Translation: This is for . . . what is her name? Then, it is for no one.) [gets a piece of paper and folds it to make an envelope] **tu** [tu'ux] **yaan le resistolo'? a k'almaj menso le beetik.** (Translation: Where is the glue? It is closed, silly, that is why.) [grabs the glue] *No lo ha abrido* [abierto]. (Translation: It is not opened.)

Quico: [Tries to open the glue] *a que chi* [sí] (Translation: It is.)

Yadira: **Masa'** [máasima'] **ma' a wojel xooki' Quico?** (Translation: You do not know how to read, right, Quico?) [Yadira goes back to writing a letter to her other cousin; reads while writing] *Cesar ama a su papá.* (Translation: Cesar loves his dad.)

Quico: [Getting frustrated with Yadira] **Waay** [ba'ax] **cartai** [carta] **le ba'ala' ka'a in jatej?** (Translation: What is this letter? I will tear it.)

Yadira: *Lee.* (Translation: Read.) [grabs the paper and reads] *Quico ama a su mamá, Quico ama a su papá, Quico ama a su ti prima, Quico ama a su tío . . . listo.* (Translation: Quico loves his mom, Quico loves his dad, Quico loves his cousin, Quico loves his uncle . . . done.)

This example reveals Yadira's bilingual strategies and how she draws from her Maya and Spanish linguistic resources: her written text is in Spanish, but most of her interactions around it are in Maya. She does not learn or use Spanish and Maya as two independent identities; instead, each influences the other.

Discussion

After engaging in a formal literacy event of writing a letter as homework, Yadira created a context to reconstruct the action of writing a letter, adapting her previous experiences and creating new understandings. In this event we observed new hybrid practices in which she took control of her learning and used print for authentic purposes she could relate to. Moreover, she tapped into her linguistic resources, Maya and Spanish, to mediate, appropriate, and transform the literacy event (Martínez-Roldán and Sayer 2006). Although her text was written in Spanish, she was not constrained by the linguistic boundaries drawn in school. She used her first language as a cognitive tool to direct her activity and as a social tool to mediate her own and her cousins' learning.

We want to highlight the creative ways Yadira negotiates and converges her school and home language and literacy practices (Reyes and Uchikoshi 2010). Yet, it is also important to recognise that her literacy practices are constrained by the limited experiences she has with authentic texts. The content of her letter shows that she has mastered only basic literacy skills, stark evidence of the systemic inequities in the Mexican educational system. Yadira is a foreigner in the literacy world (Purcell-Gates 1995). The school system is excluding her from this world by utilising two forces: an unfamiliar language and reductionist teaching practices.

In Yadira's classroom literacy instruction is reduced to drilling isolated features of written language, making the mastery of literacy more difficult. Yadira experiences something that resembles reading and writing but is not literacy (Edelsky 2006). In this contrived environment children are not encouraged to use written language to learn about the world or to communicate their thoughts and feelings. These educational practices make it difficult for Yadira to recognise the functional links between everyday literacy practices and school literacy. Even though she had previously written letters to her benefactors, she had great difficulty understanding the concept of letter writing when it was presented at school because the instruction was divorced from the functional uses of letter writing she was familiar with.

Moreover, despite the community's tenacious efforts to maintain their language and traditions, Spanish dominates and perpetuates minority language discrimination, driving homogenisation of the nation. Given the asymmetric power relationships between Spanish and Yucatec Maya, Yadira's parents consciously attempted to speak Spanish at home because they recognised that fluency in Spanish would help their children succeed academically. This illustrates the slow displacement and erosion of the indigenous language in the familial sphere. Whether created deliberately or unintentionally, the linguistic and cultural dissonance between home and school produces low literacy achievement among indigenous children.

Questions

1. What is your knowledge about the benefits of being bilingual?
2. What would you change about the literacy practices in Yadira's school, so these activities connected more with Yadira's home literacy practices?
3. How would you build on Yadira's interest in letter writing?

Further reading

Cummins, J. (2017) Teaching minoritized students: Are additive approaches legitimate? *Harvard Educational Review*, 87, 404–425.

Soltero-González, L. (2008) The hybrid literacy practices of young immigrant children: Lessons learned from an English-only preschool. *Bilingual Research Journal*, 31, 75–93.

Mary, L. and Young, A. (2017) Engaging with emergent bilinguals and their families in the preprimary classroom to foster well-being, learning and inclusion. *Language and Intercultural Communication*, 1–19.

The full text of this chapter is: Azuara, P. and Reyes, I. (2011) Negotiating worlds: A young Mayan child developing literacy at home and at school in Mexico. *Compare: A Journal of Comparative and International Education*, 41 (2), 181–194.

References

Edelsky, C. (2006) *With Literacy and Justice for All*. Mahwah, NJ: Lawrence Erlbaum Associates.

Hornberger, N. (1989) Continua of biliteracy. *Review of Educational Research*, 59 (3), 271–296.

Martínez-Roldán, C. and Sayer, P. (2006) Reading through linguistic borderlands: Latino students' transactions with narrative texts. *Journal of Early Childhood Literacy*, 6 (3), 293–322.

Mijangos-Noh, J. and Romero-Gamboa, F. (2006) *Mundos encontrados/Táantanil Yo'okol kaabil: Análisis de la educación primaria indígena en una comunidad al sur de Yucatán*. México, DF: Pomares Ediciones.

Purcell-Gates, V. (1995) *Other People's Words: The Cycle of Low Literacy*. Cambridge, MA: Harvard University Press.

Reyes, I. (2009) An ecological perspective on minority and majority language and literacy communities in the Americas. *Colombian Linguistic Applied Journal*, 11 (1), 106–114.

Reyes, I. and Uchikoshi, Y. (2010) Families and Young Immigrant Children: Learning and Understanding their Home and School Literacy Experiences. In Takanishi, R. and Grigorenko, E. (Ed.) *Immigration, Diversity, and Education* (pp. 259–275). New York: Routledge.

10 What languages do you speak? A reflexive account of research with multilingual pupils

Geri Smyth

Introduction

There are over 170 languages spoken in Scottish homes and data from the Scottish Government (2013) indicates that over 140 languages are used by pupils in schools. The most common of these after English and Scots are Polish, Urdu, Punjabi, Arabic, Cantonese and French. Of these, only Cantonese and French are offered as examinable subjects in the Scottish Curriculum, with Cantonese being available in only a small number of schools.

The title of this chapter is derived from a first encounter in a linguistically diverse primary classroom in Scotland where the author was conducting research on the languages of pupils. The class teacher asked the 11–12-year-old pupils to introduce themselves to the researcher, and they responded with answers such as:

My name's Celine and I speak French and English.

My name's Aailyah and I speak English and Swahili.

My name's Astera and I speak Farsi, Arabic and English.

Then, a boy from Afghanistan responded by asking the researcher a question:

My name's Niyusha. What languages do you speak?

Geri Smyth offers a reflexive first-person account of methodologies she developed in order to overcome barriers she faced as a researcher who does not for the most part share the first or home languages of her young research participants, and where the researcher is a speaker of the dominant societal language and the respondents are first language speakers of a less powerful language. In such situations, traditional methods of interviewing may not be relevant or reveal the most meaningful data. We include this chapter in *Learning and Teaching Around the World* because of its honest reflection on ethical issues of research with multilingual, multiethnic children in comparative primary education studies, and the practical actions researchers can take to generate meaningful data.

Research methods and research ethics in language-rich primary schools

My name's Niyusha. What languages do you speak?

I later discovered that Niyusha's home language is Pashtu and he was familiar with Qu'ranic Arabic. His knowledge of Pashtu also gave him access to other historically related languages in the North-Western region of South Asia, including Urdu, Panjabi and Hindi. Along with friends he watched rented DVDs in Hindi, which were readily available in Scotland and he could understand. He attended mosque school where he was learning to read the Qu'ran in Arabic. He understood other children in the school when they conversed in Urdu or Punjabi. In addition to now having to learn through the medium of English in school, he had started to learn French.

This 12-year-old boy from Afghanistan alerted me to the difference in our linguistic repertoires and communicative resources. As a researcher, I also became keenly aware of the relative status of our main languages and of the fact that this could have an impact on the research relationship. He demonstrated with his question that while the teacher and I may have assumed the research would be conducted in English, this need not necessarily be the case and certainly may not be the expectation of the research participants. It also brought up immediately the need for me to give very careful consideration to both data collection and subsequent analysis.

In this chapter I reflect on the methodologies I have adopted so that research respondents who do not have full command of the English language can nonetheless be fully involved in both data collection and analysis without the use of interpreters. The potential pitfalls of using interpreters have been discussed elsewhere (e.g. McKay et al. 1996; Jacobsen and Landau 2003).

In the United Kingdom, the ethical guidelines which are most relevant for educational researchers are those developed by the British Educational Research Association (BERA 2011). The BERA guidelines very clearly state that educational research must be carried out within an ethic of respect and freedom from prejudice but they make no explicit statements regarding the language usage of either researchers or participants. The guidelines also discuss cultural sensitivity although this is mostly framed in terms of research which is undertaken outside the UK. My own institution has a detailed ethical code of practice (University of Strathclyde 2013) which does mention the language involved in the research, making the assumption that researchers will be using English and indicating the need for vigilance in the choice and use of interpreters and/or translators when 'non-native English speakers' are involved in the research. This is important but does not give consideration to the possibility of alternative approaches or use of languages other than English by the researcher.

In many areas of social science, linguistic diversity seems to be subsumed in the 'multicultural guidance'. An interesting overview of these issues is provided by Salway et al. (2009) who investigated the guidance provided to members on research ethics and ethnic diversity across the 32 Learned Societies listed as members of the UK Academy of Social Sciences. Awareness and discussion of issues around multilingual and heteroglossic research practice has been growing, particularly within applied linguistics and linguistic ethnography.

Attention to language does not mean ignoring other aspects of identity and can in fact be assisted by, and in turn contribute to, an intersectional understanding of the impact of diversity in education. An intersectional approach suggests that social categories interact with each other and result in greater or less access to power, privilege and opportunity. While the concept largely arose from the black feminist movement (see e.g. Crenshaw 1991 and Hill Collins 2000) and has been most closely connected with race, gender and social class, intersectionality can be viewed as being a very relevant way of considering the complexity of structures and processes which shape the hierarchy of languages in education. Of course, language intersects with other aspects of identity including ethnicity, race, age and gender, to construct the opportunities available to individuals. Assumptions may be made about individuals' potential based on the relative status of their language and whether or not they are conventionally literate in that language (Street 2013/1995; Martin-Jones and Jones 2000).

Within the discipline of education, particularly when considering the fields of culturally responsive pedagogy (Ladson-Billings 1995), bilingual education (Cummins 2000) and multilingual pedagogies (Creese and Blackledge 2010), there is much that can be learned and applied to educational research with linguistically diverse communities. Take, for example, the use of home languages, culturally appropriate methods, and multilingual approaches to data collection. More has been written about a range of approaches to research in linguistically and culturally diverse education contexts in Smyth and Santoro (2014).

I am both a teacher and researcher with bilingual school communities, taking a practitioner approach that incorporates valuing home languages, being open to translanguaging (García and Wei 2014) among respondents and taking cultural norms and practices into account. In addition, I draw on ethnographic work that requires longer-term engagement than some other qualitative research approaches and recognises that the researcher him/herself is the main research tool. In particular, my approaches have been influenced by the work of Jeffrey and Woods (e.g. Jeffrey 2006; Jeffrey and Woods 2008) on creative learning and teaching, and I have taken Woods' (1990) tenets of creative teaching (relevance, ownership, control and innovation) into account in developing research methods. An essential aspect of educational ethnography is researcher reflexivity, written about in detail by Hammersley and Atkinson (1995) and referred to in many texts about ethnography, including Delamont (2002) and Walford (2008).

In the case of my own research this reflexivity importantly began prior to field engagement with a consideration of whose side I appeared to be on (Mac an Ghaill 1988) and the role I would adopt when researching with children. I did not wish to be seen by children as a teacher even although I was an adult in the school setting. I did not wish, despite my profession as a teacher educator, to appear to teachers to be in the school as an inspector or evaluator of their work. Thus, I have had to carefully construct the role of researcher with the people with whom I was researching, taking my language, dress and tools of the trade into account in research contexts. In the linguistically diverse contexts in which I work I must ensure that I attempt not to privilege English, and enable linguistically diverse responses.

Research activities with children

I was researching how newly arrived pupils from asylum-seeking families could demonstrate creative learning when the Scottish educational context, language and curriculum were all new to them. The research framework positioned creativity as being characterised by relevance, ownership, control and innovation (Woods 1990; Jeffrey and Woods 1997).

The main source of primary data, in addition to my field notes, was a corpus of photographs taken with digital cameras by eight groups of four pupils; each group had two newly arrived pupils from asylum-seeking families and two long-stay pupils. Over the period of a school year the groups of pupils took photographs in and around the school of anything which interested them about school and learning in Scotland. The benefit of digital photography is that the children themselves could manipulate the images and delete those they did not wish the researcher to see. The images could be (and were) subsequently developed into annotated slideshows using a range of software and IT skills such as PhotoShop and Google Translate, which were shared with the school community, enhancing the IT and communication skills of all the participants and enabling a multilingual exchange of ideas about the pupils' perspectives on learning. Children who shared a home language spoke to each other in this language prior to sharing their thoughts in English. Children who had languages with similar features (e.g. lexis) compared words for concepts related to school and decided on the best words to use in different contexts. The data thus collected included many photos of people, places and artefacts around the school accompanied by explanatory notes composed by the pupils themselves. For example, there were many photographs of the school caretaker in the data set and one accompanying commentary was *He teaches us Glasgow*. In subsequent discussions with the pupils this was explained as relating to the fact that the caretaker spent a lot of time with the newly arrived pupils telling them jokes, helping them to understand local culture, including and initiating them into the Glaswegian dialect. Thus, he acted as a cultural mediator for the newly arrived pupils and *Glasgow* here referred to many interwoven aspects of language and culture.

As an ethnographic researcher I also had to be open to plans being changed and developed by the inputs of the participants themselves. For example, the data collected incorporated not only my field notes but the field notes of the pupils who became very interested in the research process over my time in the school. I shared with pupils my photographs, interview and field note transcripts, and coded images and words. They found the process of data collection and analysis fascinating. They were particularly intrigued by and wished to discuss face to face with me the importance I placed on the photos they had taken and annotated, and my interpretations of them. My field notes of these interactions with the pupils around their photographs and commentaries contributed to the ongoing analysis.

I was struck by the ample use of non-verbal communication, especially hand gestures employed by the newly arrived pupils as they negotiated the new language of English. I was intrigued to find the number of photos which showed pupils using their hands.

I had coded this as *hand language* and explained to my pupil respondents that I used this shorthand code to mean they were using their hands to communicate when they didn't know English words. To this, Nazgol, an 11-year-old Farsi-speaking girl, responded *That's the way we talk in Iran* (i.e. with ample use of hand gestures as well as speech). Nadifa, an 11-year-old Somali-speaking girl added: *You do it Doctor Geri* (in this case indicating that I also used my hands when I was talking). I subsequently retained the code of hand language in my data analysis but modified my explanations of the code to incorporate the communicative intentions of speakers using hand gestures, as well as documenting the prominence of hand gestures in the photos.

It became abundantly clear during the course of this research that I could not impose my interpretations on the data without consultation with the young respondents as I frequently found myself allowing my preconceptions of their skills in English to dictate my analyses. The children also highlighted for me the ways in which I could sometimes attempt to be disingenuous to provoke responses and end up being unconsciously patronising, only to be rebuked by the research participants. For example, my field notes refer to me overhearing this play talk between three six-year-old boys:

Kamran (6–year–old Farsi–speaking boy) You be Saddam Hussein and we'll come and get you. (Addressed to another boy in the group.)

I asked Who's Saddam Hussein? to which Kamran replied in some astonishment: Do you not watch TV? He's a really really bad man who's killed lots of our family.

This exchange had a profound influence on the ways in which I engaged with the pupils in the future and helped to clarify for me the intersectionality of ways in which researchers from the hegemonic mainstream may unwittingly patronise or under-estimate our respondents. I also believe that my background as a teacher could sometimes lead to me asking such questions. It is important for all social researchers, perhaps particularly former educational practitioners, to be very aware of how their own identity and assumptions can influence the data gathered. Reflexivity needs to be an essential element of ethnographic work.

Much has been written in the social sciences about co-researching with respondents but this can only truly occur when researchers adopt a reflexive stance and when research practice is imagined in ways in which genuine attempts are made to address the asymmetries of power that shape researcher-researched relationships. As I have attempted to show in this chapter, field notes provided a crucial space for reflexivity, while extended engagement and dialogue with research participants allowed for some recalibration of the researcher-researched relationship and research which offered the potential for future impact on policy and practice. Methodologies which enable respondents to use forms of communication other than the written or spoken word (see also, for example, Pahl and Rowsell 2010, and Pink 2014) were able to offer powerful insights into language usage and hierarchies which might never emerge in more traditional interviews.

Questions

1. What are the ethical guidelines for doing research about or with children and young people in your country?
2. What research frameworks are you aware of that are relevant to doing research with participants who do not share your language?
3. Are there other ethical issues about researching with multilingual or multiethnic children you can think of that are not discussed in Geri Smyth's extract?

Further reading

Fields, A.J. (2010) Multicultural research and practice: Theoretical issues and maximizing cultural exchange. *Professional Psychology: Research and Practice*, 41 (3), 196–201.
Fassetta, G. (2014) Children's Agency in Research Using Photography. In Smyth, G. and Santoro, N. (Eds) *Methodologies for Researching Cultural Diversity in Education: International Perspectives* (pp. 106–121). London: Trentham Books at Institute of Education Press.
Smyth, G. and Sheridan, N. (2013) Becoming Multilingual Bridges and Barriers to Change in a Mono lingual Primary and High School. In Ragnarsdottir, H. and Schmidt, C. (Eds) *Learning Spaces for Social Justice: International Perspectives on Exemplary Practices from Preschool to Secondary School* (pp. 111–128). London: Trentham Books at Institute of Education Press.

The full text of this chapter is: Smyth, G. (2016) What languages do you speak? A reflexive account of research with multilingual pupils and teachers. *Language and Education*, 30 (2), 143–157.

References

BERA (British Educational Research Association) (2011) *Ethical Guidelines for Educational Research.* [Available at BERA. www.bera.ac.uk/wp-content/uploads/2014/02/BERA-Ethical-Guidelines-2011.pdf].
Creese, A. and Blackledge, A. (2010) Translanguaging in the bilingual classroom: A pedagogy for learning and teaching? *The Modern Language Journal*, 94, 103–115.
Crenshaw, K. (1991) Mapping the margins: Intersectionality, identity politics, and violence against women of colour. *Stanford Law Review*, 43 (6), 1241–1299.
Cummins, J. (2000) *Language, Power and Pedagogy: Bilingual Children in the Crossfire*. Clevedon: Multilingual Matters.
Delamont, S. (2002) *Fieldwork in Educational Settings: Methods, Pitfalls and Perspectives*, 2nd ed. London: Routledge.
García, O. (2009) *Bilingual Education in the 21st Century*. Malden, MA: Wiley-Blackwell.
García , O. and Wei, L. (2014) *Translanguaging: Language, Bilingualism and Education*. New York: Palgrave Macmillan.
Hammersley, M. and Atkinson, P. (1995) *Ethnography: Principles in Practice*, 2nd ed. London: Routledge.
Hill Collins, P. (2000) *Black Feminist Thought: Knowledge, Consciousness and the Politics of Empowerment*. London: Routledge.
Jacobsen, K. and Landau, L.B. (2003) The Dual Imperative in Refugee Research: Some Methodological and Ethical Considerations in Social Science Research on Forced Migration. *Disasters*, 27, 185–206.
Jeffrey, B. (2006) Creative Teaching and Learning: Towards a Common Discourse and Practice. *Cambridge Journal of Education*, 36 (3), 399–414.
Jeffrey, B. and Woods, P. (1997) The Relevance of Creative Teaching: Pupils' Views. In Pollard, A., Thiessen, D. and Filer, A. (Eds) *Children and Their Curriculum: The Perspectives of Primary and Elementary Children* (pp. 15–33). London: Falmer.
Jeffrey, B. and Woods, P. (2008) *Creative Learning in the Primary School*. Abingdon, UK: Routledge.
Ladson-Billings, G. (1995) Toward a theory of culturally relevant pedagogy. *American Educational Research Journal*, 32, 465–491.

Mac an Ghaill, M. (1988) *Young, Gifted and Black: Student Teacher Relations in the Schooling of Black Youth*. Milton Keynes, UK: Open University Press.

Martin-Jones, M. and Jones, K. (Eds) (2000) *Multilingual Literacies: Reading and Writing Different Worlds*. Amsterdam: John Benjamins.

McDowell T. and Fang, S.R.S. (2007) Feminist-informed critical multiculturalism: Considerations for family research. *Journal of Family Issues*, 28 (4), 549–566.

McKay, R.B., Breslow, M.J., Sangster, R.L., Gabbard, S.M., Reynolds, R.W., Nakamoto, J.M. and Tarnai, J. (1996) Translating survey questionnaires: Lessons learned. *New Directions for Evaluation*, 70, 93–104.

Pahl, K. and Rowsell, J. (2010) *Artifactual Literacies: Every Object Tells a Story*. New York: Teachers College Press.

Pink, S. (2014) Digital visual sensory design anthropology: Ethnography, imagination and intervention. *Arts & Humanities in Higher Education*, 13 (4), 412–427.

Salway, S., Allmark, P., Barley, R., Higginbottom, G., Gerrish, K. and Ellison, G.T.H. (2009) Social research for a multiethnic population: Do the research ethics and standards guidelines of UK learned societies address this challenge? *Twenty-First Century Society: Journal of the Academy of Social Sciences*, 4 (1), 53–81.

Scottish Government (2013) Pupils Statistics Table 1.14 Main Home Languages. www.scotland.gov.uk/Topics/Statistics/Browse/School-Education/dspupcensus/pupcensus2013.

Smyth, G. (2003) *Helping Bilingual Pupils Access the Curriculum*. London: David Fulton.

Smyth, G. and Santoro, N. (2014) *Methodologies for Researching Cultural Diversity in Education: International Perspectives*. London: Trentham Books at Institute of Education Press.

Street, B. (2013/1995) *Social Literacies: Critical Approaches to Literacy in Development, Ethnography and Education*. Abingdon, UK: Routledge.

University of Strathclyde. (2013) Code of Practice on Investigations Involving Human Beings. 6th ed. [Available at www.strath.ac.uk/media/committees/ethics/Code_of_Practice_Sixth_Edition_Nov_2013. pdf.]

Walford, G. (2008) *How to do Educational Ethnography*. London: Tuffnell Press.

Woods, P. (1990) *Teacher Skills and Strategies*. London: Falmer.

Part 3
Inclusion and exclusion

11 Indigenous ways with literacies in an Australian primary school

Kathy A. Mills, John Davis-Warra,
Marlene Sewell and Mikayla Anderson

Introduction

We include this chapter in *Learning and Teaching Around the World* for its exploration of Indigenous children's authentic multimodal meaning-making. The work is also notable for its collaborative methodology, where research participants and researchers come from very different cultures. This chapter presents data from a year-long literacy project with students aged 8 to 12 in an Indigenous primary school in South-East Queensland, Australia. The project applied participatory methods in which the research agenda and activities were negotiated with the Indigenous community. Multimodal literacy is the ability to encode or decode linguistic, visual, spatial, gestural and audio modes of meaning within texts that modify word meanings in different digital contexts and cultural contexts of use. The multimodality of communication has become a key strand of literacy research in response to the cultural diversity of global economies and the availability and convergence of new technologies. Multimodal theorists acknowledge that their investigations have been generally restricted to Western visual communication (Kress and van Leeuwen 2006: 4; Kress 2009), and the multimodality of Indigenous representations of knowledge is under-examined. Indigenous researchers have identified distinctive epistemologies of Indigenous groups (e.g. Martin 2003), and this chapter is significant for examining how the integration of such knowledge principles can be embedded in the multimodal literacy learning of Indigenous children in school settings.

The research site, aims and classroom learning experiences

Hymba Yumba Community Hub is an Indigenous independent school that had been operating for two years at the time of our field work. The students belonged to the Yuggera, Jagera and Ugarapul language regions of Southeast Queensland, including some suburbs identified as socio-economically disadvantaged areas. The student participants were of Aboriginal and Torres Strait Islander backgrounds. The Aboriginal principal and Indigenous Elders identified multimodal literacy as an area of development, and the researchers had a sustained presence in the field, which is an ethical requirement of Indigenous research. Aboriginal and Torres Strait Islander students from each of the four grade levels participated in multimodal literacy text-creation practices and semi-structured interviews. The research was conducted with students across two composite (Years 4/5 and 6/7) primary classrooms (students aged 8.5–12.5 years).

The research aim was to develop the multimodal literacy learning of Indigenous primary students through understanding the valued discourses of a school community. This is vital because Indigenous peoples take pride in the valued epistemology (i.e. nature of knowledge) and ontology (i.e. beliefs about existence) of their ancestral history, yet they must continually adapt to the Eurocentric ways of talking, doing, writing and being in institutionalised language and schooling (Kerwin 2011).

The English curriculum task for the Year 6/7 students was to retell an Indigenous Dreamtime story from South East Queensland using multiple modes and specific digital technologies. They chose the story of Nanji and Nguandi. The students used pen and tempura paint on transparency film to create a class set of artworks, with each child depicting a different scene from the narrative. The students used the iPad digital camera function to photograph the artworks, wrote the story retellings and audio-recorded the narration using iMovie for iPad. The Year 4/5 students created multimodal historical narrative poems presented as 'gamis' using the Tellagami iPad application. The students wrote poems about the first contact between the Indigenous peoples of Australia and the white colonial invaders, which they recorded as the audio narration. They created avatars they could modify for gender, skin and eye colour, hair colour and style, clothing, shoes, gestures and emotions or facial expressions. They created backgrounds from photos or other images. The teachers regularly invited the Indigenous Elders to share their cultural knowledge directly with the class as special visitors.

Findings

Transgenerational knowledge

A significant theme in the data was the children's awareness of receiving and continuing an Indigenous legacy for future generations through the digital medium. The students demonstrated a strong and continuing connection to places and traditions that were embedded in their digital narratives. Teachers said they selected Dreamtime narratives because they belong to the local geographical and language region, and because story-telling is part of a generational flow of knowledge that was vital to the community. For example, we interviewed Sophia (age 11 years) whose family taught and practised Indigenous knowledge and ways in the home:

> Interviewer: Where do you think your Dreamtime story came from . . .?
> Sophia: From generation to generation it was passed down, and then it was passed down to me. It was what they [ancestors] believed and what they saw.

Sophia uses her own phrases 'generation to generation' and 'it was passed down', to indicate a transgenerational flow that was tied to the significance of the Indigenous narratives. Her phrases (e.g. 'It was what they believed and what they saw') are lyrical.

Figure 11.1 Rainbow serpent turns the couple into coral

The visiting Indigenous Elders demonstrated to students very visibly the passing down of these dreamtime stories, and teachers drew attention to this point when introducing Dreamtime narratives. Sophia's use of the singular personal pronoun 'me' (i.e. 'Then it was passed down to me') indicates a personal acknowledgement of her place in this passage of knowledge, and implies the significance of the past for the present.

Many of the Dreamtime stories depict ancestral beings that were transformed into some physical aspect of the land, such as the dreamtime characters, Nanji and Nguandi, who metamorphosed into coral. This is represented visually in the artwork created and digitally photographed by students. For example, Figure 11.1 represents a scene in the Dreamtime narrative when Nanji and Nguandi became one with nature as they were transformed into coral under the sea by the Rainbow Serpent. The Rainbow Serpent is represented visually as the main actor, positioned both in and out of the water, and with its head and particles flowing from its mouth aimed at Nanji and Nanji. The image focuses on the symbolic connection between people, animals and other elements in nature, which is central to Indigenous ontology.

Placed knowledge

Place, the land or territory emerged as a significant concept in the children's understanding of Indigenous knowledge and their appreciation of digital storytelling.

Aboriginal narratives interconnect with particular geographical places associated with the land and nature. In Australian Indigenous culture, events inextricably belong to places, and telling stories is a way for places to speak through the narration. The following dialogue demonstrates how Joshua (12 years old) saw the digital storytelling task as personally significant in terms of place.

> Interviewer: Where did the story originate?
>
> Joshua: Fraser Island and Cherbourg, before the white invasion.
>
> Interviewer: How important is the story to you?
>
> Joshua: This story is important to me because it is part of my culture – because I have cousins that come from these Islands. I'm allowed to go dancing on those islands.
>
> Interviewer: So how about this story – is it significant to your family?
>
> Joshua: Yes, sure. My mum has been to those islands, and me, mum, and my brother and sister, and Dad are allowed to go to those places . . . It's part of our culture, plus, um, when we do our dancing, that's how we tell stories, and we also do it through singing and storytelling.

Joshua demonstrates knowledge of the place-names and geographies associated with the story of Nanji and Nguandi, and how the story belongs to the Indigenous peoples who were later taken to Cherbourg. He also denotes a time period, using the term 'white invasion' as a marker of time prior to the European colonisation of Australia. Fraser Island's significance to Joshua stands in contrast to definitions of this place driven increasingly by outsiders as a tourist destination.

The story is significant to Joshua because it is connected to his placed memories of the islands with family members, and sensorial remembering of the songs and dances associated with those places. Joshua has a larger vision of his identity than his own experiences, because this collective history of the past gives meaning to his personal digital composition experience.

The concept of place has often been regarded as a central organising principle in Aboriginal ontologies and epistemologies (Rose 2000). Aboriginal stories typically include a place-name where the events in the story occurred, because the land is not passive or inert but an active agent in events. Aboriginal Australians see the land as totality, and connections to the land are at the centre of their epistemic and community structure (Ward et al. 2003). In Joshua's interview, there is an implicit acknowledgement of an 'ecological connectivity' grounded in people and place (Rose 2000).

This connection between tribe and place demonstrates the importance of selecting traditional Indigenous stories for study in the English curriculum that have local and placed significance. Joshua conveyed an active awareness of collective practices, places, celebrations, and memories of an intergenerational legacy, which he connected with in the story of Nanji and Nguandi. The digital medium became a platform for remembering meanings attached to places of significance in Joshua's family and people.

In the gami below (Figure 11.2), Charlotte (aged 9 years) uses a painting of the tribe and the bushland as the background, pointing to the spiritual connections to the land

Figure 11.2 White kangaroo

and providing a context for the narrative of the lake as a geographical place of significance for sustaining the tribe. Charlotte explained that the figures in the background are spirits of ancestors, both good and bad spirits, represented by colours and patterns, and ancestors who died young and old, indicated by the size of the figures. Charlotte's audio poem in the gami is:

> I went to the lake one day,
> Me and my cousin went to play.
> We saw a kangaroo.
> A kind of white kangaroo.
> I saw a white man on my people's land.
> I said, 'Stay off my land'.
> He said, 'This is my land, not your land'.

The reference to the white kangaroo in the audio of the story is significant, anticipating the curious arrival of the white man, while signifying the important connections between the land, animals, and the tribe. Phrases such as 'my people's land' emphasise the collective nature of the Indigenous custodianship of the land, using the possessive pronoun 'my'. The gestures, animated by the application, were selected by Charlotte to show neither happiness nor sadness, but a 'neutral' emotion. The avatar's arms encircle her body to form a physical barricade, which accompanies the final words of the white man, 'This is my land, not your land'. The last line breaks free of the rhyming structure of the poem, creating a sense of the rupturing of traditional land ownership and geographically placed meanings.

The significance of place in terms of land ownership was a theme throughout the Year 4/5 teacher's lessons and students' gamis. The students were asked to create their gamis about the first contact between Indigenous and white races, which provided an opportunity to explore the history of the land or other issues from a non-European viewpoint. The sharing of such multimodal texts contributes to the ongoing reformulation and remembrance of Indigenous history, and its implications for understanding hegemonic relations that persist in the present, using a new mode for the interchange of ideas, antipathies, and cultural values (Simon 2012). For many Indigenous peoples, including Canadian (Battiste 2002) and Australian (Kerwin 2011) Indigenous peoples, knowledge belongs to a particular people with a particular territory and language, which is sustained from generation to generation by the Elders and the tribe.

Multimodality of indigenous knowledge

Aboriginal narratives incorporate ceremonial dances, songs, body paint, music, and associated oral storytelling. The students demonstrated an awareness of the specific cultural and multimodal practices in Indigenous communities, as illustrated in this conversation with Michael (age 9) about the ways of communicating Indigenous Dreamtime stories.

> Michael: They are passed on through culture. Like, we go up to do dancing at Stradbroke. We play didgeridoo, clap sticks, wear ochre [on skin], and wear lap-laps made of kangaroo skins.

Michael identifies the representational modes of dance and playing instruments, such as didgeridoo and clap sticks, as traditional forms of knowledge representation in Indigenous cultures. He also lists embodied forms of meaning that are also significant when dances are performed, such as wearing yellow ochre paint and lap-laps, which become part of a multimodal orchestration of symbolic meanings.

Across cultures, movement and gesture realise important ideational or conceptual meanings about the world, and dances and images can both be conceived as narrative representations that depict the recounting of actions, events, places and times. Indigenous Australian groups greatly value cultural forms of dance and music that are symbolic, spiritual and sacred. There is a rich elaboration of the symbolic and cultural meanings of movements, gestures and rhythms.

In the visual designs of their digital storytelling, the children demonstrated knowledge of embodied or living art through depiction of Indigenous body paintings using geometric designs. In Indigenous dance rituals, boys and men taking part are decorated with sacred designs that symbolise the Dreamtime ancestors. Life is acknowledged and reaffirmed through dances called 'shake- a-leg' and ceremonies. The boys in the school sometimes performed dances for the community for particular cultural events, decorated in traditional clothing and body paint. Children drew on these shared embodied meanings of practices in the school and community to make meaningful connections to the digital storytelling task.

In our project, the students received specific instruction by Indigenous artists to create images of Indigenous people that were consistent with historical forms of art in the local Indigenous culture. Students such as Sophia did not miss the significance of this: 'We learned how to draw our people'. A cursory reading of this statement might indicate that Sophia was simply relaying what she had been taught. However, her specific use of the possessive, first person, plural pronoun 'our' with 'people' indicates a sense of identification with the collective Indigenous community, of which she is a member of the group. This is counter to the hyper-individualised representation of 'self' in social and popular media.

It is important to note that Indigenous knowledge is not static and unchanging. Rather, conversations about stories, dances, and traditions reflect a sense of ongoing and 'ever-evolving community-based reflection and conversation on past, present and future identities' (Giaccardi 2012: 7). The ways in which the students retold the traditional stories for the school literacy activities were akin to the ways in which these stories are shared within the wider community: sometimes orally and at other times through the changing technologies and resources at hand.

Individual and collective knowledge and practices

The children articulated the need to take individual responsibility for moral actions, and to expect negative consequences for actions that disrespect the knowledge and practices of the Indigenous community. This was a recurring theme in the children's personal interpretations of the message of the traditional story of Nanji and Nguandi. When asked about some of the meanings of the story, Sophia (11 years old) perceived that: 'The elders were young once, and there's a consequence for everything'. Aware of the moral message of the story, she recognises a message about the relations between the young and the older members of the tribe. Aleisha (aged 10 years) also interpreted the story in terms of consequences, though demonstrating a broader recognition of the complexity of these consequences for those beyond herself in the Indigenous community.

> Aleisha: Don't run away when you have to do something, 'cause you might get another person into trouble. Like, the leading elder got killed for them (the young couple) not doing their responsibility, 'cause they ran away, and that elder that was trying to get them back and keep them safe and . . . was killed by the Great Spirit named Booloo.

Aleisha saw that Booloo had punished someone for the young couple 'not doing their responsibility' because Nanji and Nguandi 'ran away'. The collective nature of moral action and its consequence is implicit in Aleisha's statement 'you might get another person into trouble', rather than emphasising individual action and individual consequences alone. The theme of collective responsibility is implicit in the understanding that an Elder had to die as a result of the moral actions of the couple.

The emphasis on shared or collective knowledge was also a focus of the multimodal gami videos. Through the multimodal design of gamis, students remade their connections to their collective past in relation to a significant historical event: the first contact between Aboriginal Australians and the white colonisers. The gamis focused on remembering the history of white colonisation from the perspective of Indigenous people, where students positioned themselves through imagined Indigenous identities (avatars) of times past. Cultivating counter-narratives allowed the students to assert collective social identities that are typically absent in official curricula (Godley and Loretto 2013). Similarly, the sharing of counter-narratives can help build community among those marginalised by society. Digital and multimodal heritage practices can challenge the assumptions, values, and prejudices that undergird dominant narratives through creating imagined identities that contradict dominant narratives (Solorzano and Yosso 2001).

Discussion

This research aimed to understand the central themes of Indigenous knowledge in the texts and talk of Indigenous students. The primary school Indigenous student participants demonstrated an awareness, appreciation and deep respect and pride in their culture and heritage. While the multimodal texts were produced by students in response to specific schooled forms of knowledge and text requirements, the student interviews provide a sense in which the students saw these practices as personally meaningful to their lives and Indigenous identities. Key features of knowledge included the flows of knowledge from the Indigenous Elders to the students and future generations. Indigenous connections to place and to the land were central themes in the multimodal texts. The multimodal practices of dance, storytelling, art and music were depicted or woven into the students' texts and practiced in the school, demonstrating the valued semiotic forms and practices of communication. The individual and collective nature of social action and memories was also a recurring theme.

Students connected their own histories and familial stories to those of the past in a transformative way. The digital storytelling involved hybrid modes of presentation of cultural knowledge, and digital technologies became an important means for disseminating their cultural stories to others. This recognition is important to guard against the homogenising of culture or static view of culture (Keddie et al. 2013). Many forms of Indigenous knowledge and practices can be understood as dynamic and negotiated, while other forms are conserved across time and place. In the student's work, Indigenous culture encompassed practices as both historically established and yet relevant to the times, rather than exclusively fixed and unchanging. Traditional forms of visual art can be combined with digital photography, and written words with digitally recorded speech. Flows of cultural heritage in textual practices are vital to sustaining Indigenous communities. In this research, teachers introduced students to powerful forms of language, including using digital platforms and modes of distribution, to convey their message to community and public audiences.

The research has provided generative examples of culturally inclusive literacy pedagogy. It demonstrates the successful weaving of Indigenous narratives and histories, multimodal art forms, and connections to the students' placed cultural experiences through digital media production. This weaving of new media with traditional narratives is important in disrupting the cultural exclusivity that often pervades schooling in colonised countries (Castagno and Brayboy 2008; Keddie et al. 2013). This research has demonstrated how digital storytelling can be used for collective cultural remembering in the new times, as a form of cultural border crossing. It provides an example of how teachers and students can appropriate multimodal design in schools in a way that explicitly attends to the dynamic nature of Indigenous practices, to create space for a critical anti-racist approach to multimodal text production.

Questions

1. Is the Indigenous knowledge described in this research (transgenerational, connected to land and place, grounded in memory and social action, multimodal in expression) different or similar to the knowledge system you are familiar with as a learner?
2. When you were in school, was your culture and community acknowledged in school subject learning?
3. Indigenous knowledge arises from specific ways of knowing and understanding the world. How valuable is this, do you think, for children's learning?

Further reading

Jerome, P. (1999) Nanji and Nguandi. Dreaming, Series 6. Sydney: Aboriginal Nations Australia.
Jewitt, C. (2013) *The Routledge Handbook of Multimodal Analysis*, 2nd ed. London: Routledge.
Kaptizke, C. and Renshaw, P. (2004) Third Space in Cyberspace: Indigenous Youth, New Technologies and Literacies. In van der Linden, J. and Renshaw, P. (Eds) *Dialogic Learning: Shifting Perspectives to Learning, Instruction, and Teaching* (pp. 45–61). Dordrecht: Kluwer Academic Publishers.
McConaghy, C. (2000) *Rethinking Indigenous Education: Culturalism, Colonialism, and the Politics of Knowing*. Flaxton: Post Pressed.
Pahl, K. and Rowsell, J. (2006) *Travel Notes from New Literacy Studies: Instances of Practice*. Clevedon: Multilingual Matters.
Silberman, N. and Purser, M. (2012). Collective Memory as Affirmation: People-Centred Cultural Heritage in a Digital Age. In Giaccardi, E. (Ed.) *Heritage and Social Media: Understanding Heritage in a Participatory Culture* (pp. 13–29). London: Routledge.

The full text of this chapter is: Mills, K., Davis-Warra, J., Sewell, M. and Anderson, M. (2016) Indigenous ways with literacies: Transgenerational, multimodal, placed, and collective. *Language and Education*, 30 (1), 1–21.

References

Battiste, M. (2002) *Indigenous Knowledge and Pedagogy in First Nations Education*. Ontario: National Working Group on Education.
Castagno, A.E. and Brayboy, B.M.J. (2008) Culturally responsive schooling for indigenous youth: A review of the literature. *Review of Educational Research*, 78 (4), 941–993.
Giaccardi, E. (2012) *Heritage and Social Media: Understanding Heritage in a Participatory Culture*. London: Routledge.
Godley, A.J. and Loretto, A. (2013) Fostering counter-narratives of race, language, and identity in an urban English classroom. *Linguistics and Education*, 24 (3), 316–327.

Keddie, A., Gowlette, C., Mills, M., Monk, S. and Renshaw, P. (2013) Beyond culturalism: Addressing issues of indigenous disadvantage through schooling. *Australian Education Researcher*, 40 (1), 91–108.

Kerwin, D.W. (2011) When we become people with a history. *International Journal of Inclusive Education*, 15 (2), 249–261.

Kress, G. (2009) What Is Mode? In Jewitt, C. (Ed.) *The Routledge Handbook of Multimodal Analysis* (pp. 54–67). London: Routledge.

Kress, G. and van Leeuwen, T. (2006) *Reading Images: The Grammar of Visual Design*, 2nd ed. London: Routledge.

Martin, K.L. (2003) Ways of knowing, being, and doing: A theoretical framework and methods for indigenous and indigenist research. *Journal of Australian Studies*, 76, 203–214.

Rose, D.B. (2000) *Dingo Makes Us Human: Life and Land in an Aboriginal Culture*. Melbourne: Cambridge University Press.

Simon, R. (2012) Remembering Together: Social Media and the Formation of the Historical Present. In Giaccardi, E. (Ed.) *Heritage and Social Media: Understanding Heritage in a Participatory Culture* (pp. 89–106). London: Routledge.

Solorzano, D.G. and Yosso, T.J. (2001) Critical race and Latcrit theory and method: Counter-storytelling. *Qualitative Studies in Education*, 14 (4), 471–495.

Ward, N., Reys, S., Davies, J. and Root, J. (2003) *Scoping Study on Aboriginal Involvement in Natural Resource Management Decision Making and the Integration of Aboriginal Cultural Heritage Considerations into Relevant Murray-Darling Commission Programs*. Canberra: Murray-Darling Basin Commission.

12 Young British Muslims explore their experiences of primary school and 'othering'

Alison Davies

Introduction

This chapter explores the experiences of young Muslims as they negotiate their religious and cultural identities in multicultural primary schools in a small city in the eastern region of the United Kingdom. It draws from informal discussions with young people themselves reflecting on issues such as their own approach to schooling, their experiences of 'othering' (Kumashiro 2000) and how the schools they attend do, or could, promote inclusion in their classrooms. We include this chapter in *Learning and Teaching Around the World* because, whilst there is a growing body of literature about Muslims in education (see, for example, Davies 2008; Revell 2012), the voices of young people themselves are rarely heard. We also value the perspective in this chapter on the concept and practice of anti-oppressive education *for* and *about* 'others' who do not conform to the dominant culture.

In the spirit of participatory research, acknowledging children as 'experts in their own lives' (Langsted 1994), Alison Davies' study draws from discussions with 30 young Muslims, as individuals and in small groups, in their final year at primary school (age 10–11) or their first year at secondary school (age 11–12) reflecting on their experiences at primary school. The discussions took place in a madrassa (supplementary after-school classes where children learn about Islam, the Qur'an and Arabic language) and at a mosque, and, in the case of the secondary pupils, in their Islamic faith school. All the participants' names are pseudonyms.

It is important to acknowledge that these pupils' views cannot be claimed to represent the views of all young Muslims. Even within one small city there are Muslims from different Sunni and Shia traditions, intersecting with many different ethnicities and cultures, including Pakistani, Bangladeshi, Iraqi, Kurdish, Afghani, Somali and Syrian. Further, there is a danger of portraying an essentialised picture of Islam, which is often misrepresented in what is taught in schools (Revell 2012). We recognise that any summary, such as this chapter, risks perpetuating old stereotypes or creating new ones. Nevertheless, while mindful of these pitfalls, this chapter sets out what the young interviewees wanted their primary school teachers to know.

Alison Davies' study took place in the aftermath of '9/11' in 2001 and the London tube and bus bombings of 2005, as the popular perception of South Asian pupils shifted from 'well behaved' to 'troublesome and threatening' (Shain 2003; Crozier and Davies 2008). In 2011 the British Prime Minister blamed 'state multiculturalism' for allowing the growth of segregated communities (Cameron 2011) and advocated the promotion of 'British values' in schools; in the same year, long-standing dedicated state funding for the educational support of minority ethnic groups was withdrawn. In 2015 the UK-wide Counter Terrorism Act (also known as the 'Prevent' strategy) placed upon teachers a statutory duty to promote 'fundamental British values' and to report pupils deemed 'at risk' of radicalisation. The former has been criticised for exclusionist, racialising implications (Elton-Chalcraft et al. 2016) and the latter for the construction of Muslim populations as 'suspect communities' (Kundnani 2012).

The importance of religion in the lives of British Muslim pupils

It's because our culture comes from our religion . . . The same values of respecting your parents, respecting your elders, and education.

(Haris)

For those who have grown up in a liberal and increasingly secular society, the importance to young British Muslims of their religious identities can be perplexing, or indeed problematic. Modood (2010) recognises the challenge to liberalism posed by the fact that 'Muslims and other religious groups are now . . . claiming that religious identity, just like gay identity and just like certain forms of racial identity, should not just be privatised and tolerated but should be part of the public space' (Modood 2010: 42). For the primary-aged Muslim participants in this study, their religious identity was a given, and conversely, they assumed that their peers and teachers, if White, must be Christian. Many accounts of their peers' behaviour were prefaced by comments such as 'There's this boy, he's a Christian . . .' and criticisms addressed to me were qualified by 'I don't mean to be rude about your religion, but . . .' although I had not declared any faith allegiance.

The experiences they described, and their appeals to teachers of the future, indicate their endorsement of the claim articulated by Modood above, in the 'public space' of education. In particular, they sought teachers' understanding of their needs in relation to three areas: Islamic requirements that intersect with school activities; participation in the practices of other religions; and the representation of Islam in Religious Education (RE).

Islamic requirements and school activities

Kumashiro's (2000) first form of 'anti-oppressive education' is education *for* the Other, which he describes as 'improving the experiences of students who are Othered' (26). Parker-Jenkins et al. (2017) explore the movement to achieve this aim through the provision of schools with a specifically Islamic ethos. However, the young participants in this study felt that there were several accommodations that would improve their experiences in their mainstream state primary schools. The chief concern for girls was about being able to dress and to change modestly for Physical Education and swimming. Ayesha explained: 'Up to age 7 you can mix with boys, but after that you can be in class with them but not, like, showing your body.' As a result of the changing room arrange-ments and PE uniform in some schools, girls felt embarrassed, caught in conflict between being a 'good' pupil and a 'good' Muslim. According to Aqdas: 'People had to hide under the tables to get changed – it's a multicultural school but we all had to hide.' Yasmin reported such constraints were a barrier to girls' participation in physical activities:

> In PE when it's Summer you have to wear shorts, and because Muslim girls are not allowed to show their legs, but they say you have to wear shorts not leggings, or else you can't take part – and in games you can wear a tracksuit but it's really hot so most Muslim girls in my school don't take part.
>
> (Yasmin)

At Yasmin's school, Muslim girls had become excluded from PE and games, which could have been avoided by a minor amendment to uniform (permitting leggings) and reorganisation of changing facilities. In another school, Ikram described how boys changed in one classroom, and girls in another with a female supervisor, which avoided the problem. Other girls reported being compelled to do swimming (they used the word 'forced' but did not mean physical force) but were not allowed to wear a costume that would meet Islamic requirements.

A topic of high importance to both boys and girls was the food provided for school dinners. Generally, those schools with a high proportion of Muslim pupils provided varied menus with alternatives to cater for the needs of individuals, such as halal meat (from animals slaughtered according to Islamic practices) and vegetarian options. However, the quantities of each were not always well-judged:

> They're unjust with us – they give us a small portion, and the Christians, they get a big portion of their food.
>
> (Farhat)

> Sometimes, when we order something like a jacket potato with cheese . . . the dinner ladies give [you] something completely different, like un-halal.
>
> (Wasim)

At a school with very few Muslims, Yasmin reported 'I end up most of the time getting a plate of salad with a little bun'.

A more contentious issue was the duty to fast [Sawm] during the hours of daylight in the month of Ramadan. Traditional teaching is that a young person should adopt the practice from the age of puberty, which for some may occur while still at primary school. Some children elected to try fasting for a limited period from the age of 10. Participants who had fasted reported differing responses from their school. According to Farhat, 'Our school forced you to eat lunch even though it was your choice [to fast]', whereas Wasim reported, 'We have these, like, break areas where you can eat your lunch and they [lunchtime supervisors] said to be quiet for the people who are fasting so you don't disturb them.'

Learning about other religions and Islam

The second aspect of anti-oppressive education proposed by Kumashiro (2000) is education *about* the Other. The debate over whether this policy stimulates empathy or exacerbates difference has raged for over 30 years, demonstrated in Barry Troyna's classic (1987) critique of multicultural education. All the Muslim study partici-pants were happy to learn about, and show respect for, the religions of others as long as they were not required to participate in practices that are forbidden in Islam. As Kouser put it: 'At assembly we had to sit through music and songs with instruments . . . some teachers said it's all right if you don't join in the singing, but our teacher made us sing, we had no choice.' In a multicultural city, school visits to different places of worship, cathedral, mosque, and temple, were common. Most students were happy to visit and learn but felt it wrong to join in the practices. Nasiba recalled: 'When we did Hinduism [and visited the temple] we had to bow to that statue, and we were told to eat the food they had given the idols.'

In all the primary schools attended by the participants, Islam was introduced in Religious Education by teachers who were not themselves Muslims. Some teachers were commended for trying to learn, but several children reported acts of disrespect committed, no doubt, through ignorance. These included handling a copy of the Qur'an (holy book) without performing the appropriate ablutions (Wudu); placing the Qur'an on the classroom floor; and showing a video depicting images of the Prophet of Islam. Wasim explained: 'We don't know what he looks like, so we're not allowed to draw pictures.' Some pupils were upset by denial of their expertise in their own religion. Umayyah reported that her teacher: 'tells us to show something [to the class] and then we do our Salaah [set prayers] and she says "You're doing it wrong" and she shouts at you, and she's not even a Muslim.'

Experiences of 'Othering'

Being 'Othered' according to Kumashiro (2000:25) means being 'marginalised, denigrated or violated in society' as a result of being identified with a particular group. The young people in the study described racist name-calling, bullying, others being 'mean', 'rude' or 'picking on' them in relation to their Muslim identity. Some participants were ambivalent about their responses to harassment:

> Wasim: Like, they're my friends, they're not saying it in a really bad way . . . Like they're making fun of how you say it, they're saying 'Muzzies' and stuff.
> Alison Davies: And how do you feel about that?
> Wasim: I feel a little bit, like, yeah, but I ignore it.

Two of the participants, however, had moved schools as a direct result of racist bullying. Zara said, 'At my old school, it was really bad, that's why I moved to [school name] . . . They used to say "Zara, you're a Muslim" and they used to be very rude . . . they said that you are brown, go back to your country.'

Islamophobia, or racism that is specifically directed towards Muslims (Richardson, 2009), has increased significantly since the London bombings of 2005, both nationally (Tell Mama 2015) and locally (Racial Equality Council data). The 2015 statutory duty of schools to promote 'fundamental British values' appears, in some cases, to foster racism rather than inclusion. The young participants of this study feel the impact.

> In my school, the only Muslims are me and my friend and it's quite hard coping with all of them because they say different things to us and we get upset . . . they say, "Why do you like cricket" and I say, "In Pakistan they play cricket" and then they said "But we are in England not Pakistan".
>
> (Umayyah)

> Some people in my class are, like, Christians, and they're like saying that every Muslim's a bomber and all that stuff, and I get really annoyed about it and then I tell my teacher but she never really does anything about it . . . so I told them there's two-billion Muslims in the world and if everyone was a bomber you wouldn't be here right now.
>
> (Yasmin)

> A lot of stuff goes round . . . social media comes into it a lot, because Muslims are always, like, judged in a way . . . like targets, and if anything happens it's always like Muslims had something to do with it.
>
> (Abid)

Others shared their frustration and bewilderment that they, as followers of a religion of peace, were 'targets' of suspicion and vilification relating to atrocities committed by those who perverted the teachings of Islam. They are the innocent victims of oppression seen as 'the repetition, throughout many levels of society, of harmful citational practices' (Kumashiro, 2000: 41).

Complexities of 'Othering'

Haniya was born and raised in the United Kingdom and comes from a long-established Muslim community in Britain. Her grandfather came to the UK in the late 1960s along with many of his community from rural Mirpur (Northeast Pakistan), when the land of his village was inundated during the construction of the Mangla Dam and reservoir. The small sum that he received in compensation for his land, his home and his livelihood paid for a one-way ticket to the UK. The small industrial city where he settled needed workers for its factories and brick pits. The government of the day provided additional funding to schools with a significant proportion of children from immigrant families;

until 2011, Haniya's home city used the funding to provide bilingual teaching assistants, multicultural education services and resources for teachers.

In an interview, Haniya described her initial response when a number of 'new' migrants from Eastern Europe joined her predominantly British Pakistani class in her primary school:

> We had certain students who were from Slovakia, and before we knew them we were, like, OK they're foreigners, we don't need to have any interaction with them, and they're, like, a bit lower than us you could say, but once we got to know them my viewpoint quite changed and it was like, OK they're human, they're like normal people, they just can't speak English very well or they're just from a different place.

As Haniya's account illustrates, 'Othering' is a shifting process; it is neither one-dimensional nor one-directional. Haniya positioned herself as a 'native' in relation to the Eastern European 'foreigners'. Her perception of the Slovakian 'Others' changed as she got to know them. But Sumaiya recounted a different encounter between 'Others':

> There was these two girls from my school, we met at the park and then they came and they ripped my brother's shirt out there and they go "I hate Pakis, we hate you" ... they were like Czech, because we know them, and we were like "Why d'you hate us, we're just like you, you've got a different background too".
>
> (Sumaiya)

Sumaiya hoped to appeal to a common experience of 'Otherness' but was disappointed. Perhaps the most hurtful experience expressed was that of being 'Othered' by those with whom you believe you 'belong'.

> In my school, when I first joined, in Year Two [age 7], loads of the Muslims in my class, they were saying I was Christian just because of my [fair] skin colour and what I looked like and I was like "You're being racist, stop saying that about me", and I got really upset, so I stopped talking to anyone – you know those people who don't want to talk to anyone, and if you try they just run away? That was me in Year Two.
>
> (Yasmin)

The transcript does not fully convey Yasmin's emotion as she relived a distressing experience from almost four years ago. The peer relationships were eventually restored after the intervention of a Muslim teacher who spoke to the class after she found Yasmin crying.

The role of adults and policy in school

Like the teacher in Yasmin's account, teachers (who, in the children's accounts include teaching assistants) were commended for intervening in incidents of racism and bullying and were criticised for ignoring such behaviour. Wasim felt that, at his school, teachers would only intervene: 'Sometimes, if it's a really bad thing – like, it's the end of lunch and when we get in the class we say, this happened, yeah, and then they say "You should have told the dinner ladies, I can't deal with it for you".' Zara described being physically hurt by a boy in her class at lunchtime, and finding support not from the teacher but from a dinner lady:

> Anyway, I was crying [following the incident] and I said I haven't eaten my lunch, and she [the teacher] said 'Sorry, there's nothing I can do about it, did it really happen?' [then] one of the dinner ladies saw me . . . and then I go and sit right next to her she said 'How did you hurt yourself?' and she deals with it and she actually went and spoke to that boy.
>
> (Zara)

One school was singled out because: 'Racism was taken really seriously – no one used to pick on people because they knew there would be consequences' (Sahdia).

Conclusion

The pupils of this study expressed their aspiration for 'Education that is critical of privileging and Othering' (Kumashiro 2000) but their evidence supports Parker-Jenkins et al.'s (2017) conclusion that much has to change in policy and staff training before this pedagogy is consistently practised. The participants recounted many more incidents of 'Othering' and school practices that made them, as young Muslims, feel excluded. Most of these practices could be addressed, they believed, by teachers being willing to learn about their religion, and by confronting the stereotypes that are unthinkingly grafted onto Muslim pupil identities both outside and inside school. Above all, they want their teachers to create safe spaces for dialogue, to listen and to develop shared understanding.

> A good teacher, that is not biased against anyone, then she's doing it herself, she's explaining that it's fine, that everyone is different and everyone is the same.
>
> (Kouser)

This chapter set out to make audible the voices of Muslim children as they try to express the ways in which they can be unnecessarily 'Othered' within liberal, secular, school cultures. These institutions may claim to be inclusive and egalitarian, yet they can leave the children of faith and traditional cultures feeling conflicted and estranged for the most superficial of reasons. The children recorded here ask only for simple changes to teaching practices and attitudes so that they can be both good pupils and good Muslims, fully included and contributing in both aspects of their identities.

Questions

1. What are your responses to the theory of anti-oppressive education *for* 'Others' and *about* 'Others'? Have you seen these ideas applied in practice?
2. Have you had experiences of 'Othering', as a learner or an education worker, or in some other context?
3. How can we educate *about* 'Others' without creating new stereotypes?

Further reading

Revell, L. (2012) *Islam and Education*. London: Trentham/Institute of Education.
Muslim Council of Britain (2007) Meeting the needs of Muslim pupils in state schools. [Available at www.muslimparents.org.uk/downloads/MCBSchoolGuidance.pdf.]

References

Cameron, D. (2011) Speech to Munich Security Conference Munich, 5 Feb. 2011.
Crozier, G. and Davies, J. (2008) The trouble is they don't mix: Self-segregation or enforced exclusion? *Race, Ethnicity & Education*, 11 (3), 285–301.
Davies, L. (2008) *Educating Against Extremism*. Stoke-on-Trent: Trentham.
Elton-Chalcraft, S., Lander, V., Revell, L., Warner, D. and Whitworth, L. (2016) To promote, or not to promote Fundamental British Values? Teachers' standards, diversity and teacher education. *British Educational Research Journal*, 43 (1), 29–48.
Kumashiro, K.K. (2000) Towards a theory of anti-oppressive education. *Review of Educational Research*, 70 (1), 25–53.
Kundnani, A. (2012) Radicalisation: The journey of a concept. *Race and Class*, 54 (2), 3–25.
Langsted, O. (1994) Looking at Quality from a Child's Perspective. In Moss, P. and Pence, A. (Eds), *Valuing Quality in Early Childhood Services*. London: Paul Chapman.
Modood, T. (2010) *Still Not Easy Being British*. Stoke-on-Trent: Trentham.
Parker-Jenkins, M., Francia, G. and Edling, S. (2017) Education for the Other: Policy and provision for Muslim children in the UK and Swedish education systems. *Compare: A Journal of Comparative and International Education*, 47 (2).
Revell, L. (2012) *Islam and Education*. London: Trentham/Institute of Education.
Richardson, J. (2009) 'Get shot of the lot of them': Election reporting of Muslims in British newspapers. *Patterns of Prejudice*, 43 (3–4), 355–377.
Shain, F. (2003) *The Schooling and Identity of Asian Girls*. Stoke-on-Trent: Trentham.
Tell Mama (2015) Annual Report. [Available at https://tellmamauk.org/geography-antimuslim-hatred-2015-tell-mama-annual-report, accessed 1 August 2017.]
Troyna, B. (1987) Beyond multiculturalism: Towards the enactment of anti-racist education in policy, provision and pedagogy. *Oxford Review of Education*, 13 (3), 307–320.

13 Is this the right school for my gender nonconforming child?

Graciela Slesaransky, Lisa Ruzzi,
Connie DiMedio and Jeanne Stanley

Introduction

Children who have nonconforming gender identities and expressions or who are lesbian, gay, bisexual, transgender or questioning/queer (LGBTQ) are common targets of bullying and harassment. In this chapter we hear the voices of a parent, a school principal, a school counsellor and a professional development consultant in the process of working together with teaching staff to welcome and integrate a gender nonconforming child into a neighbourhood primary (elementary) school in the United States. We include this chapter in *Learning and Teaching Around the World* for its unique collective and individual narratives and for its honest depiction of the conversations, decisions and concrete actions that are involved in embedding meaningful and sustainable inclusion. The authors document and reflect on the work done over five years to transform the school into a welcoming and inclusive place for gender nonconforming and transgender children.

The main voice of this chapter is the child's mother, who is also a teacher educator. At the time the author's son Martin was about to start elementary school in the United States, more than 40% of students who participated in a National School Climate Survey (Harris Interactive & Gay, Lesbian, and Straight Education Network [GLSEN] 2005) felt unsafe at school because of their gender expression and one-quarter (26%) of the students reported having been physically harassed during the previous year because of their gender expression. A survey of elementary school students (GLSEN & Harris Interactive 2012) found that only 42% of gender nonconforming students feel safe at school, compared to 62% of their gender conforming counterparts. Over one-third (35%) of the gender nonconforming students also indicated that they did not want to attend school because they felt afraid and unsafe. It is therefore not surprising that over half (56%) of the gender nonconforming students also experienced name-calling and bullying by other students in their schools in relation to their gender expressions.

Asking the question

When my son Martin was four and a half years old, I was paying very close attention to a conversation thread in an online community of parents raising children who have gender nonconformist interests and behaviors or who are transgender. The thread was about their children transitioning from preschool to elementary school. The parents had many questions, worries, and anxieties about their children's safety in elementary school. I knew that the parents' worries about their young children's safety and well-being were reasonable and justified. Martin had one and a half more years left at his preschool, yet I found myself already worrying about him transitioning into a new school.

At that time, my daughter was in second grade at our neighbourhood school. Thus far, it had been a great school for her and for us as a family. The school is well known for its caring and effective educators and administrators, academic excellence, extra-curricular activities, clean and well-equipped environment, and an atmosphere conducive to learning. But this time it was different. We needed to keep our son safe. I began to wonder if this school would be the right school for him. I needed to know if he would be physically and emotionally safe; feel welcomed, respected, and fully embraced; and be able to focus on learning.

I decided to meet with Lisa Ruzzi, the school guidance counsellor. At the meeting, I described my son to her, illustrating how he challenged our (and society's) understanding and expectations of what it means to be a boy through his attitudes, behaviors, and desires. I introduced and explained the term 'gender nonconformity', a term that I had learned only recently myself. I told Lisa that my husband, Phil, and I were learning a lot from, and with, our children, and that there were many things we still did not know and were uncertain about, but there were some we knew for sure. We knew that we loved and fully embraced our son the way he was, despite the criticisms we were getting from others not walking in our shoes, and that we needed a school that would be affirming and protective of Martin. I told Lisa how Phil and I were learning to become "facilitative parents"; that is, parents who strive to allow their children to express themselves in their own unique gender ways while helping them to adapt to a world that will not necessarily embrace that way of being (Ehrensaft 2007). I then asked the question: "Do you think that this school is the right school for my son?" I was not exactly sure what I was expecting from Lisa, but her response felt just right. She said, "We are not ready yet, but we will work together to make sure we are ready for him." When I arrived home, I posted on the online parent community: "Great initial step! I feel hopeful and optimistic." I later learned that Lisa's sentiments about that meeting were somewhat different from mine. This is how she recalls the meeting:

> I really can't remember the exact words Graciela used to describe Martin. What I clearly remember was my reaction—a bit of panic and worry, though I was very careful not to transmit to her my concerns. She described how, when Martin was very young, he identified both as a boy and as a girl. She spoke about how, since he was three years old, most of Martin's play would be considered "girls' play," such as princess dress-up; how he pretended to have long hair by wearing a blanket or a long-sleeved shirt on his head, and many other examples of her son's interests and activities. So many thoughts flashed through my mind . . . I thought about the teasing, bullying, teacher and parent reactions, and keeping Martin safe. I was also worried that I had no previous experience with situations like this. So, when Graciela

asked if we were prepared to have Martin attend our school, I knew we were not ready yet, but I saw no reason why we couldn't be, and I knew we had a responsibility to become the right school for Martin.

Lisa informed Connie, the principal, about our conversation. This is Connie's reflection and recollection:

When I learned that a student with gender nonconforming behaviors would be a first grader at our elementary school in a year and a half, I experienced a level of professional anxiety that was both challenging and frightening. What do I know about gender identity? Am I informed enough on the subject to be able to identify and provide the support that is needed for the student, the parents, and the staff? For 39 years in education, I worked with my colleagues on creating a school climate built on respecting, embracing, and celebrating the uniqueness of everyone in the school community. But this was new to me. I thought: I don't know enough to know what I don't know.

Collaborative planning

A year before Martin would leave his preschool, my husband Phil and I met with Connie and Lisa to plan for Martin's transition into elementary school. Connie recalls that meeting in the following way:

At our parent meeting, the counsellor and I had the pleasure of listening to both parents describe their love and support of their child "just the way he is." The parents talked about his interests and talents, his loving and kind personality, his experiences in his preschool and summer camps, and their life at home. Several times in the conversation, the mom reassured us that "we were all learning together."

At that meeting, Phil and I felt grateful for Connie's and Lisa's openness and readiness to start working with us to make this a successful experience for our son and our family. Looking back, Connie remembers thinking:

There was an opportunity to plan, collaborate, and reflect prior to his arrival. We were no longer talking about a label, but instead a wonderful child whom we would be welcoming to our school family.

We all agreed that effective professional development was a critical component in this process. In particular, the success of the initial training for school staff would be important to the success of our goals.

Staff development on gender nonconformity

Jeanne Stanley, then director of the Bryson Institute in Philadelphia, Pennsylvania, led the first professional development session for the school. The Bryson Institute was founded in 2003 to provide educational training to adults about the best practices for supporting LGBTQ youth. Jeanne recalled:

> In our experience, it was unheard-of for an elementary school to ask for assistance for transgender students. No elementary school had ever requested training specifically about gender nonconforming students. I was therefore very excited to provide professional development in an elementary school setting.

The initial three-hour training session was held in the school's library for 26 teachers, administrators, and school counsellors. The session consisted of both didactic and experiential learning. The attendees were informed at the outset that the training might stretch their understanding of gender, as they would be re-examining and, at times, relearning concepts around gender that they had likely been taught since infancy. The didactic portion gave the participants an opportunity to develop a shared language and to build comfort with the topic. To this end, 'sexual orientation' and 'sexual identity' were defined and differentiated from 'gender identity'. Gender concepts were then addressed, beginning with a brief overview of biological sex terminology (male, female, and intersex). Related but separate is gender identity, which is how individuals perceive themselves as male, female, somewhere in between, or as no gender at all. A brief activity asked participants to write down when they were first aware of their gender, which was then followed by a discussion; these components were used to help the school staff understand that individuals who question their gender identity have often done so from a young age but have frequently hidden their feelings for fear of being perceived as different or being rejected. Gender roles and gender expressions were addressed in interactive exercises, which helped the participants better understand the day-to-day ways that people consciously and unconsciously express their gender. The learning then became more personalised, with each participant completing a survey about the messages that they received around gender growing up and which they receive today.

The session then turned to specific strategies for supporting gender nonconforming and transgender students in their classes and during the school day. A key point included the question of when it is developmentally appropriate to introduce gender nonconforming and transgender identities in the classroom. Developmentally, children are aware of the concept of gender by the time they are toddlers. The topic needs to be addressed in an age-appropriate way but does not have to be ignored in elementary schools. For example, it is important to emphasise throughout elementary school that we all have similarities and differences in how we express our gender and that this gender expression may go against traditional gender roles and expectations. At the conclusion of the session, the group was reminded that it takes time to expand our understanding of gender, since traditional gender beliefs are so deeply ingrained in all of us. The participants were asked to be patient with themselves while they were relearning, and to continue to learn and grow through additional professional development opportunities on LGBTQ issues.

Our involvement as parents

During Martin's first week in the elementary school, my husband Phil and I met with his teacher and gave her a packet containing a letter (see Appendix 1 for an extract) that described his personality, interests, and behaviors and provided examples of what had worked for our family in responding to other students' comments, such as "Why does Martin like pink?" or "Why does he always play with girls?" In addition, the letter offered language we found helpful in explaining gender nonconformity to Martin, his sister, and other people in his life. When Martin was very young, we learned to explain gender nonconformity in simple, concrete, and easily understandable terms. We said that there were three different ways of being a boy—there were boys who liked boys' stuff, boys who liked boys' and girls' stuff, and boys who liked girls' stuff—and that all were okay ways of being a boy. Over time, we replaced "three ways" with "many ways" of being a boy or a girl; that is, "There are many ways of being a boy (or a girl), and all are okay ways of being a boy (or a girl)." The packet also contained two articles that educators have found useful in understanding and discussing gender and gender stereotyping with their students: "Good Morning, Boys and Girls" (Bigler 2005) and "Not True! Gender Doesn't Limit You!" (Moss 2007). Finally, it included a brochure titled "If You Are You Concerned With Your Child's Gender Behaviors: A Guide for Parents" (Children's National Medical Center, Outreach Program for Children With Gender-Variant Behaviors and Their Families 2003). In addition, because of my connection to the Welcoming Schools program (Human Rights Campaign Foundation 2010), an LGBTQ-inclusive, evidence-based approach for Kindergarten to Grade 5, I was able to refer school staff to online resources (www.welcomingschools.org).

Creating a learning community

The more involved the school became with supporting Martin, the more opportunities for authentic learning experiences were created in very organic and natural ways. Led by Lisa, a group of educators began to meet regularly to deepen their knowledge and understanding of gender nonconforming and transgender children and youth. This small learning community called themselves the Welcoming Schools Committee. The momentum created by the enthusiasm and engagement of the Welcoming Schools Committee resulted in the creation of a Welcoming Schools Committees in other schools. District administrators became involved and supported district-wide oversight and coordination of policies, procedures, and practices to support schools in becoming more affirming, welcoming, and safer for gender nonconforming, transgender, and LGBQ students, families, and educators. The work of the Welcoming Schools Committees resulted in some unexpected outcomes. For example, a few families who were thought to be headed by single parents began to attend school functions and meetings with their same-sex partners. In addition, a few faculty and staff disclosed that they were gay or lesbian.

Final reflections

Guidance counselor's reflection

I believe I need to be an advocate for those children who cannot be advocates for themselves. We have a responsibility in public schools to make safe places for children to learn and thrive, and to create environments where everyone is respected. Thinking back on this experience with Martin, which I consider to be one of the most challenging, thought-provoking experiences of my life, there are some suggestions I would make to school staff who may be helping and working with students who are gender nonconforming or transgender:

- *Don't be afraid to admit you have no knowledge or experience in helping children with a specific need, and don't let that fear get in the way of helping a child.*
- *Be honest. We were not ready for Martin at school, but plans were made for staff development, teacher placement, classroom arrangement, and classroom guidance lessons.*
- *Challenge yourself. Because I did not have knowledge about students who are gender nonconforming or transgender, I wanted to learn as much as I could about the topic. We began a small study group. Other members of the staff joined us to learn more.*
- *Staff development is a very important step. Teachers need to be given information and strategies to help them make the most of teachable moments; they need to feel supported in their efforts to help create welcoming learning environments. Specific strategies were developed that were not only put into use for Martin's classroom but also for the entire school setting, so that every child could benefit from them. Some strategies included changing teacher language to be inclusive not divisive (e.g., saying "Good morning, everyone" instead of "Good morning, boys and girls"), never dividing students according to gender, and giving teachers language with which to address bullying or comments that may lead to hurtful feelings. The needs of just one student were thus translated into a wave of advocacy for many.*
- *Recognise how the work you are doing now will help other children in the future. The time we invested in learning how to help Martin was an extraordinary help to us when our next student who was gender nonconforming or transgender walked through our doors. Know you are making a difference.*

Principal's reflection

We are now ready to transition Martin to the middle school and to have him share his many gifts with his new school community. Although he will continue to face challenges related to issues of gender conformity, Martin is graduating as a happy, loving, and capable child who he has grown in his individuality and confidence.

Professional development trainer's reflection

A young student and his family changed an entire school district for the better. I hold Martin's example as a reminder to this day of how change can occur by creating opportunities for personal and professional learning. Every employee in the district has participated in two years of trainings on supporting, affirming, and understanding the intersection of students' identities, including class, ability, ethnicity, gender, gender expression, race, religion, and sexual identity. It is amazing what one student can do for so many.

Parent's reflection

My son is finishing fifth grade. In his five years at the school, as far as we know, he was never called names, bullied, or harassed. We owe it to the leadership and commitment of Connie, the school principal, and the tireless stewardship of Lisa, the school counsellor. We owe it to the wonderful teachers and other school personnel who were open to learning with us. We owe it to the vision and support of the district superintendent and the many people who contributed to this successful work. But, just as important, we owe it to Martin. It was his own doing, with his gentle, funny, sensitive, thoughtful, and insightful ways, that he gained the heart and support of his peers and educators. By learning how to negotiate difficult situations and how not to take things personally, Martin was able to create his own safe space within this school. He gets along with many kids, and his small group of friends adore him and seek his company and friendship, so much so that this year, for the first time, he decided to run for student council—and he won! I can say clearly, loudly, and with confidence: this was the right elementary school for my son.

For a list of ways to answer children's and adults' questions about gender nonconformity and sexual orientation in a developmentally appropriate way, refer to Human Rights Campaign Foundation (2010).

Questions

1. Encouraging children to ask questions is part of being an effective teacher. How confident are you about responding to children's questions about gender?
2. Good teachers know they don't have all the answers. What steps would you take to provide effective and sensitive support to a child who is questioning her or his gender?
3. The authors believe that supporting and including Martin had a much wider impact beyond helping an individual child. Do you think this idea is applicable to other kinds of children in primary schools?
4. Are you comfortable with the advice to say "children" instead of "boys and girls"? Why or why not?

Further reading

Anti-Defamation League (2016) *Discussing Transgender and Gender Non-conforming Identity and Issues: Suggestions and Resources for K-12 Teachers.* New York: ADL.

García, A. M. and Slesaransky-Poe, G. (2010) The heteronormative classroom: Questioning and liberating practices. *The Teacher Educator,* 45 (4), 244–256.

Payne, E. and Smith, M. (2014) The Big Freak Out: Educator Fear in Response to the Presence of Transgender Elementary School Students. *Journal of Homosexuality,* 61 (3), 399–418.

The full text of this chapter is: Slesaransky, G., Ruzzzi, L., Dimedio, C. and Stanley, J. (2013) Is this the right elementary school for my gender nonconforming child? *Journal of LGBT Youth*, 10, 29–44.

References

Bigler, R.S. (2005) "Good morning, boys and girls": Simple greeting can promote discrimination in young children. *Teaching Tolerance Magazine*, No. 28. [Available at www.tolerance.org/magazine/number-28-fall2005/feature/good-morning-boys-and-girls.]

Children's National Medical Center, Outreach Program for Children With Gender Variant Behaviors and Their Families (2003) *If You are Concerned About Your Child's Gender Behaviors: A Guide for Parents*. Washington, DC: Children's National Medical Center. [Available at www.childrensnational.org/gendervariance Committee for Children.]

Ehrensaft, D. (2007) Raising girlyboys: A parent's perspective. *Studies in Gender and Sexuality*, 8 (3), 269–302.

Gay, Lesbian, and Straight Education Network and Harris Interactive (2012) Playgrounds and prejudice: Elementary school climate in the United States: A survey of students and teachers. New York: GLSEN. [Available at www. glsen.org/binary-data/GLSEN_ATTACHMENTS/ file/000/002/2027–1.pdf.]

Harris Interactive and Gay, Lesbian, and Straight Education Network (2005) From teasing to torment: School climate in America: A survey of students and teachers. New York: GLSEN. [Available at www.glsen.org/binarydata/GLSEN_ATTACHMENTS/file/499–1.pdf.]

Human Rights Campaign Foundation (2010) Welcoming Schools: An LGBT inclusive guide. [Available at www.welcomingschools.org/adminis trators/.]

Moss, P. (2007) Not true! Gender doesn't limit you! *Teaching Tolerance*, 32. Montgomery, AL. [Available at www.tolerance.org/magazine/fall-2007/not-true-gender-doesnt-limit-you.]

Slesaransky-Poe, G. and García, A. M. (2009). Boys with gender variant behaviors and interests: From theory to practice. *Sex Education*, 9 (2), 201–210.

APPENDIX: Extract from a letter to teachers

As you know, Martin is a very sweet and smart child, but he is not a typical boy. Martin prefers to do many things that are usually associated with girls, and he loves to play with girls. Though we support him and love him just the way he is, we are aware that his behavior and preferences may make him subject to teasing.

It would be great if Martin was not asked to play any gender-stereotypical roles. It works best for him when he is presented with choices and is allowed to select what he prefers.

Materials we've read suggest that it would be helpful if kids are not organised or recognised as "boys" or "girls" or even addressed as "boys and girls."

The language we've learned to use with Martin is that there are many different ways of being a boy or a girl. At home, we discuss that there are different kinds of boys (or girls): boys who like boys' stuff, boys who like boys' and girls' stuff, and boys who like girls' stuff. All three ways are right ways of being a boy (or a girl).

We also tell him that not everyone is aware of the fact that there are different ways of being a boy or a girl and that we have to help others learn about it. So, when someone says something that is not nice, it is not because they are trying to be mean but because they do not know about the different ways of being a boy or a girl.

It is important that he hears from the significant adults in his life that there is nothing wrong with him. Like with any bullying victim, it is important to let him know that he is not causing the problem by being who he is, and that it's not his fault!

If someone is teasing Martin or calling him names, it would help if you (or any other adult in charge) could say something along the lines of "That's not respectful" or "We don't talk like this to our friends"—like you would do if another child was being teased for other reasons. We would ask you to allow (and actually encourage) Martin to state in his own words how he feels about the incident and express himself loud and clear, feeling proud of himself. We found the language and phrases used in the enclosed curriculum "Not True! Gender Doesn't Limit You!" (Moss 2007) very appropriate.

We cannot stress enough how strongly we feel about Martin learning to speak up for himself. If he is being teased, we have been encouraging him to speak up, such as by telling them to stop, saying that his feelings are being hurt, etc. As he grows older, it is becoming easier for him to do. But sometimes he may need some extra help.

When someone may ask him why he likes to play with girls, why he likes to play as a girl, or why he likes pink, etc., we have been teaching him to respond that "anyone can play what they want/like to play" or that "there are no girls' colors or boys' colors; colors are just colors."

Furthermore, as we learned from another boy with gender-nonconforming behaviors and interests, when someone asked him, "Why do you play with that doll? Boys can't play with dolls," he responded: "Yes, they can! I am a boy, and I am playing with them!"

14 The challenges of realising inclusive education in South Africa

Dana Donohue and Juan Bornman

Introduction

In South Africa, up to 70% of children of school-going age with disabilities are out of school. Of those who do attend, most are still in separate, "special" schools for learners with disabilities. This situation prevails despite the push for the educational inclusion of learners with disabilities in South African education policy. Following the demise of apartheid, South Africa's new constitution included an explicit section on the rights of people with disabilities. Education White Paper 6 in 2001 outlined the government's policies for a single, undivided education system for all learners, including those with disabilities, in the hopes that inclusive education would provide ". . . a cornerstone of an integrated and caring society".

Many countries have struggled with bringing inclusive education policies into practice, and the authors explore barriers that hinder the implementation of inclusion policy in South Africa, specifically examining what they characterise as the "ambiguity–conflict" model of policy implementation.

School-level barriers to inclusion

Successful inclusion depends on the attitudes and actions of school principals (Zollers et al. 1999) and the investment of other school personnel as they create the school culture and have the ability to challenge or support inclusion (Ainscow 2002). Research has found that although teachers often report that they agree with the idea of inclusion, they actually believe that the needs of learners with disabilities are best met in separate classrooms (Campbell et al. 2003), particularly those learners with greater special needs and more severe disabilities (Scruggs and Mastropieri 1996). According to Bornman and Rose (2010: 7), "[a] general lack of support and resources, as well as the prevailing negative attitudes toward disability, all contribute to the general bewilderment in South African schools towards inclusion".

Contemporary teacher education in South Africa trains teachers how to accommodate diverse learners in a single classroom (Oswald and Swart 2011). This is in line with the social model of disability that views disability centrally as a social construct created by an ability-oriented environment. Disability, in this sense, sees the problem as located not in the individual, but in a societal, economic, political (and educational) system and culture that fail to meet the needs of these individuals (McEwan and Butler 2007). The social model is rooted firmly in the human rights paradigm, arguing for inclusion and the removal of all barriers that hinder full participation of individuals with disability. Before this model of disability was widely accepted, however, teachers in South Africa were trained to teach either general education or special education. These practices have produced many teachers without the necessary skills to teach learners with disabilities, and have resulted in attitudes regarding the separate education of learners with disabilities that are strongly embedded in the South African teaching culture (Ntombela 2011).

Support (e.g. special equipment; educational provisions and accommodations such as more time during assessments; a teacher's aide to help a learner with a specific disability; one-on-one instruction) is a necessary component of successful inclusive education practices as the needs of many learners with disabilities are beyond the basic services available in typical general education classes (Lomofsky and Lazarus 2001). Yet, research involving school principals in Gauteng, the richest and most resourced province of South Africa, revealed that most learners with disabilities received specialised support services either "seldom" or "never" (Nel et al. 2011: 49).

Cultural-level barriers to inclusion

Polat (2011: 57) suggests that resources and improved infrastructure are necessary but not sufficient for inclusion and that "[c]hanging attitudinal barriers among school professionals and in the wider community . . . is one of the essential aspects of making inclusive education happen in low-income countries". The meaningful participation of children and adults with disabilities in the school and the community is affected by the cultural attitudes and values of its citizens. If a community expresses disregard and prejudice towards people with disabilities, then discriminatory practices will continue to be propagated.

Cultural attitudes about the importance of educating children with disabilities can affect whether or not parents decide to send them to school. Groce (2004) found that in various developing countries around the world children with disabilities often do not attend school because it is thought that they cannot learn or will be disruptive to other learners.

Parents also consider the financial expenditures relating to education in South Africa. Since many schools charge tuition fees, it may not be economically feasible for parents to send their child with a disability to school, particularly if they have other children of school-going age whose prospects of bringing in some sort of income are much better than those of their disabled child. For young girls, some families prefer to spare the expense of school and instead benefit from lobola, a custom similar to a dowry, which a man pays to his fiancée's family.

In the KwaZulu-Natal province of South Africa, a study of teachers, parents, children and aid workers was undertaken to determine how these various parties perceived the extent to which inclusive education was being implemented in their communities

(Maher 2009). It was found that ostracism of learners with disabilities was perceived as a barrier by all participant groups. Teachers blamed negative societal attitudes toward disability for the stigmatisation of learners with disabilities within ordinary schools and considered this a justification for maintaining separate schools. Parents and children in this same study stated that learners may be safer in special schools for children with disabilities due to the intolerant attitudes of other children and school staff. In another study, caregivers of children with disabilities who lived in the Western Cape province of South Africa expressed similar fears concerning the mistreatment of their children in ordinary schools (Masasa et al. 2005), with 72% of the respondents stating that they believed their children with disabilities were better off in special schools.

Traditional views of disability are beliefs that have been handed down through generations (Maloni et al. 2010). In South Africa (Hosegood et al. 2007) and neighbouring Zimbabwe (Jackson and Mupedziswa 1988), the traditional perspective attributes disability to family sin, witchcraft and angered ancestors. These perspectives sometimes lead to the mothers of children with disabilities being shunned and blamed for their child's disability by their families and communities (Daudji et al. 2011; Department of Education 1995), and to families hoping for their child with a disability to be "cured" (Masasa et al. 2005: 43).

Policy-level barriers to inclusion

We argue that although there are many school-level and cultural barriers to inclusion, the major factor hindering the implementation of inclusive policy is the lack of clarity in policy. It is not clear whether this ambiguity is intentional, but it has undoubtedly led to inaction by the stakeholders involved. We support a top-down theoretical approach to policy implementation (Matland 1995) and argue that the primary means by which the divide between inclusive policy and practice ultimately will be closed is through the clarification of specifically how the relevant goals can be met, with parallel enforcement of policy by the South African Department of Education.

Top-down approaches stress the importance of policy clarity, as well as the control and direction by policy-makers to systematically implement policy. Bottom-up approaches, on the other hand, highlight the importance of understanding the perspectives and experiences of target groups and service deliverers (Matland 1995; Stofile 2008). We prefer a top-down approach for inclusive policy implementation due to the many differing attitudes that create a context where there is little consensus about best education practices for children with disabilities. Hence, we believe that clear policy mandates, together with enforcement of such mandates, will be the most effective means by which inclusive policy will be realised in South Africa. Effective and clear legislation has been a primary means by which other countries (e.g. the United States) have established and supported inclusive practices (Frankel et al. 2010). Although we recognise that policy mandates are not the ultimate solution to make significant and lasting change in South Africa, we feel that reducing the ambiguity in the existing policies (i.e. stating goals more overtly as well as defining strategies on how to achieve them) and strengthening the enforcement of such policies will promote the inclusion and participation of children with disabilities within the mainstream school system.

Policy implementation challenges

Education White Paper 6 includes six broad key strategies for establishing an inclusive education system: 1) the improvement of existing special schools and the conversion of some special schools to resource centres; 2) the mobilisation of nearly 300,000 children with disabilities who are of school-going age but not currently in school; 3) the conversion of some mainstream primary schools into full-service inclusive schools; 4) the orienta- tion of staff and administration in mainstream schools to the tenets and practices of inclusive education, as well as how to make early identifications of children who may have disabilities; 5) the establishment of district-based support teams to help support educators with the process of implementing inclusive practices; and 6) the implementation of a national advocacy campaign to orient South Africans to the ideas of inclusive education, and the inclusion and participation of people with disabilities in society (Department of Education 2001: 20–23). But these six strategies lack specificity and detail, and have little guidance on how to effectively implement this policy in practice.

Jansen (2001) suggests that some South African policies are enacted for their political symbolism rather than their practicality; thus, vague policies get passed but no one is held accountable for their implementation. For example, a chief complaint of education officials in the Eastern Cape province was that the Department of Education was not committed to the implementation of the inclusive policy and had tried to rele- gate their responsibilities to others (Stofile 2008). The same study found that school officials reported having received no support or funding from the Department of Edu- cation to help sustain any progress they had made in the implementation of some of the broad strategies of the White Paper.

According to Matland's (1995) ambiguity–conflict model of policy implementation, ambiguity in policy is the result of a lack of clarity in a policy document regarding the goals or the means by which such goals will be reached. When goals are not explicitly stated, there is uncertainty and misunderstanding about the purpose of policy. Research found that education officials in South Africa were unsure regarding the goals of inclusive education, with some officials reporting they were unclear about how ordinary and special schools would be transformed into schools more suitable for inclusive education (Stofile 2008). Other officials were confused about the parameters of barriers to learn- ing and exactly how these barriers would be addressed within inclusive schools (Wildeman and Nomdo 2007).

Even more ambiguous than goals, the means by which the policies within Education White Paper 6 will be realised are not explicitly stated. Added to a lack of funding, schools lack teachers who have the capacity and knowledge to instruct a diverse body of learners in a single classroom without considerably increasing their workload. Education White Paper 6 states that "[n]ew curriculum and assessment initiatives will be required to focus on the inclusion of the full range of diverse learning needs ... since curricula create the most significant barrier to learning and exclusion for many learners" (Department of Education 2001: 31–32). How teachers are expected to accomplish the task of tailoring the curriculum to suit each learner's particular needs and pace of learning is not detailed. Training programmes that educate teachers how to accommodate and teach learners with disabilities are generally a week or two long. Teachers report that although these brief training programmes are helpful, they are insufficient (Stofile 2008).

Matland's (1995) ambiguity–conflict model suggests that policy implementation is hindered by conflict stemming from differences in opinion between various stakeholders about how the policy will be executed. According to Matland (1995: 157), "[v]irtually all [policy theorists] have emphasised the importance of delegating policy to a sympathetic agency. Placing a policy in an agency where it conflicts with existing policies and goals leads to few resources, little support, and almost certain failure." This may be a contributing factor to the lack of progress in inclusive policy. Within the Department of Education, there are various sectors that compete for limited resources.

South Africa's inclusive education policy is therefore characterised by both high conflict and ambiguity. Matland (1995: 160, 168) terms high conflict, high ambiguity policies as "symbolic implementation" policies, which almost always are associated with non-implementation and failure. Symbolic policies tend to garner attention when they are first passed but ultimately do not come to light; this same pattern is observed in the implementation of inclusive policy in South Africa.

Policy into practice

The education of children with disabilities should not be a racial issue or a political topic. Rather, it should be a human rights concern (Hay and Beyers 2011), a sentiment to which the South African government agreed when it became a signatory to the United Nations Convention on the Rights of the Child, the United Nations Conventions on the Rights of People with Disabilities, and the Millennium Development Goals. The inclusive education of a diverse body of children – including those who are diverse in terms of disability, race, gender, religion, language and socioeconomic status – allows children who are different to become acquainted with one another and helps them to discover common ground. In fact, one of the first and foremost locations where attitudinal shifts toward people with disabilities can occur is in schools, where early attitudes are formed. By learning these life lessons in childhood, children can develop into adults who are more accepting of a diverse society, which is important when living in a country as diverse as South Africa. Moreover, Engelbrecht (1999) suggests that inclusion is the primary step forward in obtaining a just and equal society.

Inclusive policies are of little meaning and use unless they are implemented and enforced. As a top-down theoretical orientation to policy implementation suggests, progress can be made with inclusive policy in South Africa if procedures are clarified, directives are given, and the appropriate authorities assume responsibility and control for its implementation. Education White Paper 6 was a monumental step forward in respect of the rights of people with disabilities in South Africa, but the policy will remain purely symbolic until real initiative and deliberate action are taken.

Most children with disabilities in South Africa are still not taught in classrooms together with their typically developing peers. However, the inclusion of learners with disabilities into mainstream classrooms, and more generally, the inclusion of people with disabilities into society, is a human rights issue – a topic with which most South Africans are quite familiar in their struggle to overcome apartheid. There are many barriers to providing quality and inclusive education to learners with disabilities in South Africa. The situation is far from hopeless, though. Inevitably, obstacles to inclusion will thwart progress in both developing and developed countries. Fortunately, these obstacles are not insurmountable, and the more children with disabilities are included in education and elsewhere in their communities, the sooner they can become productive and contributing members of society, showcasing their unique talents just like everyone else.

Questions

1. Thinking of your own country's policy on educational inclusion, how far do you consider it to be "high ambiguity and high conflict", as the authors describe in South Africa? What are the sources of ambiguity and conflict?
2. Looking at the authors' arguments, what specific actions must a government take to ensure educational inclusion policy is concretised, in terms of:
   - Training
   - Funding
   - Directives and timetables
   - Information and advocacy.

Further reading

Grobbelaar-Du Plessis, I. and Grobler, C. (2013) South Africa. *African Disability Rights Yearbook*, 1, 307–340. [Available at www.pulp.up.ac.za/pdf/2013_07/2013_07.pdf.]
Ntombela, S. (2011). The progress of inclusive education in South Africa: Teachers' experiences in a selected district, KwaZulu-Natal. *Improving Schools*, 14 (1), 5–14.
Oswald, M. and Swart, E. (2011) Addressing South African pre-service teachers' sentiments, attitudes and concerns regarding inclusive education. *International Journal of Disability, Development and Education*, 58 (4), 389–403.
Sayed, Y. and Jansen, J.D. (Eds) (2001) *Implementing Education Policies: The South African Experience*. Cape Town: University of Cape Town.

The full text of this chapter is: Donohue, D. and Borman, J. (2014) The challenges of realizing inclusive education in South Africa. *South African Journal of Education*, 34 (2).

References

Ainscow, M. (2002) Using Research to Encourage the Development of Inclusive Practices. In Farrell, P. and Ainscow, M. (Eds). *Making Special Education Inclusive*. London: David Fulton.
Bornman, J. and Rose, J. (2010). *Believe that All Can Achieve: Increasing Classroom Participation in Learners with Special Support Needs*. Pretoria: Van Schaik.
Campbell, J., Gilmore, L. and Cuskelly, M. (2003) Changing student teachers' attitudes towards disability and inclusion. *Journal of Intellectual and Developmental Disability*, 28 (4), 369–379. [Available at http://eprints.qut.edu.au/4305/1/4305.pdf, accessed 27 February 2014.]
Daudji, A., Eby, S., Foo, T., Ladak, F., Sinclair, C., Landry, M.D., Moody, K. and Gibson, B.E. (2011) Perceptions of disability among south Asian immigrant mothers of children with disabilities in Canada: Implications for rehabilitation service delivery. *Disability and Rehabilitation*, 33 (6), 511–521.
Department of Education (1995) White paper on education and Training in a Democratic South Africa: First steps to developing a new system. *Government Gazette*, 357 (16312). Pretoria: Government Printer.

Department of Education (2001) White Paper 6: *Special Needs Education – Building an inclusive education and training system.* Pretoria: Department of Education. [Available at www.education. gov.za/LinkClick.aspx?fileticket=gVFccZLi%2FtI%3D&tabid=1 91&mid=484, accessed 26 February 2014.]

Engelbrecht, P. (1999) A Theoretical Framework for Inclusive Education. In Engelbrecht, P., Green, L., Naicker, S. and Engelbrecht L. (Eds), *Inclusive Education in Action in South Africa.* Pretoria: Van Schaik.

Frankel, E.B., Gold, S. and Ajodhia-Andrews, M.A. (2010) International preschool inclusion: Bridging the gap between vision and practice. *Young Exceptional Children,* 13 (5), 2–16.

Groce, N.E. (2004) Adolescents and youth with disability: Issues and challenges. *Asia Pacific Disability Rehabilitation Journal,* 15 (2), 13–32. [Available at http://eprints.ucl.ac.uk/15132/1/ 15132.pdf, accessed 27 February 2014.]

Hay, J. and Beyers, C. (2011) An analysis of the South African model of inclusive education with regard to social justice. *Africa Education Review,* 8 (2), 234–246.

Hosegood, V., Preston-Whyte, E., Busza, J., Moitse, S. and Timaeus, I.M. (2007) Revealing the full extent of households' experience of HIV and AIDS in rural South Africa. *Social Science & Medicine,* 65 (6), 1249–1259.

Jackson, H. and Mupedziswa, R. (1988). Disability and rehabilitation: Beliefs and attitudes among rural disabled people in a community based rehabilitation scheme in Zimbabwe. *Journal of Social Development in Africa,* 3 (1), 21–30. [Available at http://archive.lib.msu.edu/DMC/ African%20 Journals/pdfs/social%20development/vol3 no1/jsda003001005.pdf, accessed 27 February 2014.]

Jansen, J.D. (2001) Symbols of Change, Signals of Conflict. In Kraak, A. and Young, M. (Eds), *The Implementation of Education Policies, 1990–2000.* Pretoria: Human Sciences Research Council.

Lomofsky, L. and Lazarus, S. (2001) South Africa: First steps in the development of an inclusive education system. *Cambridge Journal of Education,* 31 (3), 303–317.

Maher, M. (2009) Information and advocacy: Forgotten components in the strategies for achieving inclusive education in South Africa? *Africa Education Review,* 6 (1), 19–36.

Maloni, P.K., Despres, E.R., Habbous, J., Primmer, A.R., Slatten, J.B., Gibson, B.E. and Landry, M.D. (2010) Perceptions of disability among mothers of children with disability in Bangladesh: Implications for rehabilitation service delivery. *Disability and Rehabilitation,* 32 (10), 845–854.

Masasa, R., Irwin-Carruthers, S. and Faure, M. (2005) Knowledge of, beliefs about and attitudes to disability: Implications for health professionals. *South African Family Practice,* 47 (7), 40–44.

Matland, R.E. (1995) Synthesizing the implementation literature: The ambiguity–conflict model of policy implementation. *Journal of Public Administration and Theory,* 5 (2), 145–174.

McEwan, C. and Butler, R. (2007) Disability and development: Different models, different places. *Geography Compass,* 1 (3), 448–466.

Nel, N., Muller, H. and Rheeders, E. (2011) Support services within inclusive education in Gauteng: The necessity and efficiency of support. *Mevlana International Journal of Education,* 1 (1), 38–53. [Available at http://mije.mevlana.edu.tr/archieve/issue_1_ 1/4-MIJE-11–03_volume_1_issue_1_ page_38_53.pdf, accessed 27 February 2014.]

Ntombela, S. (2011) The progress of inclusive education in South Africa: Teachers' experiences in a selected district, KwaZulu-Natal. *Improving Schools,* 14 (1), 5–14.

Oswald, M. and Swart, E. (2011) Addressing South African pre-service teachers' sentiments, attitudes and concerns regarding inclusive education. *International Journal of Disability, Development and Education,* 58 (4), 389–403.

Polat, F. (2011) Inclusion in education: A step towards social justice. *International Journal of Educational Development,* 31 (1), 50–58.

Scruggs, T.E. and Mastropieri, M.A. (1996) Teacher perceptions of mainstreaming/inclusion, 1958–1995: A research synthesis. *Exceptional Children,* 63 (1), 59–74.

Stofile, S.Y. (2008) Factors affecting the implementation of inclusive education policy: A case study in one province in South Africa. PhD thesis. Cape Town: University of the Western Cape. [Available at http://etd.uwc.ac.za/usrfiles/modules/ etd/docs/etd_gen8Srv25Nme4_7965_ 1269472515.pdf, accessed 3 March 2014.]

Wildeman, R.A. and Nomdo, C. (2007) Implementation of Inclusive Education: How far are we? Occasional Paper, Idasa Budget Information Service.

Zollers, N.J., Ramanathan, A.K. and Yu, M. (1999) The relationship between school culture and inclusion: How an inclusive culture supports inclusive education. *Qualitative Studies in Education,* 12 (2), 157–174.

15 The contradictions within universal education

Why 'education for all' is still exclusionary

John Parry and Jonathan Rix

Introduction

The 'World Conference on Education for All' held in Jomtien, Thailand in 1990 laid the foundations for the United Nations' commitment to developing universal education. Its Declaration and Framework for Action represented a comprehensive international commitment to develop access to high-quality basic education for every child. However, it did not encompass the principle that all children should learn together within inclusive schools (Kiuppis 2014). Consequently, in 1994 representatives of 92 governments and 25 international organisations formed the World Conference on Special Needs Education, held in Salamanca, Spain. They declared that 'schools should accommodate all children regardless of their physical, intellectual, social, linguistic or other conditions' (UNESCO 1994: 6).

The Salamanca statement and framework for action delivered a reminder that providing education for all children is 'not about "bums on seats", but about revisiting our conceptions about schooling and the purpose of education' (Miles and Singal 2010:12). However, in the two decades post-Salamanca there has been increasing pressure on the delivery of inclusive education for all within school systems that are entrenched in a competitive market environment and a regime of standards, benchmarks and accountability (Armstrong et al. 2011). This chapter explores some of the contradictions which have emerged in the United Kingdom, the United States and Norway. The authors examine the particular legacy of previous policies, practices and provision within each state, and review the development of education in each country in order to consider the wider constraints imposed by neoliberal educational ideology upon inclusive education. We include this chapter in *Learning and Teaching Around the World* for its examination of recurrent trends, contradictions and tensions in the development of inclusion within the Education for All agenda, and for its discussion of how widening participation in established education systems often simply reconstitutes the exclusion of those who are perpetually marginalised.

United Kingdom experiences

Since Jomtien and Salamanca there has been no significant shift towards universal inclusive education. Statistics from each of the four nations of the UK show that their mainstream systems continue to accommodate a consistent proportion of the pupil population within the special school sector.

In Scotland the numbers of pupils being placed outside the mainstream in units and special schools has remained relatively constant: 7,140 pupils in 2005 and 6,735 in 2016 (The Scottish Government 2017). Significantly this consistency of placements has occurred against a backdrop of a steadily declining total school population, from over 713,000 in 2005 to 684,415 in 2016 (The Scottish Government 2017).

The data from Northern Ireland and Wales indicates a similar picture. In Northern Ireland, the number of pupils placed in special schools was 4,598 in 2008/9 and in 2016/17 had risen to 5,400 pupils, with an additional 1,800 children being educated in learning support centres attached to primary and post-primary schools (Northern Ireland Statistics and Research Agency 2017). Whilst in Wales there has been a similar percentage of drop in the number of all school types (see Table 15.1).

In England a comparable situation is evident, with a stable level of special school provision (Figure 15.1 below) and a consistent number of pupils attending (Figure 15.2 below). In 2017, the general increase in the overall school population was matched by 4,400 more young people in special schools than in the previous year (DfE 2017).

The data suggest that 'education for all' in the UK has been interpreted along the established lines of 'mainstream' and 'special'. Although many mainstream schools have engaged with the process of developing inclusive pedagogy (Dyson and Gallannaugh 2007; Laluvein 2010) the context in which they have tried to provide high-quality education for all pupils has been less than supportive. For example, Florian and Black-Hawkins' research in Scottish primary schools highlighted that teachers attempting to practice inclusively were hindered by school policies such as setting by ability and rigid differentiation which segregated children whilst fragmenting the opportunities for collaborative learning (Florian and Black-Hawkins 2011).

A study carried out by the authors, looking at two UK schools ten years apart, identified similar evidence of shifting processes and practice undermining their initial intentions to develop inclusion (Parry et al. 2013). Originally, in one school pupils identified with 'complex special educational needs' were included in a wide range of lessons and year group activities with the rest of their peers despite the base for these

Table 15.1 Number of school types in Wales

Type of school	2011	2012	2013	2014	2015	2016	2017
Primary	1,435	1,412	1,374	1,357	1,330	1,310	1,287
Secondary	222	221	216	213	207	205	200
Special	43	43	42	42	39	39	39

Source: The Welsh Government 2017.

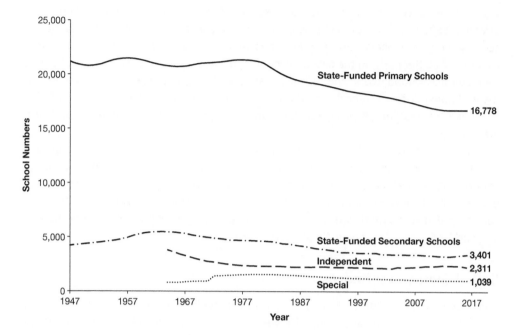

Figure 15.1 Total number of schools in England by type
Source: DFE 2017.

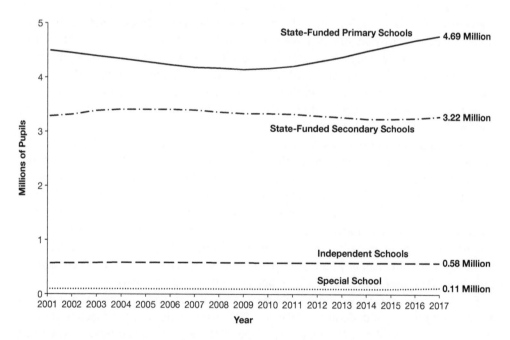

Figure 15.2 Total number of pupils attending schools
Source: DFE 2017.

students being separate from the main school. A decade later, such students only attended certain 'non-academic' lessons in the main school, and their opportunities to socialise with their peers during break times were restricted by the availability of staff to 'supervise'. Similarly, in the second school in the study, though a wide range of pupils were still accommodated in the provision, an identified group now spent more time in the Additional Support Department than in the main school. Their separation was also enhanced by Department being relocated to the basement of the school as part of a major rebuild.

Both schools attributed their increased use of separate provision for specific groups of pupils as a necessary response to a national agenda which required a focus on pupil performance and successful inspections. Such segregation became the template which both schools believed was necessary to work within in order to respond to children's educational needs but it was a template rooted in 'the institutional separation of 'regular' and 'special' schooling' (Slee 2008: 99).

United States experiences

Like many countries, the U. S. has increased expenditure on education for all and in particular upon special education. Between 1996 and 2005, 41% of all increased expenditure was on special education; and in 2017 when there was a cut in overall education expenditure special education saw an increase (Scull and Winkler 2011; Council for Exceptional Children 2017). However, familiar problems seem to remain. There has been a sustained policy development focused upon marketisation and standardisation, within a legislative framework entitled No Child Left Behind. But this would appear to have had little positive impact. In their reports on the impact of Charter Schools (U.S. schools freed from state control) the Center for Research on Education Outcomes at Stanford University (CREDO, 2009; 2013) demonstrated the lack of significant improvement and noted that any slight gains had to be set against Charters having fewer Special Education students and more focus upon the teaching of reading and mathematics (see Figure 15.3).

Standardisation approaches similarly seemed to recreate marginalisation in the name of learning for all and inclusion. Waitoller and Kozleski (2015) identified the pervasive notion of quality for all students, and how this is used to drive change, in particular through team curriculum-design, classroom observation and 'performativity' – a standardisation technology using public displays of data to judge, compare and control quality. In their study, schools used such tools as 'data walls', but the outcome was new forms of marginalisation. They demonstrated that although the intention was to move away from disability categories in discourse and practice, at meetings focused upon new data, new labels and sorting mechanisms for pupils emerged.

Evidence-based practice, another cornerstone of the standards agenda, would also seem to be problematic. Scull and Winkler (2011) speculate that approaches such as Response to Intervention (RTI) may play a role in decreasing numbers being identified with specific learning disabilities but they noted the lack of research to demonstrate the wider impact of RTI. Similarly, where some researchers feel there has been clear

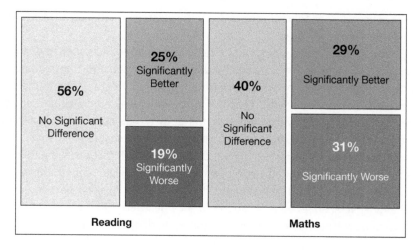

Figure 15.3 Academic attainment of Charter Schools pupils in reading and mathematics compared to local state-governed schools

research evidence the impact has been shown to be negligible. For example, McLesky and Waldron (2011) reviewed a range of practical approaches for students with learning disabilities, but noted their lack of use in either separate provision or the mainstream.

The U.S. experience suggests that the policies aiming to use the values of markets and standards do not create a new space but perpetuate the old divides between schools and within schools. They do not bring into question the old ways of working, but result in many children being left behind.

Norwegian experience[1]

Some countries have sought other ways to deal with special education. Norwegian Special Schools closed in 1993. They became advisory centers alongside the Pedagogical Psychological Service (PPS) which oversaw the assessment and funding of school provision for children with special educational needs. But this has not meant the end of segregation and separate provision. Officially, in 2010 'strengthened schools' provided segregated provision for about 0.3% of pupils, whilst 0.8% of mainstream pupils were in full-time special education and 7.6% were in part-time. However, an unknown amount of provision fell outside of official statistics. This picture does not capture the everyday classroom experience either.

The Norwegian Education Act 1998 gave all pupils the right to adapted education whilst maintaining that pupils had the right to special education if they did not, or were unable, to benefit satisfactorily from ordinary tuition. Despite many people seeing these two clauses as being in conflict, subsequent policies embedded the dichotomy. Interviewees suggested that the concepts and tensions between 'adaptive' and 'special' were formed from the 'legacy' of the previous policy context. This resulted in the belief that a young person with learning difficulties needed to be with his/her peers but, nevertheless, needed to learn something different from the rest of the class group.

The consequence was not only withdrawal from the classroom but also internal exclusion within the classroom.

The type and amount of support pupils received depended upon whether they were considered to be benefiting from 'normal' (adaptive) education. This 'normal' education seemed to emerge from a long tradition with a focus upon literacy and numeracy and 'some basic things from daily life'. Teachers questioned why pupils could not do what their peers were doing rather than whether the activity was appropriate for the class. Any deviation from the normal curriculum was regarded as 'special education'. 'Special education' became norm-referenced in relation to the pupil. It focused upon them rather than the learning environment and was often determined by guidance from the PPS.

Interviewees found it hard to delineate the practical difference between 'ordinary adaptive' and 'special adaptive' education but they believed that there was a difference and that some pupils needed the latter. The following diagram (Figure 15.4) was drawn for us:

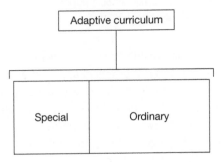

Figure 15.4 Adaptive curriculum, special or ordinary?

The research team was not able to form a clear picture of the difference. It appeared that all these concepts defined each other. However, it was equally evident that practitioners recognised their professional responsibilities and the moral force of national legislation. Interviewees explained that no teachers would question the policy or the theoretical concept of inclusion, but they seemed willing to live with the contradictions.

These policies were in turn set against the top-down pressure for schools to demonstrate higher grades in academic outcomes, as well as the previous policy contexts. Inclusion, it was suggested, had been initiated within a 'conservative' education system. Practice within this system had not changed or had only appeared to change before it reverted to previous practice. As a support teacher who had been working for two decades asked:

> *Why haven't we come further than this? . . . What is going on in the ordinary education is still the same.*

Many interviewees suggested that teaching in Norway 'used to be more or less a private thing for the teacher' that is, the teacher operated in isolation and without interference. There was a strong sense of teachers focused on good exam results rather than integrating children into their class. The longstanding response of teachers such as this one was that:

> *In general, teachers, when they face students with special needs or problems . . . don't really know how to look at the problem.*

Teachers wanted further resources to address problems. Teachers and schools became 'clever' at producing an administrative decision which resulted in special education provision and parents become very protective of their children's allocated hours of support. There seemed to be some awareness of the risks of focusing upon diagnoses and functional assessment but interviewees noted a deep respect for, and desire to listen to, 'expertise'. Many recognised that their understanding of what constituted expertise depended upon their professional training, but generally ordinary teachers were still dependent on special teachers and assessors to determine programs for pupils in their class. Frequently, they had an unease about who had responsibility for the pupil. But, perhaps ironically, support assistants working with children with special educational needs did not require any formal training and qualified teachers did not require additional training. They had the expertise of experience.

Conclusion

The issues identified above are representative of many countries (if not all) which have an established education system. The challenge of delivering inclusion in a system aiming at education for all is about 'a web of ideological positions, entrenched interests, and education and social policies' (Richardson and Powell 2011: 280), but also about the organisational location of its services and the everyday reality of mainstream provision.

It would seem that special needs education and universal education's need for 'special needs' are both reinforced and broadened by the widening of participation within schools. An unreconstituted education system, attempting to deliver education for more young people, inevitably pushes greater numbers to the margins. As a consequence, any call for Inclusive Education For All, as at Salamanca, has to be a call for the re-evaluation of our ideas about education and the systematic ways in which we deliver on those ideas. Otherwise, inclusion becomes inherently associated with Special Educational Needs. This creates a self-perpetuating cycle and undermines the chance of inclusive education achieving its educational and social reform agenda (Slee 2008). The wealth of literature which has emerged in recent years demonstrates that change needs to be system-wide, at all levels of education. It provides many ideas to enable such change, too. But despite these opportunities, separate and segregatory provision continues. The wider legacy of education seems to be the barrier. It is our reliance upon traditional ways of teaching using traditional subjects and assessment, focusing upon numeracy and literacy, within primary and secondary structures, which underlie an academic-vocational divide. It is about the bureaucratic need for funding streams, professional's processes of training, their established ways of working and their models of thinking. As one Norwegian practitioner so succinctly explained:

I guess it is a little of many things. It's got to do with workload. It's got to do with money. It has got to do with curriculum. And it also has got to do with attitudes, because people's attitudes are different . . . We are locked in and we don't have time to do this [share our competence] so, I have chosen to say it is a system problem.

(Rix et al. 2013: 145)

Questions

1. What do you think are the benefits and challenges of exploring policy and practice in other countries when you are reflecting upon experiences within your own national context?
2. In a setting or school that you know well, what tensions or issues have you been aware of between a range of policies and the development of inclusive practice? What progress made to resolving such tensions?

Further reading

Kiuppis, F. and Hausstätter, R. (Eds) *Inclusive Education Twenty Years after Salamanca*. New York: Peter Lang.

Rix, J. (2015) *Must Inclusion Be Special? Rethinking Educational Support within a Community of Provision*. London, Routledge.

This chapter was originally published as: Kiuppis, F. and Hausstätter, R. (Eds) (2014) *Inclusive Education Twenty Years after Salamanca*. New York: Peter Lang, but has been extensively adapted and updated.

Notes

1 This section is based upon research conducted in 2011 in 50 countries by the first author with colleagues from the Open University. As part of this research they conducted interviews, visited settings and explored the policy processes in Norway, Italy, Ireland and Japan (Rix et al. 2013). The underlying challenges to inclusion raised here in relation to Norway could equally be applied to these other countries.

References

Ainscow, M. and Sandill, A. (2010) Developing inclusive education systems: The role of organizational cultures and leadership. *International Journal of Inclusive Education*, 14 (4), 401–416.

Armstrong, D., Armstrong, A. and Spandagou, I. (2011) Inclusion: By choice or by chance? *International Journal of Inclusive Education*, 15 (1), 29–39.

Council for Exceptional Children (2017) Special Education Receives Slight Increase in FY 2017 Funding Bill. [Available at www.policyinsider.org/2017/05/special-education-receives-slight-increase-in-fy-2017-funding-bill-.html, accessed 29th August 2017.]

CREDO (Center for Research on Education Outcomes) (2009) *Multiple Choice: Charter School Performance in 16 States*. Palo Alto, CA: CREDO, Stanford University.

CREDO (2013) *National Charter School Study*. Palo Alto, CA: CREDO, Stanford University.

Department for Education (DfE) (2017) Schools Census – Schools Pupils and their characteristics – January 2017. [Available from www.gov.uk/government/uploads/system/uploads/ attachment_data/file/623124/SFR28_2017_Main_Text.pdf, accessed 23rd August 2017.]

Dyson, A. and Gallannaugh, F. (2007) National policy and the development of inclusive school practices: A case study. *Cambridge Journal of Education*, 37 (4), 473–488.

Florian, L. and Black-Hawkins, K. (2011) Exploring inclusive pedagogy. *British Educational Research Journal*, 37 (5), 813–828.

Kiuppis, F. (2014) Why (not) associate the principle of inclusion with disability? Tracing connections from the start of the 'Salamanca Process'. *International Journal of Inclusive Education*, 18 (7), 746–761.

Laluvein, J. (2010) School inclusion and the 'community of practice'. *International Journal of Inclusive Education*, 14 (1), 35–48.

Mcleskey, J. and Waldron, N.L. (2011) Learning Disabilities Practice Educational Programs for Elementary Students with Learning Disabilities: Can They Be Both Effective and Inclusive? *Exceptional Children*, 26 (1), 48–57.

Miles, S. and Singal, N. (2010) The Education for All and inclusive education debate: Conflict, contradiction or opportunity? *International Journal of Inclusive Education*, 14 (1), 1–15.

Naraian, S. (2011) Seeking transparency: The production of an inclusive classroom community. *International Journal of Inclusive Education*, 15 (9), 955–973.

Northern Ireland Statistics and Research Agency (2017) School enrolments – Overview [Available at www.education-ni.gov.uk/publications/school-enrolments-201617-statistical-bulletins, accessed August 22nd 2015.]

Parry, J., Rix, J., Sheehy, K. and Simmons, K. (2013) The Journey travelled: A view of two settings a decade apart. *British Journal of Educational Studies*. [Available at www.tandfonline.com/doi/full/10.1080/00071005.2013.819411.]

Richardson, J. and Powell, J. (2011) *Comparing Special Education: Origins to Contemporary Paradoxes*. Stanford, CA: Stanford University Press.

Rix, J., Sheehy, K., Fletcher-Campbell, F., Crisp, M. and Harper, A. (2013) *Continuum of Education Provision for Children with Special Educational Needs: Review of International Policies and Practices (Volumes 1 & 2)*. Trim, UK: National Council for Special Education.

Scull, B.J. and Winkler, A.M. (2011) Shifting Trends in Special Education. Ohio, OH: The Thomas B Fordham Institute.

Slee, R. (2008) Beyond special and regular schooling? An inclusive education reform agenda. *International Studies in Sociology of Education*, 18 (2), 99–116.

The Scottish Government (2017) Pupil Census 2016 supplementary data. [Available at www.gov.scot/Topics/Statistics/Browse/School-Education/dspupcensus/dspupcensus16, accessed 21 August 2017).

UNESCO. (1994) The Salamanca Statement and Framework for Action on Special Needs Education. Paris: UNESCO.

Waitoller, F. and Kozleski, E. (2015) No stone left unturned: Exploring the convergence of New Capitalism in inclusive education in the US. *Education Policy Analysis Archives/Archivos Analíticos de Políticas Educativas*, (23).

Welsh Government (2017) School Census Results. [Available at http://gov.wales/statistics-andresearch/schools-census/?lang=en, accessed 22 August 2017.]

Part 4
Teacher education and development

16 Defining 'teacher professionalism' from different perspectives

Nihan Demirkasımoğlu

Introduction

Is primary school teaching a profession? Or is it a quasi- or semi-professional role? What makes it different to other professions in terms of status and autonomy? In this chapter, the author discusses the concept of professionalism from different perspectives and how these definitions are associated with teaching.

The concept of professionalism has been controversial in different occupations. When the subject is teacher professionalism, the meaning of the term appears to change in response to external pressures and public discourses.

The concept of professionalism

The concept of professionalism can be somewhat difficult to define. For example, in daily language, it is generally used to mean an activity for which one is paid as opposed to doing voluntarily. The term is also used to classify the status of occupational groups in terms of respectability (Kennedy 2007). In the business world, professionalism is generally synonymous with success or refers to the expected behaviors of individuals in specific occupations (Tichenor and Tichenor 2005).

The need to develop and attain professional standards and benchmarking criteria for all professions has increased in global competitive work conditions. Standards can create a professional environment of best practice procedures enabling organisations to develop systems, policies and procedures; standards can also assure high operational quality (Krishnaveni and Anitha 2007).

The term "profession" has its etymological roots in Latin: professus, meaning to declare publicly. To be a professional (and in education, a professor) was to declare oneself to be an expert in some skill or field of knowledge (Baggini 2005). In 1975, Hoyle defined professionalism as "those strategies and rhetorics employed by members of an occupation in seeking to improve status, salary and conditions" (cited in Evans 2007). Later, Hoyle (2001) states that professionalism is related to the improvement in the quality of service rather than the enhancement of status. Boyt, Lusch and Naylor (2001) explain the concept as a multi-dimensional structure consisting of one's attitudes and behaviors towards his/her job and as the achievement of high-level standards. If we synthesise these definitions, it is possible to interpret professionalism as multi-dimensional, including one's work behaviors and attitudes to perform the highest standards and improve the service quality.

It is also useful to mention the distinction between the two terms "professionalism" and "professionalisation" which usually accompany each other in scholarly discourses. Professionalisation is related to "promoting the material and ideal interests of an occupational group" (Goodson 2000:182) and the attempt to gain status and influence associated with professions (Whitty 2000). Professionalism "focuses on the question of what qualifications and acquired capacities, what competence is required for the successful exercise of an occupation" (Englund 1996: 76).

David (2000) refers to five commonly cited professionalism criteria: (a) professions provide an important public service, (b) they involve a theoretically as well as practically grounded expertise, (c) they have a distinct ethical dimension which calls for expression in a code of practice, (d) they require organisation and regulation for purposes of recruitment and discipline and, (e) professional practitioners require a high degree of individual autonomy – independence of judgement – for effective practice.

Barber (1965) explains four main characteristics of professional behavior as follows: (a) a high degree of generalised and systematic knowledge, (b) orientation primarily to [professional] community interest rather than to individual self-interest, (c) a high degree of self-control of behavior through codes of ethics in the process of work socialisation and (d) a system of rewards seen primarily as symbols of work achievement.

Autonomy is one of the main features of professionalism. Forsyth and Danisiewicz (1985) state that the tasks of professionals are important, exclusive and complex, so professionals should have autonomous decision-making powers free from external pressures. Another author states that one of the major objectives and attractions of moves to professionalise teachers is to provide professional autonomy (Bull 1988).

It appears that the foci for defining and conceptualising the nature of professionalism are: "the respectability status of the occupation" (e.g. Hoyle 1975; Kennedy 2007), improvement of service quality (e.g. Hoyle 2001), "achievement of the highest standards" (e.g. Boyt et al. 2001), "self-control" (e.g. Barber 1965) and "professional autonomy" (e.g. Leiter 1978; Bull 1988; Johnson 1992; David 2000).

Teacher professionalism and professionalisation

Behind the debates about whether teaching is a professional or a semi-professional occupation, lies the question of whether teaching meets the criteria attributed to professional occupations. Traditional sociological approaches delineate key traits of a professional occupation, largely based upon law and medicine. According to this approach, while the classical occupations such as medicine and law are associated with high status and pay, other professions seek an opportunity to attain such rewards through a "professionalisation" process (Webb et al. 2004).

According to some academics, nursing and teaching are seen as "semi" or "quasi" professionals because they cannot wholly meet the criteria of professionalism commonly referred to in the literature (Etizioni, 1969; David, 2000). Likewise, Leiter (1978) states that occupations such as teaching and nursing may claim professional status but are not completely accorded this status because their individual autonomy is often under organ-isational control. More specifically, teachers are monitored by their administrators in terms of the consistency between their performance and the standards and targets set for them and for pupils. As a result of this, they are directed and shaped by the admin-istrators to achieve organisational goals, so their autonomy is restricted. Samuels (1970) supports these arguments, asserting that most school teachers do not have a high level of authority since the major decisions in educational settings are not taken by them.

Yet autonomy is, to greater or lesser extents, a component of teaching practice; autonomy can provide individual decision-making to achieve one's aims and an effect on controlling the situations related to one's work. Autonomy not only functions as a buffer against the pressures on teachers but is also a means of strengthening them in terms of personal and professional identity (Friedman, 1999). Consequently, autonomy can have an opposite function to organisational control (1978; Bull, 1988; Johnson, 1992).

Depending on the educational context, it is possible to say that definitions of teacher professionalism focus on teachers' professional qualifications such as "being good at his/her job", "fulfilling the highest standards", "and "achieving excellence". For example, Baggini (2005) claims that for today's teachers, professionalism is interpreted in terms how far teachers can overcome difficulties and to what extent they are able to use their skills and experiences related to their profession. On the most basic level, a "professional teacher" refers to the status of a person who is paid to teach; on a higher level, it can refer to teachers who represent the best in the profession and set the highest standards (Tichenor and Tichenor, 2005). Phelps believes professionalism is enhanced when teachers use excellence as a critical criterion for judging their actions and attitudes. In other words, professionalism is measured by the best and the highest standards (Phelps, 2006).

Two versions of teacher professionalism are portrayed in the literature: "old professionalism" and "new professionalism". These two views are not completely opposite to each other. Sachs (2003), who developed this classification, differentiates these two approaches: old professionalism is concerned with; (a) exclusive membership, (b) conservative practices, (c) self-interest, (d) external regulation, (e) slowness to change and (f) reactivity. The characteristics of new (transformative) professionalism are: (a) inclusive membership, (b) public ethical code of practice, (c) collaboration and collegiality, (d) activist orientation, (e) flexibility and progressivism, (f) responsiveness to change, (g) self-regulating, (h) policy-active, (i) enquiry-oriented, (j) knowledge building. New understandings of teacher professionalism provide professional space and conditions for teachers to take responsibility in their practices. Sachs calls this transition from old to new understanding as "transformative professionalism" (Sachs, 2003).

Hargreaves (2000) analyses the development of teacher professionalism as passing through four historical phases in many countries. The key features of these phases can be summarised as follows:

1. The pre-professional age: teaching was managerially demanding but technically simple, as teachers were only expected to carry out the directives of their knowledgeable superiors.
2. The age of autonomous professional: marked by a challenge to the singularity of teaching and the unquestioned traditions on which it is based. Autonomy became an important component of teaching and the principle that teachers had the right to choose the methods they thought best for their students. Also, teachers gained considerable pedagogical freedom.
3. The age of collegial profession: characterised by increasing efforts to create strong professional cultures of collaboration to develop common purpose, to cope with uncertainty and complexity and to respond to rapid changes and reforms.
4. The post-professional age: marked by a struggle between forces and groups intent on de-professionalising the work of teaching, and other forces and groups who are seeking to re-define teacher professionalism and professional learning in more positive and principled ways that are flexible, wide-ranging and inclusive in nature.

Hargreaves defines today's teacher professionalism as "postmodern professionalism" – a new era of polarised directions. In the one direction, professionalism is portrayed as an exciting broad social movement that protects and advances teachers' professionalism by enabling them to work effectively with groups and institutions beyond school; the opposite direction is characterised by moves to de-professionalise teachers who are under multiple pressures and intensified work demands (Hargreaves, 2000). Goodson (2000:182) claims that there is a considerable antipathy to teacher professionalisation, which is expressed in cost-cutting, entrenched education bureaucracies and in a range of business and corporate interests.

Ozga (1995:35) evaluates teacher professionalism in its historical and political context and interprets it as a device of professional control. Stevenson, Carter and Passy (2007) follow the same argument stating that "it is more useful to approach professionalism as an ideological construct that is neither static nor universal, but located in a particular socio-historical context and fashioned to represent and mobilise particular interests". According to Ozga and Lawn (1981), professionalism can operate "as a strategy for control of teachers manipulated by the State, while also being used by teachers to protect themselves"; additionally, Evans (2007) remarks that a common feature of new professionalism is a focus on practitioner control and proactivity that cuts both ways, pursued simultaneously by teachers themselves and external political forces.

The dominant discourses in the field of education indicate that teacher professionalism is associated with improving the quality and standards of teachers' work and their public image. "Teacher professionalism" means meeting certain standards in education and related to proficiency. However, the meaning of the term and status of 'teaching profession' is considered to be highly problematic and polarised. As Whitty states (2000), it is probably best to see the different positions as competing versions of the concept rather than seeking an essentialist definition.

Questions

1. In your country, are primary school teachers seen as professionals? Why or why not? How much autonomy do primary teachers have, and in what ways are they controlled by external forces?
2. What would make primary school teaching more "professionalised", in your view?
3. What is your own definition of a professional teacher?

Further reading

OECD (2016) *Supporting Teacher Professionalism: Insights from TALIS 2013*. Paris: OECD Publishing.
OECD (2016) *Teacher Professionalism, Teaching in Focus*, 14. Paris: OECD Publishing.

The full text of this chapter is: Demirkasımoğlu, N. (2010) Defining Teacher Professionalism from different perspectives. *Procedia Social and Behavioral Sciences*, 9, 2047–2051.

References

Baggini, J. (2005) What professionalism means for teachers today? *Education Review*, 18 (2), 5–11.
Barber, B. (1965) Some Problems in the Sociology of the Professions. In Lynn, K.S. (Ed.), *The Professions in America* (pp. 669–688). Boston, MA: Houghton Mifflin.
Boyt, T., Lusch, R.F. ve Naylor, G. (2001) The role of professionalism in determining job satisfaction in professional services: A study of marketing researchers. *Journal of Service Research*, 3 (4), 321–330.
Bull, B.L. (1988) The Nature of Teacher Autonomy. Revision of Paper Presented at the Annual Meeting of the American Educational Research. ERIC.
David, C. (2000) *Professionalism and Ethics in Teaching*. London: Taylor & Francis.
Englund, T. (1996) Are Professional Teachers a Good Thing? In Goodson, I.F. and Hargreaves, A. (Eds), *Teachers' Professional Lives*. London: Falmer Press.
Etzioni, A. (Ed.) (1969) *The Semi-Professions and their Organisation*. New York: Free Press.
Evans, L. (2007) Professionalism, professionality and development. *British Journal of Educational Studies*, 56 (1), 20–38.
Forsyth, P.B. and Danisiewicz, T.J. (1985) Toward a theory of professionalization. *Work and Occupations*, 121 (1), 59–76.
Friedman, I.A. (1999) Teacher-perceived work autonomy: The concept and its measurement. *Educational and Psychological Measurement*, 57–76.
Goodson, I.F. (2000) The principled professional. *Prospects*, 20 (2), 181–188.
Hargreaves, A. (2000) Four ages of professionalism and professional learning. *Teachers and Teaching: History and Practice*, 6 (2), 151–182.
Hoyle, E. (2001) Teaching: Prestige, status and esteem. *Educational Management Administration and Leadership*, 29 (2), 139–159.
Johnson, D.N. (1992) *Principal Vision, Environmental Robustness and the Teacher Sense of Autonomy at the High School*. ERIC.
Kennedy, A. (2007) Continuing professional development (CPD) policy and the discourse of teacher professionalism in Scotland. *Research Papers in Education*, 22 (1), 95–111.
Leiter, J. (1978) *The Effects of School Control Structures on Teacher Perceptions of Autonomy*. ERIC.
Krishnaveni, R. and Anitha, J. (2007) Educators' professional characteristics. *Quality Assurance in Education*, 15 (2), 149–161.
Ozga, J. (1995) Deskilling a profession: Professionalism, deprofessionalism and the new managerialism. In Busher, H. & Saran, R. (Eds) Managing Teachers as Professionals in Schools. London: Kogan Page.
Ozga, J. and Lawn, M. (1981) *Teachers, Professionalism and Class: A Study of Organised Teachers*. Hampshire: The Falmer Press.
Phelps, P.H. (2006) *The Three Rs of Professionalism*. Kappa Delta Pi Record.

Sachs, J. (2003) *The Activist Teaching Profession*. Buckingham, UK: Open University Press.

Samuels, J.J. (1970) Impingements on teacher autonomy. *Urban Education*, 5, 152–171.

Stevenson, H., Carter, B. and Passy, R. (2007) "New professionalism," workforce remodeling and the restructuring of teachers' work. *International Electronic Journal for Leadership in Learning*, 11 (18).

Tichenor, M.S. and Tichenor, J.M. (2005) *Understanding Teachers' Perspectives on Professionalism*. ERIC.

Webb, R., Vulliamy, G., Sarja, A., Kimonen, E. and Nevalainen, R. (2004) A comparative analysis of primary teacher professionalism in England and Finland. *Comparative Education*, 40 (1), 83–107.

Whitty, G. (2000) Teacher professionalism in new times. *Journal of In-Service Education*, 26 (2), 281–295.

17 Developing inclusive learning environments in rural classrooms in India

Freda Wolfenden

Introduction

The focus of this chapter is India, one of the world's largest educational systems. Since 2001 the government Sarva Siksha Abhiyan (SSA) programme has been working to improve access to quality schooling for all pupils; the number of children of primary school age out of school had dropped from 19 million to 2.8 million by 2013 (UIS). This is impressive, but the expansion has not benefited all pupils. For many pupils, particularly those in rural areas and from marginalised groups, school is not a productive experience and recent data indicate only half of pupils learn basic language, literacy and numeracy skills during their primary schooling (ASER 2016). This chapter analyses understandings of 'inclusion' in Indian education policy and reasons for the current disparity between policy aspirations and classroom practice.

This chapter also explores how TESS-India OER ('open educational resources' which are free to download, reproduce, adapt and modify) attempt to address this policy-practice gap and guide teachers towards more inclusive pedagogic practices (www.tessindia.edu.in). See Chapter 19 for a discussion of how other OER are used in Kenya for teacher development.

Universal school education in India: the current situation

The project of universal education in India is immense; in 2017 approximately one in every five children was born in India. But provision of formal education as a fundamental right was enshrined in Indian law only relatively recently. The Right to Education Act (GoI 2009) commits the state to provide free education for *all* children aged 6–14 based on principles of non-discrimination and equity. This Act, and the SSA programme charged with its implementation, have prompted an expansion in the number of primary schools and pupil enrolment, including a substantial growth in the enrolment of children with disabilities in multiple education settings – mainstream schools, alternative and home settings (NUEPA 2016). But behind these encouraging headlines the situation is far from equitable, with widely differing educational outcomes for children from different social groups. At least 20% of children do not complete the first five grades of primary school (UIS 2013) and irregular or sporadic school attendance is a 'huge phenomena' (UNESCO 2016: 12). A critical factor is the quality of classroom interactions: for many pupils, classrooms are dispiriting places with low learning levels and pedagogic inequality.

Recent qualitative studies of education practices in Indian schools (Ramachandran and Naorem 2013; HRW 2014) reveal multiple forms of classroom discrimination based on caste, tribe, religion, poverty, gender and disability: children from different communities are often asked to sit separately; children from Scheduled Tribes (ST) and Scheduled Castes (SC)[1] are often referred to in derogatory terms and unlikely to be considered for leadership roles in their classes; ST and SC girls, and less frequently their male peers, are often required to undertake cleaning duties around the school. The free midday meal – offered to all children in elementary schooling – is a particular site of discrimination with reports of differential access to the water pump and eating utensils (HRW 2014). Many teachers are observed to be insensitive to issues of social inclusion and equity and to make overt assumptions about the 'educability' of children from deprived social groups which are not substantiated by pupil achievement data (Ramachandran and Naorem 2013). The SSA framework directs authorities to ensure participation in education for all children but, regardless of location, children with disabilities are frequently absent and show particularly low learning gains for each year of school attendance (Singal 2016). Too frequently these children are excluded from meaningful participation in learning within the classroom and this leads to non-attendance as they come to understand how little is possible for them within the classroom. Complete withdrawal from school often follows.

The large-scale TESS-India initiative aims to disrupt such practices, to guide teachers to create more inclusive classrooms through modelling ways in which their pedagogy can become more participatory, making opportunities for productive learning *available to all* the children in their care in line with policy aspirations (Wolfenden 2015). The tools for supporting such a shift are text and video OER, collaboratively created by Indian and global experts (www.tessindia.edu.in).

The Indian education policy context: equity and pedagogy

The study of children, their care and education and the legacy of 'child centredness' date back 2,500 years in India: Charaka, a Hindu scholar from the 6–5th Century BCE, advocated play-based learning. This child-centred philosophy can be seen to continue in the writings of Indian scholars such as Tagore and Ghandi, and in recent policy.

Historically, formal education in India has been directed to the needs of upper caste male children and large social groups – most females, SC and ST children and people with disabilities were denied access to education opportunities. This elitist focus was preserved under British rule (1700s–1947) although the latter part of this period saw increased participation in formal learning by children from other castes and attempts to introduce free and compulsory education by both colonial rulers such as Lord Curzon, and nationalist leaders; Indian philosopher Sri Aurobindo proposed a *National System of Education* (1910) in which the teacher was to use his skill to guide the child appropriately (NCEE 2005). Such efforts focused mainly on boys; in 1900 there were a mere 12 girls for every 100 boys in primary education (GoI 1966).

By Independence in 1947, around 30% of children (mainly boys) had the opportunity to enrol in primary school (GoI 1966) and the new Indian Constitution made a com-mitment to free and universal primary education for girls and boys aged 6–14. This commitment was reinforced by the influential and forward-looking Kothari Commission (1964–66): 'free education up to the age of 14 for *all* children irrespective of caste, creed, community, religion, economic conditions or social status' (GoI 1966: 15). Reflecting the contemporary dominant socialist paradigm, the report sees the child, school and society as interdependent, with the child learning to become a productive citizen through the site of the school. It emphasises the education of girls, not only on grounds of social justice, but because it 'accelerates social transformation' (xiv) and similarly recommends programmes and teacher training to enable 'the handi-capped child to study in regular schools' (207). The Indian child-centred tradition is visible in the advocacy of play, creativity and active 'discovery of knowledge' in the classroom (26).

A more explicit 'child-centred' approach emerged in policies of the late 1980s / early 1990s reflecting global trends and the growth of an international neoliberal agenda. The National Policy on Education (NPE) 1986/1992 continued to view universal education as a powerful tool to move away from discriminations of the past but moved to a much greater focus on the needs of the individual distinct from those of society (Menon and Banerjee 2018). This prompted, for example, initiatives to encourage girls from socially deprived groups to attend school – conditional cash transfers, girls boarding schools and bikes for girls – within a framework which emphasises women's productive and reproductive roles. The provision of integrated education enjoyed a high visibility, encouraging shifts in attitudes towards the presence of children with disabilities in classrooms (Sharma and Das 2015).

Children are seen as active explorers of their surroundings in NPE 1986; self-directed and intrinsically motivated to understand their environment in line with Piagetian theorising. However, this conceptualisation of the child as individually distinct is in tension with prevalent notions of normative development stages of learning – minimum levels of learning specific to each stage of education which all children are expected to master.

Most recently policy (NCF 2005) outlines how the child learns and therefore how teaching should take place. Children are now placed in the context of their community but the fundamental conception of the learning child remains Piagetian, she is positioned as creative and knowledgeable, 'leading' her own learning drawing on her natural instincts to learn and explore. Teachers are encouraged to make connections between formal school knowledge and wider experiences, suggesting a broadening of what is valued as knowledge. However, the critical interrogation of local knowledge implicit in earlier policy is not mentioned nor is there any acknowledgement that local knowledge 'may contain within it biases against others' (Menon and Banerjee 2018: 222).

NCF 2005 strengthens attention on inequality in the classroom through advocating teachers' choices of learning tasks and pedagogic practices, so that classrooms are safe and welcoming for all children and all can participate. This desire to respond to the individual child's interests continues to sit uneasily with a conception of quality based on assuring similar minimum learning levels for all and the ways in which social constructions of gender, caste and disability restrict individual's ability to be agentive.

The teacher as the agent of change

The teacher's role, as articulated through policy, is to guide and facilitate individual learning pathways without determining them; acting with authority but not in the role of authoritarian – the 'humane teacher' (NCFTE 2009). The teacher is positioned as a reflective, empowered, professional who enables productive learning through bridging the gaps of caste, gender and socio-economic status; she is an agent of social transformation.

But despite policy advocacy and textbooks which include ideas such as dialogic enquiry and active learning, there is little evidence that teachers have taken up these pedagogic ideas in their classrooms. Rote learning and an emphasis on examinations and tests continue to be ubiquitous across India. Many teachers perceive their role to be limited to delivery of the prescribed content of the textbook and ignore the languages and cultures that children bring to school (GoI, 2012).

There are multiple reasons for this disconnect between policy ideals and classroom practice – lack of resources, absence of appropriate teacher training and overcrowded classrooms – but a key factor is how policy is understood and interpreted by schools. Policy is taken up by schools in ways which reflect each school's political, economic and social situation, including the attitudes and expectations of teachers, parents and the local community. Consequently, opportunities for teachers to practise in specific ways, what it is possible to be and do, are mediated by the prevalent practices in the school.

TESS-India OER (www.tessindia.edu.in) address this policy and practice disconnect by modelling for teachers ways of transacting participatory pedagogy in classrooms through exemplar activities from the pupil curriculum. The OER are not a set of scripts for teachers to follow instrumentally but instead offer teachers ideas for ways to move towards a different type of relationship with their learners. A key aim is to encourage teachers to attend to their pupils' thinking by scaffolding a process of interpreting their pupils' understanding and making decisions on how to respond to what pupils say, ask, write or do. Through the activities, case studies and videos the OER extend teachers' views of what is possible pedagogically in their classrooms. The OER offer a socially mediated version of the constructivist pedagogy of policy.

The OER challenge explicit stratification of pupils, valuing difference over age, achievement or background, thus teachers are encouraged to respect the language of each child and use it as a resource for linguistic and cognitive growth – language is frequently a factor of exclusion for ST children.

Alongside activities each text OER includes case studies of teachers undertaking similar tasks and the actions they take in response to pupils and problems in their classrooms, and prompts to encourage the teacher to reflect purposively on observations of their pupils. These reflections are at the heart of the OER and most productive for teachers when discussed with peers. Fifty-five short videos show teachers trying out learner-centred, participatory approaches from the OER in authentic classroom contexts in Utter Pradesh and Madhya Pradesh. They include examples of teachers integrating ST / SC pupils and pupils with disabilities into classroom activities and legitimising use of dialects and other languages. The videos do not present perfect or unproblematic lessons but, like the text OER, they aim to inspire teachers to experiment in their classrooms and to provoke conversation amongst teachers. They bridge new and old understandings of practice:

> We started with that video [story telling] because they [teachers} were familiar with that because right from the beginning in India you know it's an ancient way of teaching – those grandmothers and grandfathers they used to in the night time ... sit with their grandchildren and do oral stories and through that they used to teach them value[s] education. Now the same thing it was beautifully shown ... how story-telling can help in the classroom teaching ... value education, plus content, plus language.
>
> Teacher Educator, Madhya Pradesh, February 2017

Each video has a contextualised commentary[2] focusing on how *pupil learning* is being enabled, modelling how to 'notice' aspects of pupil learning that require formative action.

Learning to foster participation: Observations from a rural classroom

TESS-India OER are being used in multiple ways in response to specific needs. In Dhenkanal district, Odisha teacher educators are mentoring teachers to include activities and ideas from the OER in their lesson plans. Teachers access the OER (in Odia, the state language) through hard copies in their school and a micro-SD card in their personal mobile phone. Encouraged by the video classroom scenes and guided by the OER, teachers are trying out different ways of organising pupils in small groups and pairs, stimulating pupil talk and utilising local resources. Their children are observed to be happy, relaxed and engaged as they move on a mutual journey with their teacher towards more productive learning experiences, as this example illustrates:

> Binolini is in her fifth year of teaching in a rural primary school. Her class VII has 35 pupils, 31 pupils were present in the observed lesson: 21 boys and 10 girls including one boy with a physical disability. At the start of a science lesson, seating was by gender with the girls grouped down one side of the classroom. Furnishings were sparse with a desk and chair for the teacher, a few posters on one wall and a chalkboard; children sat on the floor. Binolini began the Ecology topic by telling a story; by connecting subject knowledge to activity outside the

school she hoped to help pupils see the purpose and relevance of their study. Then, using a technique she observed in the TESS-India video, she attempted to involve all children by using randomly generated groups of mixed gender. Each group was given a variety of vegetable products to identify and categorise before generating lists of produce from different environments; Binolini hoped to find out what her pupils knew and set the scene for the learning of a new topic. She moved around the groups, talking to pupils by name and gently prompting children to contribute to the lists. Later the groups shared their lists, taking it in turns to write on the board. Pupils were encouraged to ask questions of the other groups and to comment and correct each other's lists as they copied them – they did this a little hesitantly. Binolini then moved to an exposition on cycles in nature, using a handmade poster as a teaching aide and pupils were subsequently grouped into pairs to discuss and complete a closed written task on the cycles. Binolini's use of pair work is relatively recent but through this, and the group work, she hopes to encourage pupils to share their ideas, understand each other's points of view and then to draw on this shared knowledge in their writing.

In a discussion after the lesson Binolini described how she is feeling more confident about teaching in a more interactive way and enabling pupil dialogue: 'students are asking different type[s] of questions to me, so that is a direct inter-action between teacher and student'. Although the noise generated by pupils' talk sometimes concerns her, she is encouraged by her pupils' positive response, describing them as 'much friendlier and freer'. Binolini talked about how working with the OER had encouraged her to get to know her pupils, their views and experi-ences and the support they needed. Through observing them in group and pair work she identified those students who were not comfortable with working with their peers and supported them to integrate into the class.

Binolini is a caring teacher who through engagement with the OER activities is moving from a behaviourist to a broadly constructivist approach in her teaching. Her observations and actions currently focus on visible participation of all her pupils rather than listening explicitly for how pupils are developing knowledge and understanding during the lesson. She is focused on enabling her pupils to develop relationships, interact productively with each other and become more confident in these new ways of being in the classroom, recognising that they have the capacity to actively construct knowledge.

Conclusion

As this chapter has illustrated, transformation of Indian classrooms to make oppor-tunities for productive learning available to all pupils is a considerable task. Historic practices of exclusion based on caste, gender and disability are deeply embedded in schools and communities and reflected in the observed behaviour and attitude of many teachers. Current policy recognises the challenges but locates the problems within the classroom, tasking teachers with playing a central role as agents of change. This requires both sophisticated pedagogic skills, and motivation and momentum for change on the part of teachers. It can be difficult for teachers to start to challenge embedded practices and notions of socially differentiated and gendered expectations of children, particularly in rural areas. The TESS-India OER offer one possible tool for change; through offering authentic examples from similar rural classrooms teachers develop their understanding of what it means 'to guide learning' in a participatory and inclusive manner. The OER mediate policy and challenge teachers to consider the experiences of individual pupils and how they are situated in relation to structures of inequality around caste, gender, poverty and disability, to shift pedagogy towards quality education.

Questions

1. What is your own view of children as learners: are they individual explorers or are they shaped by normative stages of learning? How does your country's education policy describe children as learners?
2. How far can teachers be responsible for inclusion when structural inequalities flourish outside the classroom? Is it possible to have an inclusive classroom when powerful external exclusionary forces are embedded?
3. Teachers are often positioned as crucial actors in education reform. What specific challenges might teachers face in this role, especially in low-resource rural settings such as Dhenkanal?

Further reading

Agnihotri, R.K. (2014) Multilinguality, education and harmony. *International Journal of Multilingualism*, 11 (3), 364–379.

Smail, A. (2014) Rediscovering the teacher within Indian child-centred pedagogy: Implications for the global Child-Centred approach. *Compare: A Journal of Comparative and International Education*, 44 (4), 613–633.

Sriprakash, A. (2010) Child-Centred Education and the Promise of Democratic Learning: Pedagogic Messages in Rural Indian Primary Schools. *International Journal of Educational Development*, 30 (3), 297–304.

Notes

1   Scheduled Castes (SC) and Scheduled Tribes (ST) are legal categories in India who are eligible for quotas in education and government jobs.
2   TESS-India OER (text and video) have been adapted into 6 different language versions. www.youtube.com/channel/UCL9j8y4mGFyIQLvH-PvkghA

References

ASER (2016) *Annual Status of Education Report (Rural)*. New Delhi: Aser Centre.

Government of India (GoI) (1966) *Report of the Education Commission (1964–66)*. New Delhi: Ministry of Human Resource Development.

Government of India (GoI) (2009) The Right of Children to Free and Compulsory Education Act. New Delhi: Gazette of India, Government of India. [Available at http://mhrd.gov.in/sites/upload_files/mhrd/files/upload_document/RTI1.pdf.]

Government of India (GoI) (2012) *Vision of Teacher Education in India: Quality and Regulatory Perspective, Report of the High Powered Commission on Teacher Education Constituted by the Hon'ble Supreme Court of India, Vol. 1*. New Delhi: Ministry of Human Resource Development.

Human Rights Watch (HRW) (2014) *They Say We're Dirty. Denying an Education to India's Marginalised*. USA: Human Rights Watch.

Menon, S. and Banerjee, R. (2018) Construction of children. In Saraswathi, T.S., Menon, S. and Madan, A. (Eds) *Childhoods in India: Traditions, Trends and Transformations*. Abingdon, UK: Routledge.

National Centre on Education and the Economy (NCEE) (2005) *India Education Report*. Washington DC: NCEE.

National Council for Education Research and Training (NCERT) (2005) *National Curricular Framework*. New Delhi: NCERT.

National Curriculum Framework for Teacher Education (NCFTE) (2009) *Towards Preparing Professional and Humane Teacher*. New Delhi: National Council for Teacher Education.

National University of Educational Planning and Administration (NUEPA) (2016) *School Education in India: U-DISE 2015–16*. New Delhi: NUEPA.

Ramachandran, V. and Naorem, T. (2013) What It Means To Be a Dalit or Tribal Child in our Schools. A Synthesis of a Six-State Qualitative Study. *Economic & Political Weekly*, XLVIII (44), 43–52.

Sharma, U. and Das, A. (2015) Inclusive education in India: Past, present and future. *Support for Learning*, 30 (1), 55–68.

Singal, N. (2016) Education of children with disabilities in India and Pakistan: Critical analysis of developments in the last 15 years. *Prospects*, 46, 171–183.

UNESCO Institute of Statistics (2016) A pilot Study of Estimating out of School Children in India. New Delhi: UNESCO.

UIS (UNESCO Institute of Statistics) (2013) Database. [Available at http://data.uis.unesco.org, accessed 31 December 2017.]

Wolfenden, F. (2015) TESS-India OER: Collaborative practices to improve teacher education. *Indian Journal of Teacher Education*, 1 (3), 13–29.

18 Early childhood pre-service teachers engage in collegial dialogue

Kym M. Simoncini, Michelle Lasen and Sharn Rocco

Introduction

Within professional teaching standards there is the expectation teachers should be willing and able to engage in professional dialogues about practice. But this aspect of teacher professionalism is rarely examined or explicitly taught in teacher education programmes. With this in mind, the authors designed an assessment task for 47 Australian Pre-Service Teachers (PSTs) that required them to interview their supervising teachers (in the chapter identified as School Based Teacher Educators: SBTEs) about the implementation of Education for Sustainability as a cross-curricular subject in the national curriculum. The pre-service teachers then had to write a reflective account of the interview process. Analysis of these reflective accounts highlights what enables and constrains professional dialogue and learning. We include this chapter in *Learning and Teaching Around the World* for its focus on research in educational practice and its exploration of factors that promote collegial conversations.

Dialogue, reflection and participation in communities of practice

Professional dialogue – or what may also be referred to as "inquiry conversation", "reflective conversation", "learning conversation" or "professional or collegial discussion" (Cochran-Smith and Lytle 1999; Feldman 1999; Le Cornu 2006) – is "a discussion between peers that allows the other to explicitly articulate, appreciate and extend their understanding of practice" (Nsibande 2007: 4). It is widely acknowledged that professional dialogue allows teachers to grow professionally (Corrigan & Loughran 2008). Professional dialogue can play a key role in consolidating understanding of concepts shared by a professional community and, in its absence, learning is typically slower (Bereiter and Scardamalia 1993). According to Cochran-Smith (2003), professional dialogue makes possible "the *learning* of new knowledge, questions and practices and, at the same time, the *unlearning* of some long-held and often difficult to uproot ideas, beliefs, and practices" (9). The purposes of professional dialogue and reflective practice have much in common. Peer-to-peer exchange is an essential characteristic of professional dialogue and can enhance the quality of reflective practice (Rocco 2010). In fact, "dialogue coupled with reflection and moved to action creates the conditions for transformative learning" (Donovan et al. 2007: 11).

Despite its role in professional learning, there are substantial barriers to teachers participating in professional dialogue (Daniel et al. 2013). Teaching has long been characterised as an individual and isolated profession (Wei et al. 2009; Westheimer 2008). While the experienced teacher is seen as confidently independent and self-sufficient (Lortie 1975), teachers who ask their peers about practices, request advice or open up their classrooms may be perceived as less than competent or may fear a loss of privacy and security (Cochran-Smith and Lytle 1993; Lytle and Fecho 1991; Richardson-Koehler 1988). So too, advising peers about practices may well be interpreted as "presumptuous" (Richardson-Koehler 1988) in a culture wherein there are "prevailing norms of non-interference, privacy and harmony" (Carver and Katz 2004; Little et al. 2003: 189–190). Horn and Little (2010) identified numerous constraints on professional dialogue, including difficulties in making tacit knowledge explicit, issues of difference and disagreement, insufficient structural and social supports and demands of immediate and multiple tasks.

"Professional learning communities" or "communities of practice" have become increasingly popular as avenues for teacher professional development. They are "informal entities that emerge spontaneously around issues of common interest" (Welsh and Dehler 2004: 21). Such communities offer teachers professional development opportunities that "differ in quality and kind" from traditional professional development workshops and seminars (Lieberman 1995: 73), which are "often intellectually superficial, disconnected from deep issues of curriculum and learning, fragmented, and noncumulative" (Ball and Cohen 1999: 3–4). Ball and Cohen (1999) argued that "without the development of substantial professional discourse and engagement in communities of practice" (13), professional learning that "emphasizes questions, investigations, analysis and criticism" cannot be "adequately cultivated" (13).

Challenges and strategies in facilitating collegial dialogue

The pre-service teachers (PSTs) were provided with the following schedule of five questions to ask their supervising teachers (SBTEs):

1. Why do you think Education for Sustainability (EfS) is included as a national cross-curriculum priority?
2. What resources are available in the school/centre to support teachers' efforts to address EfS?
3. How do you bring EfS into your classroom practice?
4. What are some of the challenges and obstacles you face in your efforts to integrate EfS?
5. Is EfS a personal priority for you?

Pre-service teachers were encouraged to add their own questions of interest to the interview schedule. They had some prior knowledge and understanding of the topic gained through their foundational subject study, and before the interview they sourced, evaluated and compiled relevant policy and curriculum resources on EfS.

The first key challenge was of a practical nature, involving the lack of time to schedule a formal interview. It was apparent that professional exchanges experienced by the pre-service teacher were less than satisfactory.

> It was extremely difficult to find an opportunity to 'pin down' my SBTE . . . because of the heavy workload and scheduling difficulties in the first week of term . . . Before school, organising the day took precedence. After school, either parents or pre-arranged appointments were obstacles.
>
> (PST43)

> Schools are busy places . . . a 15 minute window was all that we could manage.
>
> (PST19)

> I was a little disappointed . . . It was a good lesson in making myself clear about requirements. Although I mentioned that I was required to have a collegial conversation and asked them to let me know when would be a good time, it ended up being much more informal and off the cuff than I had anticipated.
>
> (PST14)

Pre-service teachers also felt that adequate rapport had not yet been developed with their SBTEs to comfortably engage in open and honest professional dialogue about teacher perceptions and classroom practices. Some pre-service teachers reported a reluctance to initiate professional dialogue especially given that they were novices and that they had not witnessed conversations of a professional nature between teachers in the professional experience setting.

> Initiating and facilitating focused collegial conversation seemed daunting. Often professional conversations that relate to what we think about teaching and learning and what we think is important are not engaged in. Professional conversations are usually avoided and replaced by everyday conversation. This was evident when observing staff conversations.
>
> (PST17)

Nonetheless, a number of pre-service teachers reflected on enhanced confidence in fulfilling the requirements of the task through careful planning for the interview and efforts to establish a friendly environment.

> The prospect of conducting a collegial conversation made me feel nervous initially. However, after recording the sequence of steps to be taken to secure the interview, I felt more confident.
>
> (PST30)

The interview took place on my second day at school; therefore, we were still in the early stages of building a professional relationship. I endeavoured to conduct and facilitate the interview in a professional manner and focused on helping the teacher feel comfortable during the process. This was a positive and an important early step in our professional relationship.

(PST31)

Pre-service teachers also perceived the substantive focus of the interview to be challenging. They were uncertain of their supervising teacher's understanding of and commitment to Education for Sustainability. Pre-service teachers also reported a reluctance on the part of supervising teachers to engage in professional dialogue seemingly due to a lack of knowledge, experience or expertise in the area.

My SBTE seemed uncertain about what to say and aware that they probably did not have 'enough' knowledge; they seemed flustered and agitated about giving the interview.

(PST46)

I was surprised at my SBTE's resistance to the interview and the topic of EfS, as in all other areas, they were very enthusiastic and ready to share their knowledge.

(PST28)

Many pre-service teachers addressed this constraint by giving the interview questions to their supervising teachers prior to the interview, affording interviewees time to reflect, prepare responses and locate necessary resources to support the professional dialogue. Pre-service teachers who did this felt the quality of responses was enhanced.

My SBTE noted how they enjoyed having time to think and brainstorm answers to the questions by being given the interview questions in advance.

(PST20)

Pre-service teachers who did not offer the interview questions to the supervising teacher felt, in hindsight, that this strategy would have been helpful.

Benefits of collegial dialogue

First, it was evident that pre-service teachers developed teacher researcher skills. These skills included scheduling and adequately planning for an interview, and creating an environment conducive to professional dialogue. Pre-service teachers reflected on how they could more effectively conduct interviews in the future. Some pre-service teachers attributed a lack of flow in the dialogue due to the nature of the questions that they asked, their desire to get through all of the questions and their inability to respond to interviewees in a natural and informed way.

I did not create a conversation, rather I did a rigid question and answer interview. I was more concerned about making sure I asked all the questions, rather than feeding off their responses and allowing it to be more fluent. For future reference, I need make allowance for the interview to take a different direction and respond to the answers that are given.

(PST45)

I struggled to know what to say after they had answered the question and, on occasions, I believe I replied too quickly, which eliminated any chance of the teacher adding other comments.

(PST37)

My questions could have been worded differently, on a more open basis rather than a closed one. Some of the questions have a one word answer but if I had phrased the questions differently the answers could have been more informative.

(PST9)

A second key benefit was that the interview provided insight into the challenges and opportunities involved in the implementation of Education for Sustainability as a cross-curriculum subject. Supervising teachers discussed their practices and personal perspectives relating to EfS, as well as the value afforded to and investment in sustainability initiatives by the wider school community.

The interview allowed me to see some of the challenges that teachers face when implementing EfS as a cross-curriculum priority, including the difficulties associated with creating rich learning experiences as opposed to shallow integration.

(PST18, PST11)

It provided a clear insight into EfS at a personal and school level.

(PST31)

It was apparent that the interview exposed pre-service teachers to viewpoints and beliefs about EfS that diverged from their own, and the post-interview reflective activities supported a more open consideration of a range of interpretations and practices.

The SBTE and I have some different views on implementing EfS as a cross-curriculum priority but this is helpful for my learning.

(PST35)

I learned that I need to be more aware that other people can have strong opinions on issues that may not be the same as my own. This was hard to acknowledge at first but once I reflected on the conversation I felt more at ease with their opinions.

(PST2)

Third, many pre-service teachers recognised that the formal interview ensured conversation about professional practices that may not have otherwise occurred. They were appreciative of the opportunity to learn from experienced teachers; for some pre- service teachers, the interview was an inspiring exchange. There was recognition of the importance of professional dialogue in terms of its potential to provide oppor- tunity to share and enhance knowledge and practice.

> You are looking closely at the inner-workings of a practicing teacher's ideas and knowledge, which is extremely interesting, especially for a pre-service teacher.
>
> (PST40)

> I can now see the value of this process as it facilitated dialogue that would otherwise not have been raised between my SBTE and I.
>
> (PST33)

> I found that by engaging in this conversation I was learning valuable knowledge from a colleague that has experience in this field; knowledge that I will be able to use within my own teaching career.
>
> (PST11)

At their most transformative, pre-service teacher reflections were forward-looking when discussing the benefits of engaging in professional dialogue.

> This provided me with an example of what a conversation may be like between teachers ... Involvement in the interview provided me with knowledge on why communication, negotiation, time management, conflict resolution and problem solving are necessary to contribute effectively in a professional team.
>
> (PST10)

Discussion

Planning, initiating, participating in and reflecting upon professional dialogue proved to be professionally challenging yet stimulating for the pre-service teachers of this study. The task allowed them opportunity to gain insight into teacher perceptions and under- standing of curriculum developments, and implementation in classroom practices and school initiatives, through structured professional dialogue that otherwise would not have occurred. While interviewing is a skill that improves with practice, the interviewer weaknesses that were reflected upon by participant pre-service teachers, such as overreliance on closed questions and rushing to the next question instead of probing or pausing for interviewees to expand upon responses, can be avoided largely through development of interviewing and oral communication and listening skills.

Teacher engagement in professional learning through collegial discussions, along with research, is an expectation across the professional lifespan. Themes from pre-service teacher reflections suggest that professional discussions are enhanced when participants feel confident about their knowledge, understanding and capabilities in the topic area or, at least, are well prepared for professional engagement (e.g., an outline of discussion topics or questions is provided to participants in advance). Further, adequate time for collegial discussion and rapport between participants emerge as key enablers. These findings have potential implications for the promotion of ongoing teacher professional development.

It is noteworthy that the participant pre-service teachers had studied Sustainability in the first year of their programme, wherein they explored sustainability issues and underlying principles and strategies in learning for sustainability. Further, as preparation for the interview task, they had sourced and reviewed sustainability policy documents and classroom resources. In contrast, many supervising teachers had not yet participated in professional development relating to sustainability. For some supervising teachers, reference to an "interview" implied that they had to have knowledge and expertise in Education for Sustainability for the activity to be worthwhile or successful. A number of supervising teachers directed pre-service teachers to interview other staff members who were perceived to be "experts" or at least more knowledgeable than themselves in the area. Replacing 'an interview' with reference to "professional dialogue" may promote a more equal exchange of knowledge, skills and ideas.

It was also apparent from pre-service teacher reflections that, in some interviews, pre-service teachers were exposed to beliefs and practices that diverged from their own, creating tensions that presented opportunity for professional learning. As highlighted in the literature, knowledge and practice can be substantially enriched or transformed through professional conversations that explore presuppositions, ideas, beliefs and feelings (Cochran-Smith 2003; Earl and Timperley 2009). While Horn and Little (2010) also identified issues of difference and disagreement as a constraint on professional dialogue, engagement in reflective processes can support more open consideration of differing viewpoints and transformative learning wherein "sets of fixed assumptions and expectations (habits of mind, meaning perspectives, mindsets)" are made "more inclusive, discriminating, open, reflective, and emotionally able to change" (Mezirow 2003: 58).

In addition to "reflection-on-action" (Schön 1987) as a process to facilitate transformative learning, it is recognised that skilled practitioners are able to critically reflect on assumptions and restructure strategies whilst *in* the process of action in order to achieve enhanced outcomes (Cunliffe and Easterby-Smith 2004; Schön 1987). The need for reflexivity in the profession was realised by one pre-service teacher of this study, who communicated that the assessment task promoted understanding of why communication, negotiation, conflict resolution and problem-solving are necessary skills to contribute effectively to professional teams. Emphasis on reflexivity and "reflection-on-action" resonates with Darling-Hammond and colleagues' (2007) and Ball and Cohen's (1999) call for teacher education to promote the capacity to inquire and learn *in* and *from* practice.

The assessment task of this study is of value to teacher education programmes as it promotes in pre-service teachers *learning how to learn* – from others, as well as in and from practice. Guided professional dialogue enabled the participant pre-service teachers to gain insight into practices and perspectives related to Education for Sustainability, including ways of thinking and doing that diverged from, and challenged, their own. Some pre-service teacher reflections were forward-looking, identifying how professional dialogue had the potential to enhance professional knowledge and practice and collaboration in early career contexts. At their most transformative, pre-service teacher reflections revealed a deeper understanding of the knowledge and skills – beyond planning and teaching – such as negotiation, conflict resolution, problem-solving, reflectivity and reflexivity, which are essential in constituting their professional selves.

Questions

1. What are your experiences of professional conversations about education, as a novice, expert or colleague? What enabled or constrained these dialogues?
2. The evidence from this study is that professional dialogue in school is unlikely to take place unless it is planned. The authors give several reasons for this. Can you think of additional constraining and enabling factors?
3. What might be the impact of ongoing professional dialogue in the primary school, for teaching staff and for children?

Further reading

Hattie, J. (2011) *Visible Learning for Teachers: Maximising Impact on Learning*. Melbourne: Routledge.
Lieberman, A. (2012) Learning About Professional Communities: Their Practices, Problems and Possibilities. In Day, C. (Ed.) *The Routledge International Handbook of Teacher and School Development* (p. 469). New York: Routledge.
Riordan, M. and Klein, E. (2010) Environmental education in action: How expeditionary learning schools support classroom teachers in tackling issues of sustainability. *Teacher Education Quarterly*, 37 (4), 119–137.

The full text of this chapter is: Simoncini, K.M., Lasen, M. and Rocco, S. (2014). Professional Dialogue, Reflective Practice and Teacher Research: Engaging Early Childhood Pre-Service Teachers in Collegial Dialogue about Curriculum Innovation. *Australian Journal of Teacher Education*, 39 (1).

References

Ball, D. and Cohen, D. (1999) Developing Practice, Developing Practitioners: Toward a Practice Based Theory of Professional Education. In Darling-Hammond, L. and Sykes, G. (Eds) *Teaching as the Learning Profession: Handbook of Policy and Practice* (pp. 3–32). San Francisco, CA: Jossey-Bass.
Bereiter, C. and Scardamalia, M. (1993) *Surpassing Ourselves: An Inquiry into the Nature and Implications of Expertise*. Chicago, IL: Open Court.
Carver, C. and Katz, D. (2004) Teaching at the boundary of acceptable practice: What is a new teacher mentor to do? *Journal of Teacher Education*, 55 (5), 449–462.

Cochran-Smith, M. (2003) Learning and unlearning: The education of teacher educators. *Teaching and Teacher Education*, 19 (1), 5–28.

Cochran-Smith, M. and Lytle, S. (1993) *Inside/Outside: Teacher Research and Knowledge*. New York: Teachers College Press.

Cochran-Smith, M. and Lytle, S. (1999) Relationships of Knowledge and Practice: Teacher Learning in Communities. In Iran-Nejad, A. and Pearson, P. (Eds) *Review of Education*, 24, 249–305.

Corrigan, D. and Loughran, J. (2008) Mentoring for the teaching profession: Snapshots of practice. Paper presented at the British Educational Research Association Annual Conference, Heriot-Watt University, Edinburgh, 3–6 September.

Cunliffe, A. and Easterby-Smith, M. (2004) From reflection to practical reflexivity: Experiential learning as lived experience. In Reynolds, M. and Vince, R. (Eds) *Organizing Reflection* (pp. 30–46). Surrey, UK: Ashgate.

Daniel, G., Auhl, G. and Hastings, W. (2013) Collaborative feedback and reflection for professional growth: Preparing first-year pre-service teachers for participation in the community of practice. *Asia-Pacific Journal of Teacher Education*, 41 (2), 159–172.

Darling-Hammond, L., Hammerness, K., Grossman, P., Rust, F. and Shulman, L. (2007) The Design of Teacher Education Programs. In Darling-Hammond, L. and Bransford, J. (Eds) *Preparing Teachers for a Changing World: What Teachers Should Learn and Be Able to Do* (pp. 390–441). San Francisco, CA: John Wiley & Sons.

Donovan, L., Meyer, S. and Fitzgerald, S. (2007) Transformative learning and appreciative inquiry: A more perfect union for deep organizational change. *Academy of Management Proceeding*, (Meeting Abstract Supplement), 1–6.

Earl, L. and Timperley, H. (2009) Professional Learning Conversations: Challenges in Using Evidence for Improvement. Toronto: Springer.

Feldman, A. (1999) The role of conversation in collaborative action research. *Educational Action Research*, 7 (1), 125–144.

Horn, I. and Little, J. (2010) Attending to problems of practice: Routines and resources for professional learning in teachers' workplace interactions. *American Educational Research Journal*, 47 (1), 181–217.

Le Cornu, R. (2006) Reculturing the practicum through scholarly learning conversations. Refereed paper presented at the Australian Teacher Education Conference, Fremantle, 5–8 July.

Lieberman, A. (1995) Practices that support teacher development: Transforming conceptions of professional learning. In *Innovating and Evaluating Science Education: NSF Evaluation Forums, 1992–94* (pp. 67–78). [Available at www.academia.edu/1068848/Practices_that_support_teacher_development_Tr ansforming_conceptions_of_professional_learning.]

Little, J., Gearhart, M., Curry, M. and Kafka, J. (2003) Looking at student work for teacher learning, teacher community, and school reform. *Phi Delta Kappan*, 85 (3), 184–192.

Lortie, D. C. (1975) Schoolteacher: A Sociological Study. Chicago, IL: University of Chicago Press.

Lytle, S. and Fecho, R. (1991) Meeting Strangers in Familiar Places: Teacher Collaboration by Cross-Visitation. *English Education*, 23 (1), 5–28.

Mezirow, J. (2003) Transformative learning as discourse. *Journal of Transformative Education*, 1 (1), 58–63.

Nsibande, R. (2007) Using professional dialogue to facilitate meaningful reflection for higher education practitioners. Proceedings of the 30th HERDSA Annual Conference, Adelaide, 8–11 July. [Available at www.herdsa.org.au/wpcontent/uploads/conference/2007/papers/p68.pdf.]

Richardson-Koehler, V. (1988) Barriers to effective student teaching: A field study. *Journal of Teacher Education*, 39 (2), 28–34.

Rocco, S. (2010) Making reflection public: Using interactive online discussion board to enhance student learning. *Reflective Practice*, 11 (3), 307–317.

Schön D. (1987) *Educating the Reflective Practitioner: Toward a New Design for Teaching and Learning in the Professions*. San Francisco, CA: Jossey-Bass Publishers.

Wei, R., Darling-Hammond, L., Andree, A., Richardson, N. and Orphanos, S. (2009) *Professional Learning in the Learning Profession: A Status Report on Teacher Development in the United States and Abroad*. Dallas, TX. National Staff Development Council.

Welsh, M. and Dehler, G. (2004) P(l)aying attention: Communities of Practice and Organized Reflection. In Reynolds, M. and Vince, R. (Eds) *Organizing Reflection* (pp. 15–29). Surrey, UK: Ashgate.

Westheimer, J. (2008) Learning Among Colleagues: Teacher Community and the Shared Enterprise of Education. In Cochran-Smith, M., Feiman-Nemser, S., McIntyre, D. and Demers, K. (Eds) *Hand-book of Research on Teacher Education: Enduring Questions in Changing Contexts* (3rd ed., pp. 732–755). New York: Routledge.

19 Teacher education in Sub-Saharan Africa and in one school in Kenya

Macro challenges and micro changes

Kris Stutchbury, Joan Dickie and Patricia Wambugu

Introduction

This chapter looks at the challenges of primary teacher training across Sub-Saharan Africa, and how these challenges have been addressed, in small ways, in one school in Kenya, through the use of Open Educational Resources (OER).

A report from The World Bank (Bold et al. 2017) highlights the severity of problems facing education in Sub-Saharan Africa and specifically links children's poor outcomes to a lack of quality teaching. Working in the primary school sector in Mozambique, Senegal, Nigeria, Togo, Uganda, Kenya and Tanzania, the World Bank team found that, on average, children receive two hours and fifty minutes of teaching a day; large proportions of teachers do not master the curriculum of the children they are teaching; basic pedagogical knowledge is low; and the use of good teaching practices is rare. 'Good' teaching practices are defined as (Bold et al., 2017: 13):

- designing and structuring lessons, so the activities link to the learning objectives;
- frequently checking for student understanding by asking questions, and allowing time for students to review and practice what they learned, either individually or with others;
- varying the cognitive level of questions by mixing lower and higher order questions;
- providing substantive feedback to students by acknowledging correct answers in a positive fashion and correcting wrong answers.

The Teacher Education in Sub-Saharan Africa (TESSA) programme was established in 2005 to respond to these challenges by providing Open Educational Resources (OER) for teachers to use in their classrooms and for teacher educators to use in training (see Further Reading). We include this chapter in *Learning and Teaching Around the World* for its practical and sustainable model of change for teachers in the classroom. TESSA aims to address the issue of quality by providing practical examples and activities to support teachers in developing skills for learner-centred education (LCE). For information about minimum standards for learner-centred education, see Chapter 2. See Chapter 17 for an account of using OER in India.

Teacher training in Sub-Saharan Africa

Teacher education in Sub-Saharan Africa takes place in universities and colleges of education. Students can study for two years and obtain a certificate of education, which qualifies them to teach in a primary school. Three years of study leads to a diploma, which qualifies them to teach in a secondary school, and four years leads to a Bachelor in Education degree. The vast majority of teachers (if they are qualified at all) hold a certificate or a diploma. For example, in Kenya, university-trained teachers with degrees account for about 10% of the teaching workforce. Colleges of Education or Primary Teacher Training Colleges (PTTCs) award certificates or diplomas and are overseen by a university. For example, in Ghana the University of Cape Coast has oversight of 38 Colleges of Education, setting the curriculum and assessment. In Uganda, Kyambogo University has a similar responsibility for 45 PTTCs. Admission to a College of Education or PTTC requires specific grades in school exams. Many people who enter these colleges do so not because they have a particular interest in being a teacher but because that is the highest form of further education available to them based on their school grades.

There is a significant proportion of unqualified teachers working in primary schools, many of whom take 'upgrade' courses which enable them to achieve a certificate in education. The National Teachers Institute in Nigeria, for example, upgrades thousands of unqualified teachers each year through distance learning programmes. On obtaining a certificate, teachers can expect a pay rise, so there is an incentive to take these courses. Many countries also have a programme of in-service training, run at district or zonal levels. Sometimes these are school-based: for example, Zambia runs a school-based in-service training programme (although in practice the meetings often don't take place). The reality however is that training often takes teachers away from school to attend a course which usually consists of a series of lectures.

Teacher preparation courses in Sub-Saharan Africa are generally considered to be too theoretical (Dembele and Miaro-II Be-Rammaj 2003) and do not model active approaches to teaching and learning (Katitia 2015; O'Sullivan 2010). Visiting Africa, for example, we and other colleagues have experienced long lectures on the merits of group work and active participation, with several hundred students sitting passively in a large lecture theatre. Subject content for student teachers is often taught in subject faculties (for example, Maths is taught by the Maths department), while teaching methodology is taught in the Education department. The result is that pedagogical content knowledge (how to teach a specific subject) is missing from the curriculum. Teacher educators are generally people who have done well academically but will not necessarily have much teaching experience themselves. For example, someone with a diploma or a degree may become a lecturer a College of Education or PTTC without ever having taught in a primary school.

Student teachers usually have the opportunity to undertake teaching practice. The length of the 'practicum' is very variable and in many countries there is no tradition of mentoring; often the headteacher is responsible for assessing student teachers and will focus on punctuality, appearance and lesson plans rather than on observations of the student teaching or evaluations of children's learning. In our work in SSA, we have encountered situations in which the classroom teacher sees having a student teacher as an opportunity to take time off; in Tanzania we saw that a student teacher of science who was the only science teacher in the school. But in Kenya, we have seen a dedicated team of teacher educators travel extensively to visit and support student teachers. The result of this variability is that many teachers enter the workforce ill-prepared for the realities of classroom teaching.

The focus on improving teacher quality is important, but a consequence of this, and of studies like the World Bank report (Bold 2017), is to create a dialogue which positions teachers as deficient, referred to as the 'third world teacher' discourse (Tao 2016). Tao argues that teachers are often judged as unprofessional or deficient in skills based on evidence which takes little account of the realities of teachers' lives, and based on criteria derived from western models of what constitutes good practice. Within this discourse (teachers are important, but incompetent) the solutions often presented are sets of prescriptive lesson plans, setting out precisely how something should be taught, or initiatives which bypass the teacher altogether, for example, supplying tablet computers and learning packages to children. The reality is that little progress has been made in improving teaching (Schweisfurth 2011) and many improvements are not sustained. For example the Strengthening Maths and Science in Secondary Education (SMASSE) project in Kenya has trained large numbers of teachers in designing practical science activities, yet a Government report in 2014 (The Government of Kenya 2014) suggests that, after 12 years of activity, it has made no measurable impact on children's learning outcomes in Science. The situation is likely to be complex, but an evaluation of the programme in one district (Mwangi and Mugambi 2013) suggests that 'a lot needs to be done to improve the attitude of teachers. It clearly emerged that the majority of teachers are coerced to attend the INSET training' (46).

Studies from what Tao terms the 'teacher advocacy literature' (2016: 16) – investigations into the working and living conditions of teachers, and their pedagogical practices – reveal a much more nuanced picture of how teachers' lives and the context in which they work impact on their behaviour (eg Buckler 2011; Tao 2013). Tao argues that interventions are more likely to be successful if they take account of local contexts and support teachers to work more effectively in those contexts. TESSA is such an initiative, positioning teachers as active professionals seeking to improve their practice.[1] It provides practical examples of classroom practice which can be adapted. Published as Open Educational Resources (OER) the TESSA resources model the 'minimum criteria' for learner-centred education (Schweisfurth 2015) and are highly relevant to global policy agendas.

TESSA OER example

A typical TESSA activity is presented here. This activity could be done with classes of different ages; it would be up to teachers to adapt their questioning to the relevant curriculum topic – whether it is naming parts (for smaller children) or discussing adaptations or learning about types of insects (for older children).

This is not a scripted lesson plan. It addresses the teacher directly as a professional who is capable of organising a lesson based on prior knowledge of children's learning and some understanding of principles of classroom management. It does not assume the teacher is familiar with lesson sequencing, group work or open questions – there are options to seek further information as needed by the teacher. The OER presents an open-ended activity that is aligned with the curriculum. It explicitly directs the teacher to move around the classroom, talk to children, ask questions to check children's participation and their understanding. It prompts the teacher to think about the lesson after it happens in order to plan the next learning steps. The activity encourages small changes in teacher practice. Crucially, the OER is only meaningful and actionable if the teacher is engaged with the learners.

Activity: Making models of animals

In many parts of Nigeria, entrepreneurs make a living by selling lifelike models of animals. We feel that all pupils are entitled to the chance to extend this natural desire to make models to extend their study of different animals. By asking children to make models, you will also be integrating science with technology and art.

You can add to the classroom displays set up in Activity 1 by getting children to work at making models of different types of local animals like chickens, dogs or cows using appropriate materials. (See Resource 5: Pupils' models of animals for examples and suggestions.)

We suggest you organise the pupils to work in groups, three or four pupils in each group usually works well. (See Key Resource: Using group work in your classroom to help you decide how you will organise the groups.) You could organise your groups by mixing lower and higher achievers.

Encourage pupils to bring in materials for their models. As they are building the models, move around the classroom, talking to the groups; with younger pupils ask them to name the parts of the animal they are modelling – paws, tails, ears and so on. With older pupils, ask questions about the shapes and functions of the different parts of the animals – how do they help the animal move? Eat? Keep warm? Cool down? Sense that predators are near?

Think about how you could encourage your pupils to reflect on their work. Could you ask different groups to comment on the other groups' models? Make sure you allow time for pupils to talk about their work and to improve it.

Did this activity work well?
Were you surprised by the detail of the pupils' models?
Is the detail of the pupils' models accurate?
What could be improved?
Did it help pupils to see similarities and differences between animals?

Egerton Primary School and Egerton University, Kenya

Egerton Primary school is situated on the campus of Egerton University, Nakuru. It is in the Rift Valley, about four hours' drive north of Nairobi. There are nearly 1,000 children in the primary school, organised in classes of 60. The children come from what one of the teachers described as 'humble backgrounds' and it has been a struggle to involve parents. There have been significant improvements in attendance and achievement over the last six years. The Headteacher is particularly pleased that progression is much better than it was six years ago, with fewer children dropping out or repeating a year.

Egerton University is a TESSA partner institution. A component of assessment on the primary Bachelor of Education (BEd) course is to create a teaching resource that is donated to the teaching practice school, Egerton Primary. Student teachers' use of TESSA OER has produced resources such as 'word wheels', 'word pockets' and weather vanes for the primary school.

In 2010, The TESSA co-ordinator at the University introduced TESSA OER to the Headteacher of Egerton Primary School. Working with the University over time, the primary school made some changes: organising desks in tables rather than rows to encourage children to talk to each other about their work; re-casting the school as 'child-friendly'; creating opportunities for children to take responsibility for aspects of school life and have a voice through a school council; and creating a resource centre.

In 2015, we visited Egerton Primary. This is an account from the TESSA Academic Director:

> I was told 'We don't do TESSA anymore'. The TESSA OER were not in use – the hard copies had disintegrated in the Kenyan climate – and the staff and teachers were feeling overwhelmed by a big library project (started last year), the increased numbers of students and the pressure of [examinations] accountability. The conversation was really rather depressing.
>
> However, it was clear from the wall displays in the staffroom that this was a school that is thinking about itself, what it does and how it does it. There was an action plan, a 'SWOT' analysis, graphs of attendance and achievement (all going up) and a mission statement.
>
> So I asked them to think back to 2010 and tell me how their school had changed. The consensus was that it was 'completely different'. Now, they said, 'we are a child-friendly' school. On probing they said that it was introducing teachers to TESSA OER, and the teachers (with the support of the headteacher) using the OER to plan their lessons that had brought about the change. They had changed the way children sit, for example (in groups), and were much more attentive to their needs. They were much more proactive in gathering resources. (As an example they showed me the skeleton and feathers of a flamingo, mounted on a board and stored in the resources centre by the teacher who found the dead flamingo when out with his class on a nature walk.)
>
> As a result of using more active approaches to teaching, they gradually got to know the students better and understand their needs. They noticed that poor reading in P3 was preventing children from accessing the rest of the curriculum. The result was a

whole-school focus on literacy and a project to create a space in the school for a proper library. They also reported that enrolment had increased from 500 to 900, as children were finding school more enjoyable and their reputation as a child-friendly school had spread – hence the concern over large classes.

They were keen to re-engage with TESSA and introduce the OER to new teachers . . . but [this] should not disrupt teaching or place burdens on the teachers.

School-based professional development

We designed four days of school-based training over several months, using TESSA OER with a focus on pair work and questioning. Teachers were encouraged to try TESSA activities in their classrooms and report back. The Kenyan textbooks included a number of potentially engaging activities, and we included sessions on using the textbook to encourage active teaching. To gather evidence of the impact and sustainability of TESSA, we observed lessons and interviewed four teachers and the headteacher.

Some teachers commented that they were introduced to TESSA by the University in 2010, and were given hard copies of the OER, but could not manage the scope of the resources:

> . . . the material was too voluminous to engage . . .
>
> (Teacher R)

> The university brought very scary big modules which we were not able to read without losing track.
>
> (Teacher T)

This demonstrated that mediation, as well as access, is important in introducing initiatives to improve teaching. Following the school-based training sessions, these teachers talked enthusiastically about the TESSA OER and we observed them teaching some engaging, interactive lessons. The shift from their initial reluctance to use TESSA came partly from having time to find and try out activities linked to what they had to teach.

Several teachers commented on the direct relevance of TESSA OER to curriculum content. One teacher explained how the OER helped him to operationalise some training from the British Council which had focused on active teaching approaches but was not directly linked to the topics he had to teach in his class. Teacher T said that using TESSA OER was 'aligning':

> . . . really complementing what the syllabus is talking about, the social and cultural activities in Kenya . . . The TESSA material was really encouraging how to teach.

Some of his colleagues were concerned that using TESSA was something extra that they had to add on to what they were already doing. But he had been able to reassure them:

It is what you are doing in class, but now you are looking at it from a different angle.

Teacher R agreed that TESSA OER 'TESSA . . . give you ideas on how a topic can be taught'. Teachers were enthusiastic about OER on group work:

It has really improved the children in terms of leadership skills . . . in terms of discipline . . . the children were really excited . . . they wanted to present . . . fluency was really coming out.

(Teacher T)

As well as enjoying trying new approaches, teachers have seen improvements in attendance and achievement. They also reported changes to how they perceive 'slow' learners:

There was so much that I did not know . . . I came to realise that every child can learn. When these methods were introduced, I learnt that even the slow learners became interested. I learnt that children are rich in their ideas . . . they have so much to share. I am so pleased . . . I am even motivated to do it more and more.

(Teacher L)

The children are also discovering, they are finding out . . . learning can be as interesting as this . . . It has really improved retention . . . you know the absentees . . . they want to come to school . . . I am a happier teacher than before.

(Teacher T)

Even those slow ones, they love to come out . . . they want to be recognised . . . even those who don't even talk in class.

(Teacher T)

The Headteacher also confirmed that attendance and achievement were improving. We observed that small changes in practice lead to some changes in teachers' attitudes. There was evidence that teachers were more confident in active teaching; some became advocates for it, even in a context of a crowded curriculum; they felt more positive about the prospects of 'slow' learners; and they began to understand the importance of engaging learners.

Looking forward

This chapter has highlighted key challenges facing teacher education in SSA. In order to address these challenges, new models of teacher education are required: school-based models that support teachers in developing practical classroom skills, so that children and teachers can have more enjoyable and productive experiences. TESSA was conceived as a resource to develop the capacities of teachers without taking them away from school, and to improve quality consistent with the principles of learner-centred education and policy aspirations for Learner-Centred Education (LCE). Change is slow and initiatives like TESSA will not solve systemic problems. Mediation of training resources is key to their sustainability. Egerton Primary is an improving school. Staff were receptive to learning more about TESSA, so caution is required in drawing too many conclusions from our experience. However, there is evidence that school-based professional development and mediated Open Educational Resources have helped these teachers move along a continuum of Learner-Centred Education.

Questions

1. The 'good teaching' practices referred to in the World Bank report attempt to measure the quality of classroom teaching. If you had to distil 'good teaching' into a few observable and measurable statements, what descriptors would you choose?
2. See the 'minimum criteria' for learner-centred education in Chapter 2. What conditions needed to be in place for Egerton Primary teachers to begin to teach in more learner-centred ways? What did the teachers say in their interviews that reflects a learner-centred ethos?

Note

1 Teacher Education in Sub Saharan Africa (TESSA) www.tessafrica.net/ is a bank of Open Educational Resources (OER) for teachers and teacher educators, available online and contextualised for ten African countries. The OER model active pedagogy and offer concrete examples of learner-centred education. The resources cover the primary school curriculum and provide open-ended activities to try out in the classroom. TESSA OER were written by a consortium of 14 African universities. OER are published under a Creative Commons Copyright license and are free to use, distribute and adapt.

   TESSA is not an intervention. The model of change is one of evolution, not revolution. The OER speak directly to teachers, and the aim is to encourage small changes in practice that will elicit positive responses from children. Through practice and reflection, teachers can develop new attitudes and practices consistent with those modelled in the OER and promoted in government policies for learner-centred education.

Further reading

Anamuah-Mensah, J., Banks, F., Moon, B. and Wolfenden, F. (2013) New Modes of Teacher and Preservice Training and Professional Development. In Moon, B. (Ed.) *Teacher Education and the Challenge of Development: A Global Analysis* (pp. 201–211).

Murphy, P. and Wolfenden, F. (2013) Developing a pedagogy of mutuality in a capability approach: Teachers experiences of using the Open Educational Resources (OER) of the teacher education in Sub-Saharan Africa (TESSA) programme. *International Journal of Educational Development*, 33, 263–271.

Wolfenden, F., Umar, A., Aguti, J. and Amani, A. (2010) Using OER to improve teacher quality: Emerging findings from TESSA. Presented at the Sixth Pan Commonwealth Forum on Open Learning.

References

Bold, T., Filmer, D., Martin, G., Molina, A., Rockmore, C., Stacy, B., Svensson, J. and Wane, W. (2017) *What Do Teachers Know and Do? Does It Matter? Evidence from Primary Schools in Africa* (Policy Research Working Paper No. 7956). World Bank Group.

Buckler, A. (2011) Reconsidering the evidence base, considering the rural: Aiming for a better understanding of the education and training needs of sub-Saharan African teachers. *International Journal of Educational Development*, 31, 244–250.

Dembele, M. and Miaro-II Be-Rammaj (2003) Pedagogical Renewal and Teacher Development in Sub-Saharan Africa: A Thematic Analysis. Presented at the ADEA Biennial meeting, Mauritius.

Katitia, D.M. (2015) Teacher Education Preparation program for 21st Century. Which way forward for Kenya? *Journal of Education and Practice*, 6, 57–64.

Mwangi, N.I. and Mugambi, M. (2013) Evaluation of Strengthening of Mathematics and Science in Secondary Education (SMASSE) program. A case study of Murang'a South District, Kenya. *International Journal of Education, Learning, and Development*, 1.

O'Sullivan, M. (2010) Educating the Teacher Educator – A Ugandan case study. *International Journal of Educational Development*, 30, 377–387.

Schweisfurth, M. (2015) Learner-centred pedagogy: Towards a post 2015 agenda for teaching and learning. International *Journal of Educational Development*, 40, 259–266.

Schweisfurth, M. (2011) Learner-centred education in developing country contexts: From solution to problem? *International Journal of Educational Development*, 31, 419–426.

Tao, S. (2016) *Transforming Teacher Quality in the Global South: Using Capabilities and Causality to Re-Examine Teacher Performance*. Basingstoke, UK: Palgrave MacMillan.

Tao, S. (2013) Why are teachers absent? Utilising the Capability Approach and Critical Realism to explain teacher performance in Tanzania. International Journal of Educational Development, 33, 2–14.

The Government of Kenya (2014) *Education for All 2015 National Review: Kenya*. World Education Forum, Incheon, Korea.

20 Learning Assistants in Sierra Leone

Community support for future teachers

Martin Crisp and Kimberly Safford

Introduction

Auxiliary support staff in primary schools are known by different titles: teaching assistants, classroom assistants, classroom helpers or teachers' aides. They are recognised, in many countries, as important sources of support for children and for teachers. Teaching assistants often go on to further study and training to become qualified teachers, building on their practical experiences of supporting learning in classrooms. But in many parts of the world this support role and pathway to becoming a teacher are less familiar or unknown.

This chapter reports on the Learning Assistant (LA) programme in Sierra Leone, a component of the UK Government-funded Girls Education Challenge. The LA programme has enabled hundreds of young women to train as teachers in remote rural areas where schools are understaffed and there are few female teachers. The programme provides a route to teaching through a combination of distance study to enter teacher college and in-school work experience where LAs support teachers and children in rural classrooms.

The research described in this chapter used an ecological approach, exploring the support systems that LAs have. The interview data show the significance of the community in developing and motivating future teachers in remote rural areas, where there are many challenging circumstances.

Sierra Leone is located on the Atlantic coast in West Africa, bordered by Guinea to the north and Liberia to the south. Its population in 2015 was just over 7 million (Statistics Sierra Leone 2016). A decade-long civil war ended in 2002. During this time, education in Sierra Leone was significantly disrupted, particularly in rural areas; after the war, the challenge of reconstructing the country's education system was a monumental task (see Novelli and Higgins 2017: 34). In 2014, an Ebola outbreak had a further catastrophic effect on education, including the closure of all schools for almost a year, and the deaths of many teachers and school leaders. In 2014, 41% of Sierra Leonean young people between the ages of 15 and 24 had not completed primary education (Education Policy and Data Center 2014).

Within this wider context, Novelli and Higgins (2017) highlight two policy areas relating to post-conflict education in Sierra Leone that are particularly relevant to the LA programme. First, they contend that although national and international policies to address gender inequities in Sierra Leone through expanding girls' access to education have, at face value, achieved success, such policies have not adequately tackled more deeply rooted socio-cultural constraints within education and society more widely. Novelli and Higgins argue that the lack of job opportunities for young people impacts more negatively on girls than boys, and they criticise the majority of interventions relating to girls' education for failing to 'inform and equip boys and girls, through education, to challenge deep-rooted patriarchal cultural attitudes and practices' (38). A telling example of this inequity is the scarcity of women teachers and head teachers in primary schools in Sierra Leone. Second, Novelli and Higgins highlight low morale amongst teachers due to constraints on their 'personal and professional agency resulting from their daily exposure to conditions of precarity and vulnerability' (39) including, for many, grossly inadequate and overcrowded classroom spaces.

Terms used in this chapter

FAWE: Forum of African Women Educationalists, a Non-Governmental Organisation (NGO) that promotes educational opportunities for girls and women

FAWE District Supervisor: Person with overall responsibility for the Learning Assistant programme within a district (approximately 100 LAs)

FAWE Social Worker: Person with responsibility for the day-to-day wellbeing and progress of Learning Assistants within a local area (typically between 10 and 20 LAs)

Paramount Chief: Elected male member of local government responsible for an area (Chiefdom) within a District

'Mamie Queen' Women's Leader: Female elected to represent, promote and uphold women's rights and interests within a community

WASSCE: West African Senior School Certificate Examination, the examination required to pass out of secondary school and enter tertiary education

The LA programme and research

The Learning Assistant programme was developed with the aim of increasing the numbers of female teachers in primary schools in rural areas of Sierra Leone. Recruiting more women into teaching is critical for improving gender equity in education, and providing important role models for increasing and sustaining girls' participation in and completion of primary schooling. The programme aimed to do this by recruiting young women who did not complete their school education to follow a work/study pathway to teacher training: working as LAs in primary schools in their own communities alongside studying modules in English and maths in preparation for the Teacher Training College entrance exam. LAs who pass the exam become Student Teachers and continue to work in their schools as they study the Teacher Training College distance programme, which includes regular residential schools, to become fully qualified teachers. The LA programme was designed by the UK Open University (OU) and delivered in partnership with FAWE. The programme started in 2013 but was interrupted by the Ebola outbreak in 2014: 550 young women initially registered for the programme in five districts. In 2016, 483 LAs had passed the Teacher Training College entrance exam to become Student Teachers.

Research was carried out in 2017 in two districts of Sierra Leone, in two locations: a remote agricultural community and a rural township. Eighteen people were interviewed. The LAs interviewed represented a range of ages, backgrounds and family statuses; two LAs were interviewed in greater depth. People who help the LAs were also interviewed to gain a holistic understanding of the roles, relationships and activities that have collectively contributed to the success of the programme (see Figures 20.1 and 20.2).

Our research highlights how individual determination and tenacity are attributes of successful LAs, many of whom overcame considerable hardships to participate and succeed in the programme. But it is also evident that such individuals did not succeed

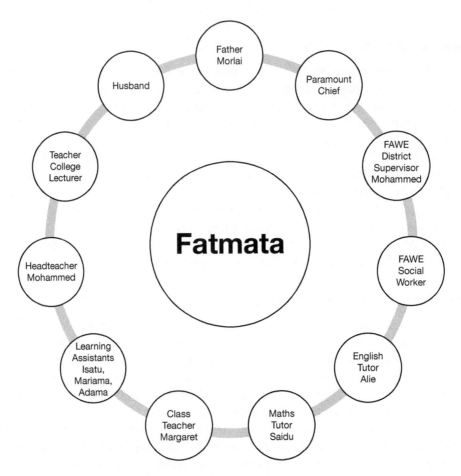

Figure 20.1 Learning assistant Fatmata and her support community

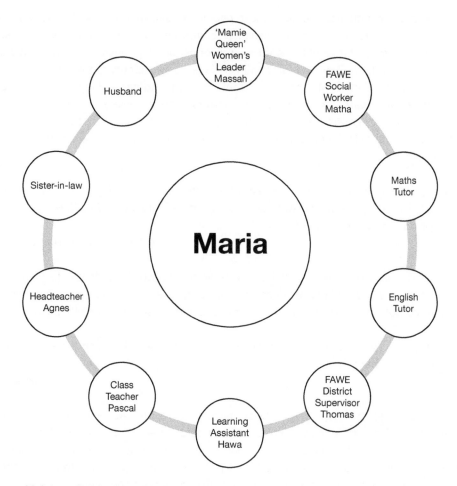

Figure 20.2 Learning Assistant Maria and her support community

in isolation. A clear picture emerges from the research of how LAs are supported by a constellation of people in roles that are formal and informal, paid and voluntary, new and traditional. Furthermore, the encouragement and involvement of such people is generating a culture of collective learning and community development. The following themes were identified as contributing to the sustainability of the Learning Assistant programme.

Community selection

> Because it was owned by the community, the community gave it a lot of support.
>
> (FAWE District Supervisor Thomas)

An innovative element of the LA programme is the community selection process. FAWE assembled a committee of high-status people in each village to identify and recruit suitable candidates. Some of these people are shown in Figures 20.1 and 20.2. This process helped to inform and sensitise communities about the nature and purposes of the programme, and inducted a range of people in professional and traditional roles to support its implementation and provide ongoing support to the LAs.

FAWE Social Worker Martha went from home to home, talking about the LA programme and searching for potential recruits. She conveyed to candidates and families how the programme could raise the aspirations of women who had left education and were economically and educationally 'idle', and improve perceptions of them in the community:

> So, people give you names . . .'Prostitutes', many names . . . If you put seriousness [into it], this programme will take you from zero to hero and make you very important in this community.
>
> (FAWE Social Worker Martha)

Other people in selection committees were on the lookout for potential LAs. 'Mamie Queen' Women's Leader Massah identified one candidate at an adult literacy workshop. Massah did not know how to write her name, and had to sign the workshop register.

> This young lady wrote my name for me . . . So I thought: If I push her she will try, she will be educated.
>
> (Massah)

Being selected by the community conferred status on LAs, and increased their motivation and determination. The selection process created a network of people to monitor the LAs inside and outside school, to provide encouragement and practical support. Headteachers saw the recruitment process as an opportunity to benefit their schools, their communities and the futures of the candidates themselves.

> Had it not been for [the LAs] this school would be understaffed . . . a school like this accommodating over five hundred pupils, having only four paid-up teachers . . . There is no way we can cope with this kind of situation.
>
> (Headteacher Mohammed)

The daily presence of high-status people with an ongoing interest in the LAs' progress has been a sustaining aspect of the programme. LAs know these people are paying attention to them and have a reputational stake in their success.

'Total engagement'

> Just after Ebola . . . I moved to all the communities with my team, in fact we slept there with all of them . . . those days created a big change in [communities'] mindsets: 'We were thinking that you'd gone, but thank God you are back'.
>
> (FAWE District Supervisor Thomas)

FAWE staff reported being on duty constantly, answering calls from LAs on issues ranging from distribution of bursaries to reassuring husbands who were suspicious about their wives' activities. District Supervisor Thomas described his work as 'total engagement', a term that is equally applicable to many of the other people supporting the LAs. Taking Fatmata (Figure 20.1) and Maria (Figure 20.2) as examples, it is of note that the majority of the people in each young woman's support community are not paid by the programme. Instead they support LAs as part of their normal roles. Some of these roles are professional and formal, such as headteacher, class teacher and teacher college lecturer. Other roles are traditional and more informal, such as the 'Mamie Queen' Women's Leader and the Paramount Chief. The support of husbands, parents, siblings and in-laws is also important.

This ongoing support is underpinned by a high level of commitment to ensuring the success of LAs. English and maths tutors, for instance, often provided additional weekly tutorials, and sometimes paid LAs' transport costs and provided food to enable them to attend tutorials. Headteachers also sometimes provided food, as well as responding to other emerging needs, for example, allowing LAs to bring their small children into school and to continue to teach and study if they became pregnant.

LAs said they have been able to call regularly on family and friends to look after their children while they are away from the house. Some domestic chores would be redistributed to mothers, sisters-in-law, siblings and older children. Hawa also highlighted the importance of peer support from the other LAs:

> I will sit by my friends . . . ask them question. They explain to me so I'll recall when I go home . . . So, I will decide to go to them and ask them if I am lost, any question.

> (Hawa)

Exposure

> Some of these young girls have never gone to the big towns. In fact, they have never mixed together in a larger group . . . it is really helping them. It exposes them to meet other people, other places. Like when they go for the seminars, even when they go for their tutorials . . . Wider communities. Meet people of other, higher status.

> (Headteacher Agnes)

Few LAs had travelled outside their local area before they joined the programme, and most had not ventured outside their small villages. Encountering new places and situations, and meeting people such as registrars, lecturers, hotel staff and FAWE officials, brought LAs into new relationships with other professionals and para-professionals. Such exposure has promoted mobility and raises aspirations. LAs report feeling part of a network of teachers and students, and have become more confident to try new things, and to talk to people with whom they might previously have been too shy to speak.

These new relationships enable LAs and those who support them to develop new or enhanced responsibilities, as students, mentors, para-professionals and experts.

Class teacher Margaret, the only female teacher in her remote rural school, takes on a mentoring role and acts as a role model to the young women, which extends beyond their responsibilities as LAs to include their deportment and conduct outside of school.

> Whether in school or outside, it is bad, you should not quarrel because you are a role model . . . I told them how to behave. If you are a teacher you do not behave like a farmer again.
>
> (Class Teacher Margaret)

For LAs, the realisation that professional people are willing to help them can be life-changing. When Fatmata entered the Teacher College, she found it 'difficult and strange' because she had been out of formal education for so long. A lecturer took Fatmata under her wing.

> Miss J said 'Fatmata, call to me at night' . . . I went there every night . . . She cajoled me, she encouraged me, teach me every day. She made me to be capable of being in [the Teacher Training College].
>
> (Fatmata)

Social, professional and academic exposure has increased LAs' capabilities when they work in their schools, and helped them to develop professional relationships with Class Teachers. It has given them confidence to ask questions and see themselves as learners. Teachers such as Pascal, who supports the LA Maria, see themselves as important role models of adults as learners.

> You [must] have the courage to ask others. It's not bad when you ask, it does not mean you are stupid when you ask . . . you'll not be debating 'Am I doing the right thing?'
>
> (Teacher Pascal)

Pascal said he can see Maria developing her own teaching style, and he appreciates having another adult in the classroom.

> She's going to relieve me more from standing there alone. And also, it's going to give the children, you know, like a mixture in the sense they are not just hearing one voice.
>
> (Class Teacher Pascal)

Exposure can also cause problems. When LAs started going to teacher colleges and other meetings, teaching in schools and interacting with a range of other people, there was discord in some homes.

Interactions with husbands became distanced. Some women think they are no longer at the same level as their husbands. One LA has taken her husband to the police. It all started when she started Teacher College.

(FAWE District Supervisor Thomas)

Therefore, the important role of men, in voluntary and paid roles, in sustaining the LA programme must be acknowledged.

Men supporting female empowerment

Our hopes are onto them because they are women ... this is putting them on a higher level ... nowadays you have these footballers, you have Ronaldo, you have Messi, and all the young boys want to be like them ... and these women as well, they are [like] footballers.

(Paramount Chief)

Men such as FAWE District Supervisors, chiefs, headteachers and tutors have lent their status and leadership to the LA programme, and expressed a deeply felt belief in the value of girls' and women's education and a commitment to actively supporting female empowerment. For Fatmata, one of 16 children, these supporters include her farmer father who, although very poor, has made considerable personal sacrifices to send all of his children to school. He expressed great pride in his daughter's achievements.

[I] can see changes in her in terms of her physical appearance, she knows how to dress. [As farmers] we were not able to dress her. That makes me happy ... Also the attitude changed. ... She is now able to meet with people and greet in a gentle mood ... She talks in low tones and she does not get annoyed easily and I am sensing a lot of respect in her for humanity ... she is learning patience.

(Morlai, Fatmata's father)

Many of the LAs' partners have been supportive, including providing practical assistance such as looking after young children while their mothers are in tutorials or residential schools. However, convincing some husbands of the worth and authenticity of the programme has been challenging. Influential men are therefore important 'levers' in persuading men opposed to their partners' or daughters' involvement. For example, FAWE District Supervisor Thomas has sometimes had to validate the whereabouts and activities of LAs when they are away from home at tutorials or study camps, occasionally dramatically:

I told [a husband] 'I'll go and show you the class'. I sat on top of his bike and went to the college [study camp] ... I said "look at your wife sitting down!" He was ashamed. I said "I want you to ascertain that I am not bringing them here for un-seriousness . . . feel free to trust them . . . when they are here 8 to 5, it is purely education".

(FAWE District Supervisor Thomas)

In addition to class teachers, the distance-study English and maths tutors of the programme are respected men of status in their communities. In Fatmata's village, the English tutor is principal of a secondary school as well as a local politician, and the maths tutor is a secondary school vice principal and maths teacher. Both men considerably exceeded their paid duties as tutors to support the LAs. For example, they met with husbands, urging them to let their wives be educated so that 'two frogs can croak together', as one of them put it. He added that he had a long-held vision of supporting women's education that the LA programme had enabled him to achieve.

Conclusion

Before they were 'Just look at this, she is just giving birth to a lot of children without doing anything'. But now I'm part of this programme, they call us 'Teacher' . . . We have respect now in the community.

(Maria)

The personal impact on individual LAs has been significant. All talked about their increased confidence, feelings of competence, efficacy and ambition. Participation in the programme has moved them out of educational inactivity, from insecure petty trading and street selling, subsistence farming, and in some cases literally 'doing nothing', to being active high-status members of their communities. These changes are evidenced in a range of ways: pride in personal appearance and comportment, punctuality, confidence to speak, work ethic, teaching skills, planning, reorganisation of domestic responsibilities, devoting time to study, language development, subject knowledge, understanding children, and overall comportment. Supporters of LAs confirm these developments. The changes that Fatmata's father sees in her community interactions, described above, are reflected in comments by others. Headteachers noted that LAs feel more secure, respected, happier, noticed and cared for. There is a sense of LAs now being 'inside' the professional context of the school and the learning context of the Teacher Training College, enabling them to act as role models inside and outside schools.

You see pupils coming close to them, talking to them like sisters or mothers . . . some pupils cannot explain to us, the Headteacher or the men [teachers], but they will go close to the women and speak to them.

(Headteacher Mohammed)

The personal transformation of LAs is having a wider positive impact. 'Mamie Queen' Women's Leader Massah described the LAs as 'special people' in the community. She is confident to send them to represent the village in meetings because 'they can address people comfortably'. Massah also attributed a decrease in domestic and community violence to the LAs' greater sense of self-worth and being respected more by others. They are a new group of high-status women in communities who promote a culture of learning and personal aspiration.

In interviews, Learning Assistants spoke of their ambitions to become financially responsible, to contribute to the home and family, share financial burdens with husbands and thereby gain respect from husbands and others.

> If you have your own job . . . no [one] can say 'This woman is doing nothing' . . . when your husband provides everything you are just sitting there . . . But if he brings two thousand [Leones] and you bring one thousand, you're able to manage a home. He will have respect for you . . . I am able to support my children too . . . if we inform ourselves now to be educated, we will be side by side working.
>
> (Maria)

A key element contributing to the sustainability of the Learning Assistant model is the shift in the perception that it is possible for mothers to work and study without being held back by the demands of childcare. There are many examples within the programme of family and other community members taking care of children while Learning Assistants are away or studying at home; women can continue the programme whilst pregnant or with infants, and Learning Assistants with young children and younger siblings can attend the schools where they work.

The LA programme has not just resulted in sending nearly 500 young women to Teacher Training Colleges. It has acted as a catalyst to a more deep-rooted transformation within communities by shifting the balance (between young and old, male and female) and strengthening community leadership. The LAs are emerging as younger, high-status individuals who are recognised and intrinsic – not extrinsic – to their villages. This development is already reaping benefits. Many school leaders in rural areas have relied on unqualified 'community' teachers who are not on government payroll and therefore often unreliable. In LAs, schools have found a local supply of future teachers who will remain in the area, and additionally help to establish a culture of learning and aspiration – for girls and young women in particular. The contribution of LAs has also acted to raise morale of school staff by alleviating the effects of overcrowded and inadequate teaching spaces as discussed by Novelli and Higgins (2017).

We argue that the LA programme disrupts a 'generic globally structured educational agenda designed by donors and global actors' (Novelli et al. 2014: 3) by getting meaningfully inside what is feasible, and indeed needed, in specific contexts. The evidence from our research suggests strongly that the success of LA programme, and its acceptance within its communities, has been enabled by engaging from the outset with key individuals and stakeholders in education.

In addition to the personal learning and development of the LAs themselves, the programme has also extended the professional and personal development of key high-status people who support them. For example, by regularly visiting the beneficiaries in their schools, the Chief and Women's Leader have been prompted to reflect on their own roles in supporting girls and young women in their communities. School staff reported how mentoring and supporting LAs has enhanced their own personal learning and professional development. Across the range of LA programme participants, the aspects of learning and growth described encompassed respect, patience, good listening, facilitation, problem-solving, how to interact with people and enabling others to speak and act. In this respect, the LA programme contributes to the formation of a coherent community of practice as defined by Wenger (1999), through mutual engagement and joint enterprise.

In a wider sense, the LA programme in Sierra Leone can be seen as an innovation in authentic community transformation that has strengthened and expanded a professional class in a sustainable way. Networks of new and traditional roles have been harnessed to support individual beneficiaries, transforming young women viewed previously as failures into successes.

Questions

1. To what extent is the Learning Assistant programme a model that could be transferred across cultures and countries?
2. Are there any elements of the programme that might need to be adjusted to make it appropriate for any contexts that you are familiar with?
3. How might a 'Learning Assistant' classroom support role be developed to ensure its sustainability, as a pathway to teaching or as a role in its own right?

Further reading

Crisp, M., Safford, K. and Wolfenden, F. (2017) *It Takes a Village to Raise a Teacher: The Learning Assistant Programme in Sierra Leone*. [Available at http://oro.open.ac.uk/49603/.]
Novelli, M., Higgins, S., Ugur, M. and Valiente, O. (2014) *The Political Economy of Education Systems in Conflict-Affected Contexts*. London: Department for International Development and University of Sussex.
Tarry, E. and Cox, A. (2013) *Teaching Assistants in International Schools*. London: John Catt Educational.

References

Education Policy and Data Center (2014) Sierra Leone – National Education Profile 2014 Update. [Available at www.epdc.org/sites/default/files/documents/EPDC NEP_Sierra Leone.pdf, accessed 26 July 2017.]
Novelli, M. and Higgins, S. (2017) The violence of peace and the role of education: Insights from Sierra Leone. *Compare: A Journal of Comparative and International Education*, 47 (1), 32–45.
Novelli, M., Higgins, S., Ugur, M. and Valiente, O. (2014) *The Political Economy of Education Systems in Conflict-Affected Contexts, Brighton*. [Available at www.gov.uk/government/uploads/system/uploads/attachment_data/file/469101/political-economy-conflict-affected.pdf.]
Statistics Sierra Leone (2016) *2015 Population and Housing Census: Summary of final results, Freetown*. [Available at www.statistics.sl/wp-content/uploads/2017/01/final-results_2015_population_and_housing_census.pdf.]
Wenger, E. (1999) *Communities of Practice: Learning, Meaning and Identity*. Cambridge: Cambridge University Press.

Part 5
Local, national and global intersections

21 Is the grass always greener? The effect of the PISA results on education debates in Sweden and Germany

Johanna Ringarp and Martin Rothland

Introduction

What does a country do when its schools and educational system in general do not produce the results the country believes they are capable of? This chapter describes the political debates that comparative international studies such as the Programme for International Student Assessment (PISA) gave rise to in Germany and Sweden. As a result of the PISA scores, both countries have gone outside their borders in order to find new models and policy norms. The authors analyse whether or not the debate on educational policy in the two countries plays a role in *policy borrowing*. Germany looks to the north, primarily to Sweden – the country at the forefront of pedagogy – but also to Finland. At the same time, Sweden is in the process of dismantling just those parts of its educational policy that have aroused interest and admiration in other countries, especially Germany. Who is learning from whom? And is the grass always greener on the other side?

A rude awakening? Points of departure for debates on PISA in Sweden and Germany

In most European countries, including those with the highest rankings, the PISA results set off a debate, often couched in critical terms, about their respective educational systems. In the first PISA assessment in 2000, the German students' results were well below the average of the Organisation for Economic Co-operation and Development (OECD). This came as a shock to Germany and produced a national crisis in a country that for years had viewed itself as the 'great' education country. While the Swedish students' results were better than those of the German students, they did not rank near the top. Leading the study were the Finnish students, who have continued to achieve excellent results in PISA assessments (OECD 2000, 2003, 2006).

In both Sweden and Germany, the results of the studies have been the catalyst for school policy discussions. In Sweden, the debate has dealt primarily with the teaching profession and the quality of teacher education. Germany's weak results gave rise to a more sweeping discussion of the country's educational system: the debate centred on the sad state of education, and how '*das Land der Dichter und Denker*' ('the land of poets and thinkers') could fail so miserably.

Policy borrowing with a view on the education sector

Many people view policy borrowing as a natural consequence of globalisation; even though Steiner-Khamsi and Stolpe (2006) do not equate the two, they believe that it is customary for policy makers in one country to refer to reforms in other countries when they want to carry out changes in their own. With regard to the field of education, the OECD assessments such as PISA, for example, have been very important for the implementation of *policy borrowing in education.*

The concept of 'borrowing' has been criticised by some researchers, who have proposed alternative terms, such as 'travel', 'copying', 'assimilation' and 'transfer' (see the discussion in Phillips and Ochs 2003). While the concept may be controversial, the definitions of what it concerns are, for the most part, similar. It deals with a form of transformation or transfer of a *policy* from one country to another, in this case, within the field of education. The introduction of a new policy itself can then be explained in four fairly easy stages, which Phillips and Ochs (2003) call 'cross-national attraction', 'decision', 'implementation' and, finally, 'internalization'. The first stage, *cross-national attraction*, deals with a country's impulse to change the system. The reason for the inclination to change may derive, in part, from the educational sector's negative results in external assessments – for example, PISA – and in part from general dissatisfaction with the current educational system among teachers, students and parents. Regardless of the reason, according to the model put forth by Phillips and Ochs, individuals look for inspiration and solutions in the world around them in order to cope with the situation. The next stage in the model deals with *decisions* and the measures that the government and other authorities resolve to launch in order to bring about change – for example, they might choose to develop a new type of school or a fresh approach to education in the country. Once the decision is made, we enter the next phase, which involves the *implementation* of the new policy in the country. In order for this to be carried out, there must be a strong conviction within the government that something is wrong in the educational sector and that in order for the situation to be rectified, a change must take place. Second, if there is consensus regarding the solution, it is up to the players within the field to see to it that the reform is pushed through. The last stage, *internalisation*, deals with assimilating the new policy and ensuring that all the various parts of the educational system apply it.

Thus, if the model is executed, it can lead to a reform of the educational system. In this way, a country's ideas and concepts can be implemented in another country with the help of policy makers. However, the execution is not always easy; most often, in the *implementation* phase, educational policy makers miss the fact that a particular system's success depends on specific national or local contexts. When the system is then transferred to another country, there is no guarantee that it will work equally well (Gabisonia 2007). Therefore, some further reform, designed to adapt the system to the new country's needs and conditions, is required. For instance, if it is true that a negative external review, such as poor results in international assessments, can be a powerful rationale for *educational borrowing*, which earlier studies have demonstrated (see, for example, Ochs 2006; Berényi and Neumann 2009; Grek et al. 2009), then it is interesting to look at the way in which Germany and Sweden conducted themselves after the PISA results were announced.

Study trips to the PISA 'Wonderland': a German look at the Swedish educational system

It was as if Germany's self-image splintered when the PISA results, which were below the average for the countries studied, were made public (Hermes 2003). In spite of the fact that earlier international comparative studies had indicated a similar trend, one thing now became clear: the country had fallen from its pedestal (see, for example, Helwig 2002; Ingenkamp 2002). While Germany improved its standing somewhat in PISA 2003, this did not either ease the anxiety or bring an end to the discussion. Of course, the situation had improved, but much still remained to be done in order for the country to regain its standing in the field of education.

After the first assessment in 2000, Germany's interest in Sweden, 'the pedagogic wonder to the north', grew. On the one hand, Germany needed to acquire a broader global perspective in the internal debate on education (Weigel 2004). On the other, even before the PISA studies, Sweden had been viewed as a leader in the field of pedagogical development and the design of educational systems (Engel 2003). One consequence of this was that teachers, union members, researchers and politicians took study tours to both Finland, the country at the cutting edge, and to Sweden (Eibeck 2002). These study tours, also described as a 'pilgrimage to the PISA wonderlands' (Schwarz 2002), produced numerous articles and reports. What was it about Swedish education that so fascinated these travellers? They all reacted positively to the joy of reform and the courage it took for Sweden to introduce an all-day comprehensive school that welcomed everyone, including children with physical disabilities (Schnack 2002; Schwarz 2002; Eikenbusch 2003). In Sweden, concepts such as solidarity, equal opportunity and every individual's right to an education were not just empty words; they were a reality (van der Groeben 2003). At the same time, Swedish students were producing excellent results (Schmerr 2002).

The high degree of Swedish school autonomy, deregulation and the barely visible bureaucracy also engendered admiration. From a German perspective, decentralisation and deregulation were viewed as something positive, both for the school as an organisation and for the pedagogical work in the schools (Engel 2003). In addition, the German 'pilgrims' viewed the opportunity given to individual Swedish schools to select the pedagogy on which to base their instruction as both interesting and positive (Seelmann-Eggebert and Richter 2006).

The reality behind the Swedish educational system

The Swedish PISA results did not bring on the same rude awakening. In part, this probably had to do with the fact that they were better than the German ones and more in line with the country's image of its level of educational attainment. Nor did any in-depth debates or even a description of the PISA study in general and the Swedish results in particular appear in professional pedagogical publications. Instead, discussions took place in the media, both on the front pages of newspapers and through political initiatives of politicians and teachers' unions, for the purpose of raising the status of the teaching profession.

Thus, the autonomy of the teaching profession was linked to the students' results by, among other things, comparing the status of Swedish teachers with that of their Finnish colleagues. It was felt that Finland's excellent results were based in part on the fact that Finnish teachers enjoy an elevated status, in spite of their low salaries (Uljens 2005). This status brings with it a growing number of applications for teacher training that, for its part, produces competent, certified teachers. In Sweden, on the other hand, the number of certified teachers decreased from 90% in 1992/93 to below 80% a decade later (Persson 2006).

Ironically then, German educators travelled to a country whose educational policy was in a state of change. Sweden had had a compulsory comprehensive, mixed-ability system of education since the 1960s. But by 2007 it was acknowledged that the nine-year compulsory school had not become a school for everyone; on the contrary, many students left school without a complete education, often because they were routinely moved up to the next grade without having met the goals for the previous grade. The notion was put forward that the lack of discipline in Swedish schools had impacted on the students' poor showings in the PISA international studies. A behaviour intervention plan that included written evaluations, detention, parent–teacher meetings and limited suspension were all suggested as ways to help the teachers and school administrators improve discipline in the classroom, as well as student achievement (Folkpartiet 2006; 2009). One political party proposed a different educational system, under which part of the Swedish academic upper secondary school would have a more practical orientation (Folkpartiet 2006; 2009); in many ways, this proposal was similar to the German apprentice system.

Those who worked in the school system did not exactly greet the proposals from the political parties with open arms. For example, the Swedish Union of Teachers expressed scepticism at the behaviour intervention plan, which they feared would only lead to students currying favour with them (Hansson 2007). However, some of the proposals, among them the 2007 bill on 'Improved Order, Security and Quiet Study Time in Schools' were implemented (Utbildningsdepartementet 2007a). Here, it should be noted that previously teachers could also punish students through the use of detention or suspension from class; now the teachers' right to expel students from school if they misbehaved was articulated more clearly. Furthermore, in the society as a whole, there was a growing initiative to increase the teachers' disciplinary authority (Skolverket 2007b).

Additional proposals for changes to the Swedish educational system included internships (Socialdemokraterna 2009) or a probationary year for teachers (Folkpartiet 2009). This can be compared with Germany, where teacher education is divided into two parts: after studying at university, students enter into a two-year practical training programme. Concurrent with the practical segment, they take courses at a

Studienseminar. These seminars are not connected to a university; rather, they are teaching bodies that are part of the German government, and the instructors are qualified teachers whose task it is to train future teachers (Terhart 2005).

Perhaps it is not so surprising that, in spite of German expectations and its admiration for Sweden, the latter is not an education paradise. On the other hand, what may be surprising is the fact that the Swedish government had begun to change just those parts of the educational system that international observers had looked up to. The Swedish educational system has gone from being one of the most centralised in the West to one of the most decentralised in the twentieth century, one in which even private schools can carry on and make a profit with government funding (see Lindblad et al. 2002; Utbildningsdepartementet 2007b; Skolverket 2009). According to the National Agency for Education, this streaming has entailed obvious segregation in both the standard of attainment and among the students. Under the neighbourhood principle that applied previously, all students, regardless of their socio-economic background, attended the same school; today, this principle has been replaced by one in which students attend individualised, streamed schools (Skolverket 2009; see also Arnesen and Lundahl 2006). There is no question that the Swedish educational system idealised by German educators had disappeared without the Germans even noticing. The country they thought they visited no longer exists. Instead of an educational policy that embraced a goal of one school for everyone, a radically different policy, one with deregulation, decentralisation and privatisation as catchwords, emerged in Sweden (Bjarnason and Persson 2007).

Who learns from whom?

We return to the question that was posed initially: Have discussions about educational borrowing taken place in Sweden and Germany following the results of the PISA studies? Our answer is 'yes' and 'no'. But we are of the opinion that the two countries have only achieved the first or, possibly in the case of Sweden, the second phase of the Phillips and Ochs model, that is the *cross-national attraction* and *decision* phases.

The debate initiated by the external PISA assessments dealt with the need to begin change work. But with regard to Germany, for example, no real transfer in educational policy has occurred. Instead, the debate has resulted in both a more theoretical pedagogical debate and a practical approach in the form of study and informational trips for teachers and other individuals in the field of education. Accordingly, Sweden's function as a model for Germany has more to do with serving as a point of departure for public debate than as a model for changes in the German educational sector. In conclusion, we have determined that much remains to be done before one can talk about real *educational borrowing* in Germany and Sweden as a consequence of the PISA results.

Questions

1. In your own country, have you had knowledge or experience of an internationally comparative assessment such as PISA or TIMMS (Trends in International Mathematics and Science Study)? How did your country perform in these comparative assessments?

2. Has your country had an experience of educational assessment 'shock', such as Germany? What was the impact? Was there 'policy borrowing' from other, more successful, nations?
3. How useful are internationally comparative assessments, in your view?

Further reading

Grek, S. (2009) Governing by Numbers: The PISA 'effect' in Europe. *Journal of Education Policy*, 24 (1), 23–37.
Steiner-Khamsi, G. (2003) The Politics of League Tables. *Journal of Social Science Education*, 1. [Available at http://www.jsse.org/2003/2003-1/tables-khamsi.htm.]

The full text of this chapter is: Ringarp, J. and Rothland, M. (2010) Is the grass always greener? The effect of PISA results on education debates in Sweden and Germany. *European Educational Research Journal*, 9 (3), 422–430.

References

Arnesen, A.-L. and Lundahl, L. (2006) Still Social and Democratic? Inclusive education policies in the Nordic welfare states. *Scandinavian Journal of Educational Research*, 50 (3), 285–300.
Berényi, E. and Neumann, E. (2009) Grappling with PISA: Reception and translation in the Hungarian policy discourse. *Sísifo*, 10, 41–52.
Bjarnason, D. and Persson, B. (2007) Inkludering i de nordiska utbildningssystemen: En socio-historisk bakgrund [Inclusion in the Scandinavian educational system: A socio-historical background]. *Psykologisk Pædagogisk Rådgivning*, 44 (3), 202–224.
Eibeck, B. (2002) Reise ins Pisa-Wunderland Schweden [Journey to Sweden, the PISA Wonderland]. *Welt des Kindes*, 80, 42–43.
Eikenbusch, G. (2003) Alle sind gleich – aber jeder ist anders . . . Erkundungen zur Kultur der Individualisierung und Differenzierung in Schweden [Everyone is alike but everyone is different . . . investigations into the culture of individualization and differentiation in Sweden]. *Pädagogik*, 9, 10–14.
Engel, H. (2003) Schulverwaltungsreform in Schweden: Ein Modell fur Deutschland? [School administration reform in Sweden: A model for Germany?]. In von Döbert, H., Kopp, B., Martini, R. and Weiß, M. (Eds) *Bildung vor neuen Herausforderungen: Historische Bezuge – rechtliche Aspekte – Steuerungsfragen – internationale Perspektiven* (pp. 332–338). Neuwied: Luchterhand.
Folkpartiet (2006) Mer ordning i skolan: 9 förslag från folkpartiet [More order in schools: 9 proposals from the Liberal Party]. [Available at www.folkpartiet.se/upload/61590/Ordningsomdöme.pdf.]
Folkpartiet (2009) Dags att sikta ännu högre: Skolgruppens förslag till ny utbildningspolitik [It's time to set our sights even higher: Proposals for a new educational policy]. [Available at www.folkpartiet.se/ImageVault/Images/id_5453/ImageVaultHandler.aspx.]
Gabisonia, T. (2007) A Literature Review on the Causes and Stages of the Education Borrowing or Nature of Education Borrowing. [Available at www.scribd.com/doc/28792700/Nature-of-Education-Borrowing.]
Grek, S., Lawn, M., Lingard, B., Ozga, J., Rinne, R., Segerholm, C. and Simola, H. (2009) National policy brokering and the construction of the European education space in England, Sweden, Finland and Scotland. *Comparative Education*, 45 (1), 5–21.
Groeben, A. van der (2003) Schule(n) in Schweden: Eindrucke einer Bildungs-Reise [School(s) in Sweden: Impressions of an educational journey]. *Neue Sammlung*, 43, 203–210.
Hansson, M.E. (2007) Betyg på barnens uppförande [Grading children's behaviour]. *Svenska Dagbladet*, 16 April. [Available at www.svd.se/stockholm/nyheter/artikel_218491.svd.]
Helwig, G. (2002) PISA-Schock [PISA shock]. *Deutschland-Archiv*, 35, 369–372.
Hermes, L. (2003) Die OECD-PISA Untersuchung in Deutschland: Nationales Ungluck oder heilsamer Schock? [The OECD-PISA study in Germany: National disaster or beneficial shock?] *Karlsruher Pädagogische Beiträge*, 55, 35–54.

Ingenkamp, H. (2002) Die veröffentlichte Reaktion auf PISA: Ein deutsches Trauerspiel [The published reaction to PISA: A German drama]. *Empirische Pädagogik*, 16, 409–418.

Lindblad, S., Lundahl, L., Lindgren, J. and Zackari, G. (2002) Educating for the new Sweden? *Scandinavian Journal of Educational Research*, 46 (3), 283–303.

Ochs, K. (2006) Cross-national policy borrowing and educational innovation: Improving achievement in the London borough of Barking and Dagenham. *Oxford Review of Education*, 32 (5), 599–618.

Organisation for Economic Co-operation and Development (OECD) (2000) Knowledge and Skills for Life: *First results from PISA 2000*. Paris: OECD. [Available at www.oecd.org/dataoecd/44/32/33691620.pdf.]

Organisation for Economic Co-operation and Development (OECD) (2003) *First Results from PISA 2003: Executive summary*. Paris: OECD. [Available at www.pisa.oecd.org/dataoecd/1/63/34002454.pdf.]

Organisation for Economic Co-operation and Development (OECD) (2006) *PISA 2006: Science competencies for tomorrow's world. Executive Summary*. Paris: OECD. [Available at www.oecd.org/dataoecd/15/13/39725224.pdf.]

Persson, A. (2006) Nöjda som lärare, missnöjda som anställda: Skolexistens mellan mening och missnöje [Satisfied as teachers, dissatisfied as employees: School existence between meaning and dissatisfaction]. In Petersson, H., Leppänen, V., Jönsson, S. & Tranquist, J. (Eds) *Villkor i arbete med människor: en antologi om human* servicearbete (p. 4). Arbetslivsinstitutet (Department of Technology and Change).

Phillips, D. and Ochs, K. (2003) Processes of policy borrowing in education: Some explanatory and analytical devices. *Comparative Education*, 39 (4), 451–461.

Schmerr, M. (2002) Was macht Schweden anders? Eine Reise zu den Schulen des Nordens [What makes Sweden different? A journey to the schools of the north]. *Die Deutsche Schule*, 94, 282–289.

Schnack, J. (2002) Warum hat Schweden die Nase vorn? [Why is Sweden the leader?]. *Pädagogik*, 1, 57–58.

Schwarz, P. (2002) Blick nach Norden: Pilgerfahrt in die skandinavischen PISA-Wunderländer: Finnland und Schweden [The view northward: A pilgrimage to the Scandinavian PISA wonderlands: Finland and Sweden]. *Pädagogische Beiträge: Unterricht und Schulleben in Rheinland-Pfalz*, 2, 4–7.

Seelmann-Eggebert, G. and Richter, R. (2006) Von den Schweden lernen: Impressionen einer Studienreise nach Göteborg [Learning from Sweden: Impressions of an educational journey to Gothenburg]. *Die Ganztagsschule*, 46 (4), 151–157.

Skolverket (2007) *Trygghet Och Studiero i Skolan* [Security and quiet study time in school]. Stockholm: Skolverket.

Skolverket (2009) *Vad Påverkar Resultaten I Svensk Grundskola? Kunskapsöversitk om Betydelsen av Olika Faktorer* [What influences the results in Swedish nine-year compulsory school? Knowledge overview of the importance of different factors]. Stockholm: Skolvert.

Socialdemokraterna (2009) *Beslut om framtida skoloch utbildningspolitik* [Decisions on future school and educational policy]. [Available at www.s-info.se/press.asp?press_id=3266.]

Steiner-Khamsi, G. and Stolpe, I. (2006) *Educational Import in Mongolia: Local Encounters with Global Forces*. New York: Palgrave Macmillan.

Terhart, E. (2005) Die Lehrerbildung [Teacher education]. In Cortina, K.S., Baumert, J., Leshinsky, A., Mayer K.U. and Trommer, L. (Eds) *Das Bildungswesen in der Bundesrepublik Deutschland: Strukturen und Entwicklungen im Überblick*. Hamburg: Rowohlt.

Uljens, M. (2005) PISA-resultaten i Finland: Perspektiv på och förklaring till Framgången [PISA results in Finland: Perspectives on and exposition of success]. [Available at www.vasa.abo.fi/users/muljens/pdf/PISA.pdf.]

Utbildningsdepartementet (2007a) Förbättrad ordning, trygghet och studiero i skolan [Improved order, security and quiet study time in schools]. [Available at www.regeringen.se/content/1/c6/07/54/53/cb7f8c62.pdf.]

Weigel, T.M. (2004) Die PISA-Studie im bildungspolitischen Diskurs: Eine Untersuchung der Reaktionen auf PISA in Deutschland und im Vereinigten Königreich [The PISA study in the educational policy discourse: A review of reactions in Germany and the United Kingdom]. Trier: University Trier.

22 Creativity and education in the European Union and the United Kingdom

Dominic Wyse and Anusca Ferrari

Introduction

The importance of creativity in children's learning has increasingly been recognised from diverse sources, including drives for greater national economic prosperity and enlightenment visions of young people's education. One facet of creativity in education is its visibility in national curriculum policies and programme documents. The research in this chapter analyses the place of creativity in the national curricula of (at the time of writing) the 27 member states of the European Union (EU 27) and in the United Kingdom, and compares this information to the responses of 7,659 teachers to a survey.

The place of creativity in education

If we accept that originality and value are two definitional concepts in relation to creativity, this raises a series of questions about how they might be reflected in early years and primary/elementary education. Although it is possible for children and young people to have revolutionary ideas that are both original and valuable to wider society, it is perhaps more appropriate to interpret originality and value in their more everyday meanings (Runco 2003). The adoption of what has been called a democratic view of creativity (NACCCE 1999; Craft 2011) recognises the potential of all individuals to be creative (Esquivel 1995). Creativity in this perspective is an attribute that can be developed and therefore learnt, and its output reflects something new and of value. However, as with major creative work of historical significance, the judgements involved are rarely straightforward. The thinking and products of children are often original and valuable for the children themselves, but not in comparison with larger norms (Runco 2003). This leads to a re-thinking of the concept of value, as it is the learners themselves, and their educators, who might judge the value of their creative expression (Runco 2003; Craft 2005; Jones and Wyse 2013). Research indicates that when educators make judgements about creativity, for example in relation to music teaching, they draw on their experience in both teaching and in their subject discipline (Odena and Welch 2009). In addition to drawing on experience, educators' judgements are influenced by basic beliefs about creativity, such as whether it is innate or not. Kokotsaki's (2011) research with student teachers of music found that their understanding of creativity was intuitive rather than explicit, and that national curriculum documents needed to include working definitions and explicit guidance to support such teachers. The focus on the everyday, democratic conception of creativity, that is concerned with the agency of teachers and learners, has been described as 'little c creativity' (Craft et al. 2001), as opposed to 'big C creativity', which describes exemplary achievements in a given domain and entails some refashioning of the domain it contributes to.

Extending our understanding of the way that originality and value are manifest can also be enhanced by consideration of whether creativity is domain-specific or domain-general. There are two main lines of thinking: one strand of scholarship concentrates on whether people who are creative in a given domain are likely to be creative in another domain or if creative endeavour reflects 'islands of creativity' firmly attached to a given domain (Silvia et al. 2009; Baer 2010). Another strand of scholarship has tried to establish whether creativity is a phenomenon that crosses disciplines, or if instead creativity differs significantly across different disciplines (NACCCE 1999). Findings on both strands are contrasting and inconclusive. Scholarship of creativity in education has moved to view creativity as being relevant to any domain or area of knowledge. This has been linked with rejection of creativity as the preserve of the arts alone (Runco 1999; Sharp 2004; Beghetto 2007) and cautions against creativity's role being solely concerned with self-expression (summarised in Sternberg and Lubart 1999) that is best manifest through artistic performance. However, overall there is a lack of clarity in relation to creativity as a cross-cutting phenomenon or as entailing some specific attributes particularly applicable to the arts, something that scholars in the field regard as worthy of further attention (Baer 2010).

Creativity in national curricula

According to the analysis of frequency, creativity was included in national curriculum texts of European countries but there were notable differences between countries. Occurrences of creativity ranged from 0.04 per thousand words in the Netherlands and Poland to 1.78 in Northern Ireland (see Figure 22.1 for the ratios of occurrences across Europe). There was no European country where the search term was not present. The reference to creativity in all of the EU 27 national curricula suggests that policy-makers and curriculum developers recognise the relevance of creativity for education. If we accept ratios of occurrence as an indicator of the importance of creativity then it is also clear from the ratios that its importance varies widely across different states. This reflects to some degree the extent to which creativity is deemed to be an educational priority in national curricula or not.

Creativity occurred far more frequently in the curricula for arts-related subjects than in other subjects (see Table 22.1). The term occurred almost twice as much in arts than in the any other subject group. The idea that creativity is a feature of all disciplines did not appear to have been reflected in the ratios of its occurrence across national curriculum subjects. The higher occurrence of the term in the arts subjects group could reflect a perception about the 'natural' place of creativity in the arts, and a lack of alignment with the theory of creativity as relevant for all subjects.

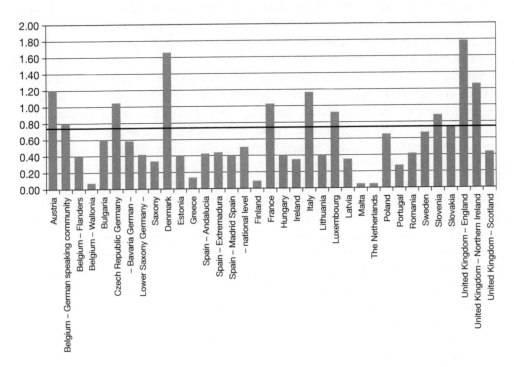

Figure 22.1 Ratios of occurrence (per thousand words) of creativity in national curriculum texts in the countries of Europe

Source: JRC (see Chachia et al. 2010).

Table 22.1 Ratios of the inclusion of the term creativity in school subjects

Subject group	Ratios
Arts	1.66
ICT	0.85
Physical education	0.54
Languages	0.50
Social sciences	0.24
Other	0.28
Natural sciences	0.20
Mathematics	0.17

A common semantic context for creativity in curriculum texts was as a thinking skill and related to problem-solving, however curriculum text developers did not in general refer explicitly to creativity when drawing specifications for subjects such as the natural sciences and mathematics, which might be expected if creativity is conceived mainly as a thinking skill.

Creativity was not commonly cited across the subject group of languages, including national language. The national curricula for these subjects contain areas such as literature, writing, and sometimes creative writing, disciplines where creativity might be assumed to be central and therefore where one would expect to find higher relative occurrences of the term. Instead, connections with creativity were more frequent in the visual arts and music than in languages and literature.

The content analysis of the EU 27 revealed that creativity was more frequently present in UK curriculum texts than other European countries. Northern Ireland had the highest ratio of all EU 27 (the analysis did not include Wales' Framework for Children's Learning for 3–7 year-olds [Department for Children, Education, Lifelong Learning and Skills, 2008] which is notable for having a separate area of learning devoted exclusively to creativity).

Primary education in the UK has long been regarded as notable for its creative elements. One aspect of this was the child-centred education attributed to primary schools in the 1960s, 1970s and 1980s (characterised memorably in the 1967 Plowden Report). In this same period, schools and local education authorities attracted attention internationally for their innovative and creative approaches, including topic-based learning, the integrated day, and creative writing. The *Creative Partnerships* initiative in England from 2002 to 2011 was further evidence of a commitment to creativity (see Arts Council England 2012). Summing up the implications of some 20 years of advances in research on creativity and motivation, Hennessey (2010) recognised the influence of the British infant classroom model of the 1960s on the open classroom of the 1970s in the United States. Hennessey regards the infant classroom approach as the ideal practical realisation of the optimal conditions for creativity.

Creativity and subject areas: an example from England

One area of debate in the creativity research has been the extent to which creativity is a feature of different subjects or areas of learning. The analysis of the primary national curriculum texts for England revealed that the lowest ratio of occurrence was in the programmes of study for geography and history, respectively at one occurrence each. The single occurrence of the term for history and geography was not part of the programmes of study but appeared in the foreword to the national curriculum which applies to all subjects, promoting the aim of enabling pupils:

> . . . to foster their creativity [and] give teachers discretion to find the best ways to inspire in their pupils a joy and commitment to learning that will last a lifetime.
>
> (Department for Education and Employment 1999: 3)

Mathematics also had a low ratio 0.13 (2 occurrences); one of the two was in the subject title page, and read as follows:

> Mathematics is a creative discipline. It can stimulate moments of pleasure and wonder when a pupil solves a problem for the first time, discovers a more elegant solution to that problem, or suddenly sees hidden connections.
>
> (Department for Education and Employment (DfEE) and The Qualifications and Curriculum Authority (QCA) 1999: 60)

The idea that mathematics is a 'creative discipline' is a strong claim, and one that you would expect to see represented in the detail of the programmes of study. However, in the details of the knowledge, skills and understanding that pupils were to acquire, creativity did not appear. There seems therefore to be a gap between the general claim that mathematics is a 'creative discipline' and its realisation in the specific knowledge and abilities that learners have to develop. It could be argued that an aspect of creativity was implied in the requirements for 'problem-solving' that appear in the programmes of study. However, although solutions to problems might require a creative approach this was not explicitly suggested in the document. Instead pupils were to experience 'trying alternative approaches'. Original ways of solving issues were not specified, instead pupils were to be taught to use 'appropriate tools, methods, approaches, solutions' rather than develop their own approaches and test them.

The research revealed a mismatch between creativity stated in general aims for UK curricula and the subsequent details of programmes of study in subject areas. The general aims often strongly advocated the place of creativity but this was not matched by the place of creativity in the detail of the programmes of study for most subjects, although creativity was more prevalent in the arts subjects. The importance of general national curriculum aims in relation to nations' aspirations for their citizens, and the extent of the fit with programmes of study, is part of a wider challenge for curriculum developers (White, 2004). It is necessary for general aims to be rigorously and coherently represented in the detail of programmes of study to enhance and focus pupils' experiences of creativity for the benefit of their learning.

Teachers' perceptions of creativity

There was very strong agreement from the survey respondents that creativity is not only relevant to arts subjects. Eighty-six per cent of EU respondents disagreed with the statement that creativity is only relevant to visual arts, music, drama and artistic performance (56% disagree and 31% strongly disagree). The responses to the same question for the UK (out of the 98 respondents) were 47 disagree, 46 strongly disagree. Teachers from the EU believed that creativity can be applied to every school subject (96%). Ninety respondents from the UK agreed or strongly agreed with the statement that creativity is a skill that can be applied to every school subject, and 94 respondents agreed or strongly agreed with the statement that creativity is a skill that can be applied to every domain of knowledge.

The survey addressed the two fundamental concepts in relation to defining creativity: originality and value. There was strong support within the EU27 that creativity is the ability to produce something original: 79% of respondents agreed or strongly agreed; within the UK there was majority support for this idea (59 respondents agree or strongly agree; 12 neither agree nor disagree; 24 disagree or strongly disagree); to the question that creativity is about finding connections between things that have not been connected before, 69 agreed or strongly agreed; 25 neither agreed nor disagreed; 1 disagreed). Similar ranges of responses were seen in relation to creativity as the ability to produce something of value (56 respondents agreed or strongly agreed; 25 respondents neither agree nor disagree; 15 disagree, or strongly disagree). Value as a more problematic concept than originality was evidenced by responses to the statement that creativity can be assessed (agree or strongly agree 40, neither agree not disagree 41, strongly disagree or disagree 14). The process of assessment, just like the process of determining value, requires a judgement to be made.

The idea that creativity is a trait that only some people have was strongly rejected by respondents: 88% of EU teachers agreed with the statement that everyone can be creative. From the UK, 95 out of 98 responses agreed or strongly agreed with the statement that everyone can be creative. Related to this, 85 responses disagreed or strongly disagreed with the idea that creativity is a characteristic of eminent people only. However, there was less certainty about the related idea of creativity being an inborn talent: 64 responses disagreed or strongly disagreed with this idea but 29 agreed or strongly agreed. This was related to the responses about whether creativity can be taught: 64 responses agreed or strongly agreed but 30 responses neither agreed nor disagreed, or disagreed. These responses suggest that respondents believed strongly that everyone can be creative, but there was uncertainty about the extent to which this is a product of inborn talent or something that can be taught.

The categories of critical thinking, independence and curiosity are key aspects of fostering creativity. The question 'How often do you foster the following skills and abilities in your students?' showed some interesting responses from the UK. The number of responses suggesting that the teachers always or often fostered these three skills and abilities in students was high (critical thinking, 73 responses; independence, 92 responses; curiosity, 91 responses). The tension between developing creativity and developing other skills that are both necessary for creativity but also a potential barrier to creativity if emphasised too strongly, was perhaps evident in the similarly high responses to the following categories: fostering basic skills, 82 responses; accurate recall, 53 responses; discipline, 80 responses.

Discussion

The inclusion of explicit reference to creativity in all national curricula of the EU27 is an indication that creativity is valued by policy-makers and curriculum developers. But the wide range of ratios of occurrences of creativity suggests that creativity is valued differently in the national curriculum policies of different countries and states. It is likely that creativity will have a more significant impact on pupils' learning if the choices made to include creativity in national curricula are coherent throughout different types and sections of texts (e.g., general documents into programmes of study for subjects, and primary level through to secondary level).

The predominant location of creativity in the arts subjects of the national curricula in the EU27 contrasts with a strong trend in the creativity research field suggesting that creativity is a feature of all subjects and disciplines. This representation in the curriculum texts also contrasted with the opinions of the teachers in their view that creativity was not only relevant to the arts. One implication of this finding is that a closer match between national curricula and creativity research could be achieved if greater attention was paid to the location of creativity in curriculum texts in order to ensure greater balance of attention to creativity across curriculum subjects. However, it can also be argued that the role of creativity in artistic composition and enactment is qualitatively different, for example, from the creativity of problem framing and solving that is an important part of maths and sciences, and that this qualitative difference may be a sufficient rationale for the higher inclusion of creativity in arts subjects. Whichever view is taken by policy-makers means that a more explicit rationale for the inclusion of creativity, and definition of creativity, is required in curricula to ensure greater cohesion and rigor.

The lack of attention to creativity in the subject group of languages should perhaps be of concern to educators and curriculum developers. Although the learning of the vocabulary and grammar of languages may not require an emphasis on creativity, one important element of writing in particular is the creative process of the writer who makes choices over elements, particularly when writing story and poetry forms but also in non-fiction writing. Furthermore, the theory of reading as a transaction (Rosenblatt 1985) suggests that comprehension of texts is not only a literal process but also an active two-way process of transaction between texts and reader that can require creative thinking. To take another example, the dramatic realisation of play scripts also requires creativity to achieve impact on audiences. One possible reason for the lack of attention to creativity in the language subjects may be an overemphasis on functional literacy intensified as a result of the growth of high-stakes testing of attainment in this area.

The higher ratios of occurrence of creativity in UK national curricula, compared to the EU27, parallel the historic attention to creativity in the UK. Creativity in the UK has most frequently been attributed to primary and early years education, for example through child-centred approaches such as the British Infant school model and the integrated day, a form of cross-curricular thematic planning deriving, in part, from children's interests. But the findings of our study show that creativity has become more prevalent in secondary national curricula in the UK than in primary curricula. This could represent a move towards the rationalist perception of the primary years as first and foremost the place for the development of functional knowledge, skills and understanding in preparation for secondary schooling. If this is the case it runs counter to the evidence that creative thinking is a feature of children's development from the early years on-wards that can be supported through appropriate curricula.

Across Europe, policy documents suggest that creativity is still regarded as a key goal of education. Recommendations to foster 'creative ways of teaching and learning' and 'creative thinking' continue to appear in policy documents (European Commission 2012), while the aim of 'enhancing creativity and innovation at all levels of education' is foreseen in the strategic framework for European cooperation in education and training (European Commission 2009). Although the remit of educational policies lies with the member states, the Commission could highlight the ambiguity of the use of creativity and work towards a more coherent approach to creativity in the curriculum.

Questions

1.   What is the place of creativity in the primary school curriculum of your country? Is creativity aligned more with some subjects than others?
2.   The research found the historic emphasis on creativity in UK primary education has decreased, perhaps because of a growing emphasis on learning basic skills. Does an emphasis on learning literacy and numeracy inhibit creativity, in your view?
3.   How important are policy documents in terms of what happens in the classroom? For another perspective on this, see Chapter 14.

Further reading

Kampylis, P. (2010) Fostering creative thinking: The role of primary teachers. *Jyväskylä Studies in Computing*, 115, S. Puuronen, Finland, University of Jyväskylä.
Wyse, D. (2017) *How writing works: From the Invention of the Alphabet to the Rise of Social Media*. Cambridge University Press.

The full text of this chapter is: Wyse, D. and Ferrari, A. (2015) Creativity and education: Comparing the national curricula of the states of the European Union and the United Kingdom. *British Educational Research Journal*, 41 (1), 30–47

References

Amabile, T. M. (1990) Within you, without you: The Social Psychology of Creativity, and Beyond. In Runco, M.A. and Albert, R.S. (Eds) *Theories of Creativity* (pp. 61–91). London: Sage.
Arts Council England (2012) *Creative Partnerships: Changing Young Lives*. London: Arts Council England and Creativity, Culture and Education.
Baer, J. (2010) Is Creativity Domain Specific? In Sternberg, R.J. and Kaufman, J.C. (Eds) *The Cambridge Handbook of Creativity*. Cambridge: Cambridge University Press.
Banaji, S. and Burn, A. (2006) *The Rhetorics of Creativity: A Review of the Literature*. London: Arts Council England.
Beghetto, R.A. (2007) Creativity Research and the Classroom: From Pitfalls to Potential. In Tan, A.G. (Ed.) *Creativity: A Handbook for Teachers* (pp. 101–114). Singapore: World Scientific.
Chachia, R., Ferrari, A., Ala-Mutka, K. and Punie, Y. (2010) *Creative learning and innovative teaching: Final report on the study of creativity and innovation in education in the EU member states*. Brussels: Joint Research Centre.
Craft, A. (2005) *Creativity in Schools: Tensions and Dilemmas*. London: Routledge.
Craft, A. (2011) *Creativity and Education Futures: Learning in a Digital Age*. Stoke-on-Trent: Trentham Books.
Craft, A. and Jeffrey, B. (2008) Creativity and performativity in teaching and learning. *British Educational Research Journal*, 34 (5), 577–585.
Craft, A., Jeffrey, B. and Leibling, M. (2001) *Creativity in Education*. London: Continuum.
Department for Children, Education, Lifelong Learning and Skills (2008) *Framework for Children's Learning for 3 to 7-year-olds in Wales*. Cardiff: Welsh Assembly Government.

Department for Education (2013) *The National Curriculum in England: Framework Document*. London: DfE.

Department for Education and Employment (DfEE) and The Qualifications and Curriculum Authority (QCA) (1999) *The National Curriculum. Handbook for Primary Teachers in England. Key stages 1 and 2*. Norwich, UK: Her Majesty's Stationery Office (HMSO).

Department for Education and Skills (DfES) (2003) *Excellence and Enjoyment: A Strategy for Primary Schools*. London: DfES.

Department for Education and Skills (DfES) and the Qualifications and Curriculum Authority (QCA) (2004) *Religious Education: The Non-statutory National Framework*. London: DfES.

Esquivel, G.B. (1995) Teacher behaviors that foster creativity. *Educational Psychology Review*, 7 (2), 185–202.

European Commission (2009) Council conclusions of 12 May 2009 on a strategic framework for European cooperation in education and training ('ET 2020'), 2009/C 119/02.

European Commission (2012) Rethinking education: Investing in skills for better socio-economic outcomes, COM(2012) 669 final.

Hennessey, B. (2010) Intrinsic Motivation and Creativity in the Classroom: Have we Come Full Circle? In Beghetto, R. and Kaufman, J. (Eds) *Nurturing Creativity in the Classroom* (pp. 342–365). Cambridge: Cambridge University Press.

Jones, K. and Thomson, P. (2008) Policy rhetoric and the innovation of English schooling: The case of creative partnerships. Journal of Education Policy, 23 (6), 715–727.

Jones, R. and Wyse, D. (Eds) (2013) *Creativity in the Primary Curriculum* (2nd ed.). London: Routledge.

Kokotsaki, D. (2011) Student teachers' conceptions of creativity in the secondary music classroom. *Thinking Skills and Creativity*, 6 (2), 100–113.

NACCCE (1999) All our futures: Creativity, culture and education. [Available at http://sir kenrobinson.com/pdf/allourfutures.pdf, accessed 4 February 2014.]

Odena, O. and Welch, G. (2009) A generative model of teachers' thinking on musical creativity. *Psychology of Music*, 37 (4), 416–442.

Plowden, B. (1967) *Children and Their Primary Schools*. London: HMSO.

Rosenblatt, L. (1985) Viewpoints: Transaction versus interaction: A terminological rescue operation. *Research in the Teaching of English*, 19 (1), 96–107.

Runco, M.A. (1999) Implicit Theories. In Runco, M.A. and Pritzker, S.R. (Eds) *Encyclopedia of creativity* (vol. 2, pp. 27–30). San Diego, CA and London: Academic.

Runco, M.A. (2003) Education for creative potential. *Scandinavian Journal of Educational Research*, 47 (3), 317–324.

Sharp, C. (2004) Developing young children's creativity: What can we learn from research? *Topic*, 32, 5–12.

Silvia, P.J., Kaufman, J.C. and Pretz, J.E. (2009) Is creativity domain-specific? Latent class models of creative accomplishments and creative self-descriptions. *Psychology of Aesthetics, Creativity, and the Arts*, 3 (3), 139.

Sternberg, R.J. and Lubart, T.I. (1999) The concept of creativity: Prospects and Paradigms. In Sternberg, R.J. (Ed.) *Handbook of Creativity* (pp. 3–15). Cambridge: Cambridge University Press.

White, J. (Ed.) (2004) *Rethinking the School Curriculum: Values, Aims and Purposes*. London: Routledge Falmer.

23 New teachers and corporal punishment in Ghanaian primary schools

Alison Buckler

Introduction

School-based corporal punishment is still legal in 76 countries (SRSG 2012). A large-scale survey of children in Ethiopia, India, Peru and Viet Nam reported that 50–90% of children had witnessed a teacher administering physical punishment in the week prior to the survey (Ogando Portela and Pells 2015). While others have highlighted that some teachers, parents and even children believe that corporal punishment is linked to improved learning (Parkes and Heslop 2011; Morrow and Singh, 2014), Ogando Portela and Pells' longitudinal research found that corporal punishment at age 8 is associated with poorer learning outcomes at age 12 (see also UNICEF 2014).

This chapter is about two things. First, it is about how children are disciplined in Ghanaian primary schools. Second, it is about the experiences of Ghanaian educators on the cusp of becoming professional teachers, how their identity, intentions and imagined capabilities for teaching are navigated and negotiated through interactions with pupils and teachers in the 'real world' of the school. It draws on data from a wider study of student-teacher learning in Ghana,[1] but presents a vignette of one student-teacher called Dominic in his third year of teacher training.

The majority of prospective primary-level teachers in Ghana study at residential colleges and work towards their Diploma in Education. The programme – known as the 'in-in-out' model – consists of two years at college studying subject knowledge, educational theories and methods, followed by one year, the 'out-programme', working as a practice-teacher in a school. Dominic was enrolled at a college in the south of Ghana and for his out-programme had been posted to a rural school 40km away, although traffic and road conditions meant that it could take up to two hours to travel between them.

The research was framed conceptually through a socio-cultural lens (Wenger 1998) and analytically using Amartya Sen's capability approach (1999). Other work (Buckler 2015) describes how this framing was used to understand how student-teachers' development of professional capability – moving deeper into the practice of becoming a teacher – depends on the relationships they have developed within the formal and informal environments of teacher training, but also that these relationships shape how professional capabilities are identified, negotiated and pursued. This chapter illustrates this framing by showing how Dominic's perceptions of professional capability in relation to discipline shifted during the out-programme. It is presented in three sections, which correlate with the generation of data through observations and interviews at three points during the 2014–2015 academic year. Through these sections, Dominic's articulations around corporal punishment are considered alongside international, national and local perspectives.

November

> The teachers here carry the cane and say it is the only language that Ghanaian children understand. No, no, no, it's not the only language they understand. Now, there is this student, he is very difficult in class so I have taken him as my friend and I think this is one way of amending their behaviour. Some of them are stubborn so I try to get close to them and find out why. You have to learn about them and learn why they are disturbing in class – maybe there are challenges at home – and see how you can help them to react differently . . . it's about building a relationship with them and taking time to become their friend . . . If you befriend them they feel they can relate to you and there is no need to use the cane.

Corporal punishment[2] is legal in Ghana, although there are regular calls for the government to ban it (Kyei-Gyamfi 2011). In 2011, the Constitution Review Commission suggested that greater clarity be provided in relation to disciplining children but did not recommend changing the law. In 2012 and 2016 reports were filed with the African Committee of Experts on the Rights and Welfare of the Child, which accepted recommendations to ban corporal punishment, but in their most recent report, the Global Initiative to End All Corporal Punishment of Children (GIEACPC 2017) suggested that while the government was committed to law-reform there were no clear plans to mobilise these recommendations.

Ghana is not unusual in this respect. In fact, despite almost all countries globally signing up to the United Nations' Convention on the Rights of the Child, which emphasises protection of children from 'all forms of physical or mental violence, injury or abuse' (UN 1990:7), only eight percent of children live in countries in which these guidelines have been enshrined in law (UNICEF 2014). In Ghana the law is rooted in the 1998 Children's Act, which states that 'correction of a child' must be justified and reasonable (Ghanaian Government 1998).

Ghanaian Government directives aim to limit the use of physical punishment in educational settings, and outline severe repercussions for perpetrators. The Ghana Education Service's Child Friendly School Standards document states that school should be a 'safe environment . . . free from intimidation, violence and abuse including corporal punishment' (see GIEACPC 2017). The Teachers' Code of Conduct (GES 2008) states that children 'should be free from . . . harmful or degrading punishment and any type of violence' (4) and that 'physical harm inflicted on pupils/students . . . constitutes a gross violation of the child's rights' (8). Teachers should not 'administer any act of corporal punishment, or any act that inflicts physical pain . . . or causes physical harm to their pupils/students', 'threaten any pupil/student with harm with intent to put that person in fear of harm', and teachers should 'intervene to stop a fellow teacher from perpetrating physical violence or abuse on another pupil/student' (ibid). However, these directives contradict other documentation such as the Code of Discipline for Schools which aligns with the Children's Act's stipulation on 'justifiable' correction and authorises the headteacher, or a person authorised by the headteacher, to administer up to four strokes of the cane (Kyei-Gyamfi 2011).

The confusing policy and media narrative over the legality of corporal punishment (Dery 2017), combined with widely held acceptance, maintains the practice. A 2006 study reported that 43 percent of mothers and care-givers in Ghana believed physical punishment was appropriate (MICS in Kyei-Gyamfi 2011). CAMFED research found that 64 percent of teachers said it must be tolerated, while 94 percent of parents and 92 percent of students were in favour of school-based corporal punishment (GNA 2011).

February

> It's not like we are teachers, they don't respect us like teachers so we need to think of ways to get respect . . . so I just became very strict. I had to. But we only use the cane when the children get really out of hand . . . I set some homework and less than half of the class had done it, maybe 19 out of 60 and I was very angry. So I had to make them aware that I was as strict and as serious as any other teacher so I actually did cane those who had not done their homework. I think they were sorry and I told them the next time I would cane them again and they are better now. The fear is enough now and I can continue my approach of trying to get close to them.

Dominic had been posted to a rural government school with oversight from a wealthy Presbyterian church which owned the land. Unlike many schools in similar locations in Ghana, it had smartly painted classrooms surrounding a manicured field. But the field was rented out for corporate events and the children were not allowed to play on it – their break-time was confined to the concrete steps between the field and the school buildings. Fresh from the college and keen to 'make a positive change in these children's lives' Dominic and his fellow student-teachers raised money to buy netball posts. But within hours of them being erected on the field, the headteacher instructed the care-taker to remove them. Dominic's colleague found the posts broken behind one of the classrooms. The incident was never discussed between the student-teachers and the staff. The essence of this situation, where the student-teachers were uninformed about, unhappy with, or frustrated by, an aspect of their experience on the out-programme, but felt unable to challenge, or even discuss the issue publicly, was replicated multiple times in the data. Three further examples are presented to give a sense of the context in which Dominic was working:

Student-teachers are supposed to observe the teachers, and have their own teaching observed by their mentor. But in Dominic's school the student-teachers were mainly left on their own to teach. During the pilot-research and the three days spent shadowing Dominic over the year, there were no examples of him working alongside his mentor:

'In terms of learning it would be ideal if we could be in the classroom with the mentor. But we don't have that kind of culture here'. Dominic had a 'good relationship' with his mentor and didn't want to 'spoil it by raising the issue'.

Because the student-teachers live on-site, they have to contribute to the electricity bill. But the bill includes electricity used for the corporate events, which require lighting and sound-systems running for several hours at weekends. The student-teachers complained to a teacher who said she would raise it with the principal but she never did, so the student-teachers continued to pay the bill: 'we did everything we could'.

At certain points in the year a tutor came from the college to assess the student-teachers. During one visit Dominic was marked down for not covering everything in his lesson plan. Actually, he had covered it in the previous lesson, but he didn't explain this because *'it would be wrong to contradict a tutor'*.

School-based experiences, as part of the teacher preparation process, are widely advocated as a key component of the drive to improve teaching quality in low-income contexts (Commission for Africa 2005; Moon 2013). Across Sub-Saharan Africa, intended benefits of the school-based component are written into policy, for example in South Africa: 'Time spent in the workplace is considered to be very important and should provide the authentic context within which student-educators experience and demonstrate the competence developed in the . . .curriculum' (DoE 2000). In Ghana the out-programme aims to 'deepen principles in methodology . . . and reflection which leads to a dynamic, developmental concept of "professional competence"' (GES 2001, in Eshun and Ashun 2013), although subsequent reports highlight challenges around the logistics of the out-component[3] and recommend cutting it from three to two semesters (GES 2015). Since 2015, teacher education in Ghana has been supported by the UK Government-funded T-TEL[4] programme, which maintains the importance of the out-programme:

> Teaching-practice is an essential component . . . to develop the required professional skills and competencies, and a positive attitude towards the teaching profession. Teaching-practice also provides the right environment for student-teachers to familiarise themselves with all the processes of the school setting, and to observe examples of good practice.
>
> (T-TEL 2016:5)

Of course, not all student-teachers face the lack of opportunities for professional dialogue that Dominic and his colleagues did. Chapter 24 of this book describes the experiences of a student-teacher in the Gambia who worked with the principal to implement school-wide changes in policy and pedagogy. In a survey of student-teachers in Nigeria, Nwanekezi et al. (2011) found that the majority reported positive relationships with teachers and a willingness to obey school rules and school authority. Many, however, experience a 'reality shock' (Akyeampong and Lewin 2002: 344) amidst expected conformity to established practices, rigid hierarchies of seniority (Westbrook et al. 2009) and a lack of support, which can compromise professional identities and intentions. So, what does it mean for student-teachers such as Dominic when the 'authentic context', 'good practice' and the 'competences developed in the curriculum' are at odds? And when the 'positive relationships' student-teachers have with the teachers are dependent on them not challenging contradictions between rules and authority? How might student-teachers develop professional capability within a context in which they struggle to articulate capabilities they aspire to?

June

> So what I have learned is that punishment – like caning – doesn't really work. You can punish them over and over again but their behaviour won't change. We were taught in the college about other forms of punishment, and they do not work either. I thought that if you give the child a reward their behaviour will change over time. But that doesn't happen either ... When I am a professional teacher I will try not to use the cane, but if things get bad, if it calls for it then I will need to use it. Sometimes no punishment will work, but if they are used to the cane you have to use it – and even just carry it around with you – to show that you are serious.

In an older study of Ghanaian teachers, Akyeampong and Lewin (2002) found that the longer a teacher had been in the profession, the more likely they were to promote the cane as a form of discipline. They suggested that training programmes didn't adequately cover alternative methods or approaches, and that school contexts weakened teachers' beliefs. Dominic's college did cover alternative methods of discipline, which shaped his sense of what it meant to 'be' a teacher. However, in the school an alternative sense of what it meant to be a teacher appeared to be fixed and resistant to change, and there were no spaces – physical, in terms of time or in terms of appropriateness – where opportunities for student-teachers and teachers to discuss alternative practices or alternative ways of being could arise. The student-teachers were not included in staff meetings, and teachers never visited the student-teachers in their accommodation, where they spent their breaks. As seen above, attempts made by the student-teachers to open up these spaces were not welcomed by the teaching staff.

The socio-cultural framing of this study draws on the idea of learning as a 'process of becoming' (Wenger 1998: 215): students develop as teachers through the possibilities enabled by relations within the learning environment. The capabilities framing adds that possibilities for being changed and for making change – based on a shared sense of what is valued and what is not – are shaped through negotiation within the community. Learning is a movement towards participation in valued ways of being a teacher (see also Murphy and Wolfenden 2013). Dominic's last quote suggests that by the end of the year his valued ways of 'being' a teacher involved being serious and strict, and the cane – more than just a means of discipline – embodies the local cultural script around what a teacher is and does and has the potential to do.

Examples which resonate with Dominic's experience, where student-teachers feel their own knowledge is 'oppressed' (Dahl 2014: 159) and where innovative teachers are 'punished by the system' (Asare and Nti 2014: 8) are widely reported across Sub-Saharan Africa. However, there are recent reports of programmes which emphasise student-teacher voice, and create spaces for professional dialogue between tutors, student-teachers and mentors. A teacher preparation programme in Kenya, for example, introduced a participatory action-research module. An evaluation reported that student-teachers were able to 'raise their voices' in the usually 'somewhat disempowering context of teacher training' (Dahl 2014: 172). A school-based apprenticeship model of teacher development in Malawi explicitly incorporated 'interactions with others' and built in opportunities for discussion and reflection between apprentices and mentors. A report acknowledged that the quality of these discussions depended on the commitment of the mentor, but there were several examples of mentor-teachers reflecting on discussions with the apprentices and making changes to their own practice (Safford et al. 2013).

These examples emphasise recognition of the understanding that changes in teaching and learning at school-level require relational change within teacher education (Schwille et al. 2007), and suggest the need for broader epistemological shifts that challenge the assumed relationship between seniority and expertise. But this chapter concludes with an example of how Dominic and his colleagues exercise capability around the edges of this assumed relationship and contribute to the currently limited literature on creative ways student-teachers can 'adapt the knowledge and skills they have acquired through formal training' (Adu-Yeboah 2011: 4) and 'think outside the box as they scrutinise and critique their own teaching and that of other teachers' (Asare and Nti 2014: 8):

> If other teachers are caning, it isn't my place to tell them to stop. So my colleagues and I came up with a plan. What we do is save up punishments until the mentor is in the room. Then we use other methods that aren't painful or violent, or we show the mentor that we are trying to understand the child rather than just cane them. So in a way we are trying to teach [the mentors] by showing them new ways without challenging their authority.

Questions

1. Is corporal punishment in schools legal or illegal in your country? What directives are there for teachers in relation to discipline? Does current policy reflect your own experiences of school?
2. There is much evidence that many people across the world believe corporal punishment is acceptable. But the Global Initiative to End All Corporal Punishment of Children (GIEACPC) suggests that repeated polls, when questions are phrased differently, yield very different results. Can you design a short survey to understand people's views on corporal punishment? Reflect on the wording of the questions and the kinds of responses they might return.
3. What are the different pathways to teaching in your country? In what ways is dialogue between student-teachers and tutors/mentors facilitated in these pathways? See Chapter 18 for an account of professional dialogue.

Further reading

Global Initiative to End All Corporal Punishment of Children (GIEACPC). [Available at www.endcorporal punishment.org/.]

Notes

1 Funded by the Spencer Foundation (USA), Grant No. 201500089.
2 UNICEF (2014:4) defines corporal punishment as 'any punishment in which physical force is used and intended to cause some degree of pain or discomfort, however light'.
3 Including student-teachers not being able to find accommodation, long distances between colleges and schools limiting opportunities for supervision from college tutors, and inadequate incentives or support for mentoring.
4 Transforming Teacher Education and Learning.

References

Adu-Yeboah, C. (2011) Teacher Preparation and Continuing Professional Development in Africa: Learning to teach reading and mathematics and its influence on practice in Ghana. Draft Country Report, TPA Project, University of Sussex. [Available at www.sussex.ac.uk/webteam/ gateway/file.php?name=report-ghana-1july2011.pdf&site=320.]

Akyeampong, K. and Lewin, K. (2002) From student teachers to newly qualified teachers in Ghana: Insights into becoming a teacher. *International Journal of Educational Development*, 22, 339–352.

Akyeampong, K. and Stephens, D. (2002) Exploring the backgrounds and shaping of beginning student teachers in Ghana: Toward greater contextualization of teacher education. *International Journal of Educational Development*, 22 (3–4), 262–274.

Asare, K.B. and Nti, S.K. (2014) Teacher Education in Ghana: A Contemporary Synopsis and Matters Arising, *SAGE Open*, April–June, 1–8.

Buckler, A. (2015) Conceptualising and mapping student teachers' perceptions of themselves as agents of social justice: A case study from Ghana. Paper presented at the UK Forum for International Education and Training (UKFIET), University of Oxford, UK, 15–17 September 2015.

Commission for Africa (2005) *Our Common Interest*. [Available at www.commissionforafrica.info/wp-content/uploads/2005-report/11–03–05_cr_report.pdf.]

Dahl, K. (2014) 'From worse to better': How Kenyan student-teachers can use participatory action research in health education. *Educational Action Research*, 22 (2), 159–177.

Dery, S.K. (2017) *Corporal punishment is illegal – GES warns*, Graphic Online, 03 March 2017 [Available at www.graphic.com.gh/news/education/corporal-punishment-is-illegal-ges-warns.html.]

DoE (2000) *Norms and Standards for Educators*, South African Department of Education. [Available at www.gov.za/sites/default/files/20844.pdf.]

Eshun, I. and Ashun, E. (2013) The effect of the 'out' programme of the 'In-In-Out' policy of teacher education in Ghana: Implication for human resource development. *Journal of Education and Practice*, 4 (13).

GES (2008) *Teachers' Code of Conduct: Rules of Professional Conduct for Teachers in Ghana*, Ghana Education Service, USAID, DEVTECH and CEDEM.

GES (2015) [Available at www.moe.gov.gh/assets/media/docs/Challenges1-Educational%20 Reforms(Jophus).pdf.]

Ghanaian Government (1998) Act of the Parliament of the Government of Ghana: The Children's Act.

GIEACPC (2017) *Corporal punishment of children in Ghana*. Report prepared by the Global Initiative to End All Corporal Punishment of Children.

GNA (2011) 94 percent of Ghanaian parents endorse corporal punishment – survey. GhanaWeb 18 August 2011. [Available at www.ghanaweb.com/GhanaHomePage/NewsArchive/94-per-cent-of-Ghanaianparents-endorse-corporal-punishment-Survey-216625.]

Kyei-Gyamfi, S. (2011) Corporal Punishment in Ghana. In Ame, R.K., Agbenyega, D.L. and Apt, N.A. (Eds) *Children's Rights in Ghana: Reality or Rhetoric?* Lexington Books.

Moon, B. (2013) *Teacher Education and the Challenge of Development: A Global Analysis*. London and New York: Routledge.

Morrow, V. and Singh, R. (2014) *Corporal Punishment in Schools in Andhra Pradesh, India. Children's and Parents Views*, Working Paper 123, Oxford, Young Lives.

Murphy, P. and Wolfenden, F. (2013) Developing a pedagogy of mutuality in a capability approach: Teachers' experiences of using open educational resources (OER) of the Teacher Education in Sub-Saharan Africa (TESSA) Programme. *International Journal of Educational Development*, 33 (3), 263–271.

Nwanekezi, A.U., Okoli, N.J. and Meziebobi, S.A. (2011) Attitude of student-teachers towards teaching practice in the University of Port Harcourt, Rivers State, Nigeria. *Journal of Emerging Trends in Educational Research and Policy Studies*, 2 (1), 41–46.

Ogando Portela, M.J. and Pells, K. (2015) *Corporal Punishment in Schools: Longitudinal Evidence from Ethiopia, India, Peru and Viet Nam*, Innocenti Discussion Paper No.2015–02, UNICEF and Young Lives, Florence. [Available at www.younglives.org.uk/sites/www.younglives.org.uk/files/Corporal%20Punishment%20in%20Schools.pdf.]

Parkes, J. and Heslop, J. (2011) *Stop Violence Against Girls in School: A Cross-country Analysis of Baseline Research from Ghana, Kenya and Mozambique*. London: Action Aid/Institute of Education.

Safford, K., Cooper, D., Wolfenden, F. and Chitsulo, J. (2013) 'Give courage to the ladies': Expansive apprenticeship for women in rural Malawi. *Journal of Vocational Education and Training*, 65 (2), 193–207.

Schwille, J., Dembe le, M. and Schubert, J. (2007) *Global Perspectives on Teacher Learning: Improving Policy and Practice*. Paris: UNESCO.

Sen, A. (1999) *Development as Freedom*. Oxford: Oxford University Press.

SRSG (2012) Tackling Violence in Schools: A Global Perspective. Bridging the Gap Between Standards and Practice. Office of the Special Representative of the Secretary General, New York: United Nations.

T-TEL (2016) [Available at www.ttel.org/files/images/Publications%20section/Section%20stock%20photos/Student_Handbook1%20(2).pdf.]

UN (1990) The United Nations Convention on the Rights of the Child. [Available at https://downloads.unicef.org.uk/wpcontent/uploads/2010/05/UNCRC_united_nations_convention_on_the_rights_of_the_child.pdf?_ga=2.24201082.1983327304.1513781766–99485388.1513781766.]

UNICEF (2014) *Hidden in Plain Sight? A statistical analysis of violence against children*. New York: UNICEF. [Available at http://files.unicef.org/publications/files/Hidden_in_plain_sight_statistical_analysis_EN_3_Sept_2014.pdf.]

Wenger, E. (1998) *Communities of Practice: Learning, Meaning and Identity*. Cambridge: Cambridge University Press.

Westbrook, J., Shah, N., Durrani, N., Tikly, C., Khan, W. and Dunne, M. (2009) Becoming a teacher: Transitions from training to the classroom in North West Frontier Province, Pakistan. *International Journal of Educational Development*, 29, 437–444.

24 The Gambia

The intersection of the global and the local in a small developing country

Michele Schweisfurth

Introduction

Little educational research has been published on The Gambia, the smallest country in Africa. The Gambia has a strong commitment in policy to inclusive and emancipatory education, and this chapter illustrates how contextual factors have shaped its education policy in relation to Learner Centred Education (LCE) and to the practical implementation of LCE. Minimum standards for LCE are presented in Chapter 2.

We include this chapter in *Learning and Teaching Around the World* for its analysis of policy in relation to education generally and to pedagogy specifically. Whilst policy in The Gambia creates considerable space for Learner Centred Education, there is little direct reference to pedagogy – LCE or otherwise – in policy documents; this situation is characterised in Chapter 14 as a 'high ambiguity–high conflict' model of policy implementation.

Michele Schweisfurth asks important questions about the implementation of education policy within global agendas for quality and learner-centredness: There is a lot of reference to trained teachers, but trained in what? There is attention to the need for instructional materials, but what will the nature of these be? The curriculum is intended to emphasise problem-solving skills, but can it do this without teachers working within a Learner Centred Education framework? What does 'excellence' or 'active teaching' mean, and what do they look like in a low-resource classroom? The chapter also refers to 'emancipatory' and 'preparation' narratives which focus on different purposes of education. Is education meant to liberate and empower children, or is it to prepare children for the future world of work? Are these narratives mutually exclusive?

The Gambia shares many features with other countries in Sub-Saharan Africa. It has high levels of poverty and underdevelopment. Like the rest of the continent, it has a colonial history and was a British colony until independence in 1965. As with many colonies, its borders were determined by Europeans, and The Gambia is surrounded by Senegal, a former French colony. Along with agriculture, The Gambia, as with other SSA nations, is reliant on aid and subject to global and bilateral agreements, assistance and pressures – not least in terms of education.

The Gambia is diverse. There are five major ethnic groups and several others, each with its own language and traditions. English remains the official language and is the medium of instruction beyond early primary schooling. While the population is 90 percent Muslim, there is a substantial Christian minority and traditional 'animist' beliefs are widely held across all groups. Intermarriage between groups is common and most people speak several local languages. The capital, Banjul, and the furthest regional capital, Basse Santa Su, do not look distant on a map, but getting from one to the other on poor roads, even travelling short distances, can be challenging, and Basse feels worlds apart in terms of infrastructure, resources and even climate.

All of these factors have implications for trends in education generally, and for Learner Centred Education (LCE) specifically. Small states such as The Gambia are vulnerable to global pressures and influences of all kinds. They are more likely to be subject to external cultural influences for a number of reasons: the prevalence of imported goods and media, since diseconomies of scale make local production diffi-cult; the dominance of larger countries in regional co-operation schemes; the presence in numbers of foreign tourists; dependence on aid and expertise from elsewhere; and the lack of availability of higher-level local education, again because of economies of scale, necessitating overseas training of high-level local personnel.

The data of this chapter were collected between 2000 and 2011 and include: a series of workshops on Learner Centred Education at The Gambia College, the sole provider of teacher education in the country; action research into perceptions of democracy and democratic education, and into the impact of the LCE workshops on the attitudes and teaching practice of the participants; interviews with college staff and students; lesson observations in the College; observations of student teachers in their placement schools; a survey conducted across the College to gather opinions regarding teaching and learning and College management; staff and student case studies; workshops with inspectors, advisors and education officers in each of The Gambia's six regions that focused on the relationship between democracy and quality in education, with LCE as a key factor in the relationship; national workshops and interviews with policy-makers and educational leaders.

Education policy context

Quality of schooling is an ongoing concern in The Gambia. The Education Policy 2004–15, and the Education Sector Medium-Term Plan 2008–11 set out a range of goals and strategies to meet them, within a framework of guiding principles stating that education will be premised on:

i.   Non-discriminatory and all-inclusive provision of education underlining in particular, gender equity and targeting of the poor and the disadvantaged groups.
ii. Respect for the rights of the individual, cultural diversity, indigenous languages and knowledge;

iii. Promotion of ethical norms and values and a culture of peace;

iv. Development of science and technology competencies for the desired quantum leap.

(DOSE 2004: 13)

The values expressed within these principles create plenty of space for Learner Centred Education: respect for rights, a focus on the individual, a recognition of difference, and peacebuilding. Likewise, the basic aims of education can be seen to open spaces for LCE:

i. Promote a broad-based education at the basic level for lifelong learning and training

ii. Mainstream gender in the creation of opportunities for all to acquire literacy, livelihood skills and the utilisation of these skills in order to earn a living and become economically self-reliant members of the community

iii. Develop the physical and mental skills which will contribute to nation building – economically, socially and culturally in a sustainable environment

iv. Encourage creativity and the development of a critical and analytical mind

v. Further an understanding and appreciation of the contribution of science and technology to development

vi. Cultivate sound moral and ethical values in the development of life skills

vii. Develop a healthy body and an appreciation of the value of a healthy mind in response to life-threatening diseases like HIV/AIDS, malaria and tuberculosis

viii. Create an awareness of the importance of peace, democracy and human rights, duties and responsibilities of the individual in fostering these qualities

ix. Foster an appreciation of and respect for the cultural heritage of The Gambia

x. Promote a sense of patriotism: service, loyalty, integrity and dedication to the nation and humanity.

(DOSE 2004: 13–14)

Most of these goals could be promoted through Learner Centred Education, and indeed some might argue that only LCE could do so effectively. Certainly, goal four reflects a non-transmission model of education. Many of the values underpinning the principles align well with LCE and an emancipatory narrative for education. In tandem with this emphasis on the individual, rights, equity and peace are a number of other imperatives around preparation for the world of work, with the references to science and technology showing awareness of the role that technology will play in the future and how this will help the country to develop. The references to patriotism and respect for cultural heritage might raise questions regarding the references to a critical and analytical mind: is questioning of nation and culture acceptable? What if cultural practices undermine other goals?

While policy creates space for LCE, there is little direct reference to pedagogy – LCE or otherwise – in the policy documents. It is generally supportive, while not being directive. There is one notable exception:

> While the textbook will continue to be a basic teaching/learning tool, it is now becoming obvious that there will be an urgent need to acquire, develop and make available other teaching/learning tools and technologies which are more likely to shift methodology from chalk and talk/lecture, rote memorisation to active engaged and collaborative learning. Such a shift will provide opportunities for learners to develop their own concepts. To this end, the use of new technologies . . . will be promoted.
>
> (DOSE 2004: 36)

It is salient to note the linking of LCE and new technologies. Electricity is rare in Gambian schools, let alone computers. But technological change is rapid in The Gambia (and similar countries). Over the period 2000–2007, when I was regularly visiting The Gambia to conduct workshops and fieldwork, the proliferation of mobile phone use was extraordinary. Initially, they were rare novelties: towards the end of this period, negotiating rules with workshop participants over appropriate use of mobile phones was essential as almost all the teachers, headteachers, lecturers and inspectors had them and used them often.

There are several key priorities in policy, within which pedagogy is a kind of shadow cast by the objectives which are held to the light. There is a lot of reference to trained teachers: but trained in what? There is attention to the need for instructional materials, but what will the nature of these be? There is considerable awareness shown of the need for improved assessment and for continuous assessment, but what will these assess, and how? The curriculum is intended to emphasise problem-solving skills, but can it do this without teachers working within an LCE framework? 'The pursuit of excellence in the teaching and learning process of the education system for the transformation of the Gambian economy will be emphasised' (DOSE 2004: 35) – but what does excellence mean in this context? While the relevant guiding principles provide a framework for these which might encourage LCE, the relationship is indirect. Pedagogy is more often implied than explicit in written documents, although Learner Centred Education is often advocated indirectly in them.

Influences on practice

Beyond the policy documents, key individuals in the Gambian policy arena expressed views which help to illuminate both the motivations behind the LCE directions and the challenges in implementing it. The interviews shed light on the policy-practice interface in this context. Teachers feel great pressure to cover the entire syllabus thoroughly, as one teacher educator noted: 'They have to complete the syllabus within a specified period . . . We have periods of 45 minutes. If we ask teachers to adopt learner centredness, before the students have started enjoying what they are doing, they have to stop.'

A Deputy Permanent Secretary describes policy moves in the direction of LCE as 'a truism', with all of the policy-level respondents pointing to strong commitment at government level. As elsewhere, LCE is seen in part to be a response to learners' changing needs, as noted by one Ministry Director: 'Awareness is increasing. Students need to learn more. They are not tied to that rigid method of focusing on the teacher. This is more of the free society, and we are all moving towards that.' Another pointed out that this is not just a recent phenomenon: 'For a long time we have not been helping our learners to become independent. Interact, solve problems on their own … they need to become independent lifelong learners. Just trying to take in what they can in a day or a cycle and remembering it for exams, that is not appropriate.'

In interviews, teachers, teacher educators, headteachers and inspectors were broadly in favour of more 'democratic' approaches in the classroom. However, among the challenges, as in so many developing country contexts, are resources. Classroom conditions vary but many are severely under-resourced both in terms of hard furnishings and learning materials. Policy prescribes a textbook student ratio of 1:1, but in reality, infrastructure and other challenges make this difficult to achieve. As one senior official noted: 'Large class size encourages teachers to use vertical presentation. The teacher is a demigod. The students are at the receiving end, taking everything from the teacher.' As for the new technologies advocated above: these are present in few schools, and basic infrastructural issues mean that for the most part these are aspirational rather than reality. Electricity is not consistently available, in or outside of schools. The economic and resource contexts also shape the effectiveness of monitoring and support. School inspectors in remote parts of the country reported travel difficulties in visiting rural schools due to poor roads, petrol shortages, vehicle maintenance – and even the weather. Therefore, the reach of official monitoring and support is constrained and teachers and administrators in rural schools can feel out of touch with Banjul, even in this small country.

Ultimately, it is teacher agency which makes the difference, as one policy-maker noted: 'It is mainly teachers who decide. They look at the curriculum and the syllabus. In the end, they choose from the methodologies available to them.' Attention to sustainability is emphasised by other policy agents, and rather than depending on donor-driven projects, there have been moves to establish local professional development initiatives, with senior teachers working with junior teachers and clusters of schools joining forces, in order to 'institutionalise' changes. Whether the senior teachers have LCE expertise as well as general experience, is an open question implied by one senior official:

> We know the shift isn't easy, because if people have been doing the same thing over and over and they come back to teach the way they were taught, changing their mindsets might be very difficult. Support and training are needed together, so that when they are trying out new ideas you are there to help them.

Creative use of appropriate technology by teachers well-trained in LCE and motivated to use it might be able to get around these material resource constraints. However, this is where the issues really start to bite. There is a substantial shortage of qualified teachers, especially in rural areas, and their motivation is hard to secure without the basic provision of a living wage. It is estimated that 65 per cent of trained and qualified teachers live and work abroad as a result of low morale, 'deplorable' conditions and very few incentives to keep their profession, especially in rural areas (UNICEF 2017).

International development aid has gone some way to improving working conditions for teachers, and has also provided some training, but this will need to be reinforced through other measures in order to be sustainable. And training depends on trainers. Observations of lessons at The Gambia College led to the conclusion that there was a great deal of chalk and talk, even when the topic was about more learner-centred pedagogies. Even the relatively participatory lessons were strongly teacher-led, in a question-and-answer format. And these were usually dominated by the more vociferous students. In a survey at the College, 91 per cent of permanent staff felt that they regularly experienced active teaching and learning in classes; however, only 59 per cent of students felt that they did. As one policy agent noted: 'The lecturers themselves need to be trained on this. Strengthen the teacher training and then train them well on this new active and collaborative learning.'

There are also questions about how the notion of 'active teaching and learning' is locally understood in this context. Cultural attitudes to the status of children help to shape the context for Learner Centred Education in The Gambia. As in many African societies, respect for elders plays an important role (see Tedla 1995). The relationships of equality demanded by LCE mean that deference for elders may restrict open dialogue and critique. As one trainee teacher reported: 'Right from the home, there are things children aren't allowed to do; they must respect and obey elders.' Part of this is driven by concerns about discipline and fear that children might abuse newly endowed rights; 17 out of 45 respondents to a questionnaire at a workshop on education for democracy indicated that their communities were concerned that greater democracy in schools would lead to indiscipline, compared to 15 who felt this was not a concern. A manifestation of this belief in authority and control was the prevalence of corporal punishment (technically regulated against but used by some in practice), and in the same workshop, only 11 out of 45 felt it should be completely abolished. For some respondents, these issues related to principles of Islam; according to one teacher educator, 'Individual freedom or rationality is limited to the dictates.'

However, The Gambia, as a typical developing, prismatic society, is changing, and multiple views co-exist in society and even within individuals. Both teachers and learners noted that relationships are, overall, becoming less authoritarian and beliefs more subject to interrogation, as a manifestation of more 'modern' attitudes, and global influences. Recent policy initiatives have developed within a human and child rights framework, against sexual harassment of students, and corporal punishment. There was also a strong awareness expressed in interviews of the need for respect for local cultures, even when learning about cosmopolitan notions of democratic and learner-centered education. In our work in the country, my colleagues and I were encouraged to learn more and to be flexible in our views of what constituted good practice.

The context of national scale has implications for educational change. Policy-making and implementation in The Gambia are moved by individuals. In a bigger system, the impact of one person, unless they are a dictator or have particular structural or personal power, is likely to be diluted. This is less true in a small state. Centrally and regionally, the Ministry of Basic and Secondary Education, and the Standards and Quality Assurance Department, are comprised of a small number of people, each potentially being quite influential. Even a single teacher can become a national star if they are doing the right things and come to the attention of the right people. This can, potentially, facilitate educational change. Additionally, people frequently also fulfil several roles: they may, for example, act as an inspector on behalf of the Ministry, while working in a school, again enhancing the potential for impact (or inertia, depending on the individual).

What is true for people is also true for institutions. As there is only one qualified teacher status-granting teacher training institution in the country, whether or not it is on board with LCE, and lecturers' capacity to model as well as to teach it, will be major factors in how well teachers are inducted into these ways of working. Policy-makers noted the limited capacity of this sole college to address substantial pedagogical change. The smaller number of key stakeholders also adds a personal dimension to relationships, as most people in positions of authority in the education sector in the country know each other. Given that in traditional African cultures there is a tendency to work through the particularity of relationships in any case, this is magnified by the small state factors. Particular individuals' attitudes to LCE and efforts to promote it (or not) will be consequential in moving the agenda.

Action research into the impact of LCE workshops illustrated a number of the contextual factors relevant to the implementation of LCE in The Gambia. The researchers could work collaboratively with the Ministry and Inspectorate because of contacts in key roles. There were potentially greater opportunities for impact, because of the scale and networking reasons, and other international organisations with similar goals were working in the same sector, multiplying the effects. Participants, most of whom had previously experienced little LCE directly, were exposed to it through the workshop formats, in which there was open sharing of, and respect for, viewpoints; this was singled out repeatedly in feedback as a major factor in whatever successes the projects might claim. Any impact on practice was no doubt facilitated by our regular visits; individuals, while not at all accountable to us, knew that we were interested in their work in a sustained way, and observing it. The small-state nature of loyalty no doubt had a role as well, through our interpersonal connections to people of influence. The small number of participants who were particularly inspired had the opportunity to be change agents in their own working environments and beyond, facilitated by all the same factors.

An illustrative case-in-point is Amat, a student trainee teacher who participated in the first LCE workshop in the early 2000s. He implemented learner-centred approaches in his own classroom during his teaching practice 'practicum' and, through a receptive headteacher and deputy headteacher, went on to bring changes to the whole school in terms of behaviour policy. A few months later, he was running LCE workshops in neighbouring schools. It is hard to imagine something similar happening in a larger, more bureaucratic context. His case also illustrates the mediation that occurred as the central concepts and practices of LCE were adapted – reflectively or spontaneously – for The Gambian context. He used materials from the workshop, but in ways which incorporated more typical local practices. For example, in the original workshops, learner-centred ways of working (such as agreements to ask questions when in doubt) were negotiated with all participants to form a learning contract, which was posted visibly in the seminar room. In Amat's class, these were not so much negotiated as made transparent and then agreement sought. This was a step towards more learner involvement: at least learners knew what was being demanded, and had a chance to voice their views, even if they did not actively participate in shaping the learning environment in that way. Amat's workshop was observed in a neighbouring school, where the chanting of choral answers could be heard through classroom windows from multiple lessons. Workshop materials, which were in their initial incarnation activity based, were being used as teaching aids, but largely through lecture methods. However, the attentive atmosphere and engaged questioning which followed suggested that this worked very well in this context.

This natural tendency for mediation is backed up in interviews; as one policy-maker noted:

> [teaching here is] a blend of paradigms . . . learner-centred teaching revolves around a lot of ideas. In the Gambian context we use a blend of theory and what is applicable in practice . . . [LCE] is already established in schools but varies from subject to subject, teacher to teacher and environment to environment . . . it is contextualised based on the subject being taught and the environment of the teacher.

Another was specific in terms of what is appropriate in terms of LCE and what is not:

> The Gambian view of learner-centered is: how do we make sure teaching and learning is interactive, learners apply what they are learning so they can apply it during the learning and outside of the classroom? The extreme view of learner-centered, where learners can choose what they learn, we know we can't do that now . . . as a nation where the opportunities for employment are not vast, learners are using their educational attainment to get jobs. Learning is not just for education's sake, it is for someone to use to get certificates and employment. Employment in the Gambia is mainly government, so what is taught is really controlled.

Conclusions

There are a number of specific and general lessons to be learned from the Gambian case. It illustrates a number of commonalities across similar SSA contexts, which are likely to affect the implementation of Learner Centred Education. We find policy which is accommodating but not mandating of LCE. We find challenges of teacher and teacher educator capacity, where teaching is not a particularly desirable or motivating profession, and where there has been little experiential exposure to LCE practice. We find mixed messages regarding culture, as the global and the local, and the traditional and the modern, meet and mix. LCE is seen as part of the modern, global world, and this brings with it both resistance and desire. Policy messages reference the emancipatory narrative, and yet there is evidence of oppressive behaviours by government and reluctance on the ground to change norms of adult-child relationships. The 'preparation for work' narrative receives somewhat less policy space than the emancipatory narrative, but policy-makers in their reflections use preparation for work to de-radicalise LCE.

Such apparent contradictions are common in, but not unique to, prismatic societies such as The Gambia. Crucially, we see that where LCE is embraced whole-heartedly it has local manifestations in its practice that could be seen as a starting step on a continuum towards its more widely recognised forms. Or, it could be something new and particular to The Gambia. What is called learner-centred may include particular elements of LCE – more participation in discussions, for example – but under tight teacher control and selectively inclusive. There are also interesting specifics about the Gambian case because of the scale of the country and how this intersects with the professional development of key individuals and how they influence the direction of education and the spaces for facilitators of LCE.

Questions

1. The chapter suggests that Learner Centred Education might look different in different cultures and countries. Do you agree, or do you think there are some elements of LCE that should apply to any context?
2. The chapter suggests that smallness of scale presents opportunities to embed Learner Centred Education. What would this imply for large-scale policy implementation programmes?
3. If you have the opportunity to read the education policy of your country, or another country, can you find any specific or detailed information about how goals for educational quality will be achieved in practice?

Further reading

Alexander, R. (2008) *Education for All, The Quality Imperative and the Problem of Pedagogy*. Brighton, UK: Consortium for Research on Education Access, Transitions and Equity.

Davies L., Harber, C. and Schweisfurth, M. (2002) *Teacher Education for Democracy*. Birmingham: CIER/CfBT.

Harber, C. (2002) Education, Democracy and Poverty Reduction in Africa. *Comparative Education*, 38 (3), 267–276.

The full text of this chapter is: Schweisfurth, M. (2013) Chapter 6 in *Learner-centred Education in International Perspective: Whose Pedagogy for Whose Development?* London: Routledge.

References

DOSE (Department of State for Education in The Gambia) (2004) *Education Policy 2004–2016*, Banjul: DOSE.

Tedla (1995) *African Thought and Education*. New York: Peter Lang.

UNICEF (2017) Real Lives: Curbing the Attrition Rate of Teachers – The EFA/FTI Programme in The Gambia. [Available at www.unicef.org/gambia/reallives_5590.html, accessed 21 November 2017.]

25 Globalising education and the shaping of global childhoods

Nicola Ansell

Introduction

Throughout the world, a common feature of children's lives is education. Most children today spend a very large part of their childhoods in school, and schooling is becoming a defining feature of childhood in most societies. We conclude this Reader with Nicola Ansell's discussion of four key sets of actors and processes that have contributed, and continue to contribute, to the globalisation of children's education. The issues that the author examines relate to many of the themes and topics in *Learning and Teaching Around the World*, such as the 'gold standard' of colonial education, gender and schooling, teacher training, Indigenous education and international comparative assessments.

Education, as distinct from schooling, has always been a global phenomenon insofar as every society has sought to educate its young people. In the past, societies developed their own distinctive systems for raising young people and inculcating in them the knowledge, skills, attitudes, and values that were deemed appropriate to their context. Practices varied and in some instances this education would be delivered entirely through informal means: the family, kin, and community would teach children and youth in non-institutional settings, as and when they were seen to be ready for, or to require, particular knowledge or skills. In other societies these informal practices were combined with more formalised processes of education, which might take the form of regular attendance at school, madrasah, or a more concentrated preparation for initiation into adult life. In most societies education systems were not only distinctive but differentiated: the education provided for children differed by gender and by social class, delivering the learning that was perceived to be most appropriate for their anticipated adult lives.

Today, mobility and migration bring children from diverse national and cultural backgrounds together in schools, particularly in urban communities and, as Chapter 2 by Dryden-Peterson illustrates, in refugee education contexts. In the present chapter by Nicola Ansell, the emphasis is not on young people migrating for education but on the ways in which education itself moves around the world. The author skilfully traces the historical arc of the globalisation of children's education over the past two centuries, as schooling systems, practices, and ideas have been exported globally in the service of four broad agendas: missionary activity, colonialism, international development and neoliberal corporate capitalism. These are not distinct processes pursued by distinct actors; rather they are complex, changing, often contradictory, and strongly interrelated. As education has become globalised, increasingly uniform experiences are delivered to children worldwide. Through intersecting transnational processes, systems of education have been exported and become rooted in very varied social and cultural contexts. The globalisation of systems of education is therefore a prime means through which childhoods are shaped, children's lives produced, and in turn through which societies are transformed.

Religious motives and colonial powers

From the late-eighteenth to the mid-twentieth centuries, a similar form of schooling spread from Europe to most parts of the world. In many societies, a large proportion of children were drawn into an institution that had been unheard of among earlier generations. There were two key sets of actors and motivations behind the dissemination of this form of education: Christian missionaries, eager to win converts, and colonial authorities, with goals relating to politics and trade. The schools not only embodied their creators' intended motives but also their social values and expectations, and thereby impacted on everyday patterns of childhood and the capacities, ideas, and expectations of children.

Education has long been used by proselytising religions, most notably Islam and Christianity, as a means of winning religious converts. Over the course of more than 700 years, Koranic schools or madrasahs have been established across much of Asia and Africa. These have served to assist in spreading Islam from its Middle Eastern origins and continue to be used to win allegiance to the religion. By the thirteenth century, for instance, the presence of madrasahs had grown in Baghdad, Damascus, Cairo, and India (Kong 2013). Today they are found globally, and while in some cases they retain a largely religious purpose, in other situations, they provide both spiritual and secular education. Christian missionaries have similarly established schools around the world in order to propagate Christianity. The European conquest of the Americas was accompanied by the establishment of mission schools. In eighteenth-century colonial northern Peru, for instance, the Catholic church established primary schools in Indigenous communities and boarding schools for Indigenous youth in the cities, which were envisaged not only as a way of Christianising the young people but also as a means of turning rebellious subjects into dutiful and productive citizens (Ramirez 2008).

During the nineteenth century, education played a key role in spreading the Christian religion through Africa. Missionaries wanted people not only to hear about the new religion but also to be able to read the Bible. In India, Christian missionaries hoped that promulgating Western scholarship, saturated with Christian morals, would help them 'prove' the falsehood of Indian religions (Bellenoit 2016). Most mission stations therefore included elementary schools, where children of Christian converts were taught basic literacy and church doctrine (Wolhuter 2007). The education that was introduced mirrored that provided to children of the lower classes in Europe, where school was increasingly viewed as the appropriate place for children (Ansell 2017).

The education of children in mission schools had significant effects on the structure of society. Gender relations, in particular, were reshaped through education. In many parts of the world, girls were a particular target for schooling. Christian missionaries played a key role in developing mass female schooling in India, for instance, and achieved better outcomes for girls than the secular education provided by colonial authorities (Lankina and Getachew 2013). In Korea, where women had been excluded from formal education, the first formal educational institution for women was established in 1886 by a Methodist missionary (Rowe and Byong-Suh 1997). In south-eastern Nigeria in the late-nineteenth and early-twentieth centuries, the Church Missionary Society used schooling to convert Igbo young women. The emphasis of missionaries on girls' education was not concerned with securing gender equality, however. Rather, it is argued, the focus on girls' schooling was more closely related to perceived male interests and needs. Leach (2008), for instance, suggests that early-nineteenth-century missionaries in West Africa saw the education of girls as essential to the furtherance of Christianity. Educated girls, they believed, would provide moral and practical support to men in the new monogamous family, raising their children as Christians. Missionary education also intervened in the construction and sustenance of racial hierarchies. In South Australia, for example, Presbyterian missionary education represented a system of disciplinary control over Indigenous bodies, minds, and souls, and helped secure the racial order (Schultz 2011).

From the late-eighteenth to the mid-twentieth centuries, education was used as an instrument of European colonial policies to support economic and political agendas (Whitehead 2005). Schooling was expected to make populations more governable and to create workers and consumers for the colonial economy (Wolhuter 2007). London (2002) reports how, in Trinidad and Tobago, the colonial curriculum and pedagogical practices were intended to promote attributes that would benefit the colonial state – notably habits of obedience, order, punctuality, and honesty, and a willingness to occupy the lowest rungs on the occupational and social ladder. Colonial administrations in Africa provided education of just sufficient quantity and quality to train the clerical workers they required (Wolhuter 2007). Literacy widely became the basis for secular authority: written laws, treaties, and deeds needed to be accessible to at least part of the local population (Topping 1987). Schooling also served to incorporate populations into a monetary economy. Colonialists sought to create a pool of labor to produce goods for the colonial export market. Not only did education produce workers with the necessary skills and dispositions; it produced a demand for employment as wages allowed families to pay school fees in the hope that their offspring would secure higher status work in future years (Martin 1982).

Relations between colonialists and missionaries were often uneasy. An example of tensions may be seen in Rhodesia (now Zimbabwe). The first mission school was founded at Inyati in 1883, but until British colonial rule began in 1890, missions had little success in teaching or evangelising. With economic and political change in the 1890s, people embraced education. While the missionaries established schools to enable people to read the Bible, the colonial state wanted cheap pliable labor and was not convinced that this required education. A member of the Rhodesian legislature in 1905 explained that an "uneducated native was the most honest, trustworthy and useful" (cited in Ansell 2017). Unable to prohibit missionary education, the state, from 1899, employed a system of grants-in-aid in order to control schools. In return for British government funding for teachers' salaries, mission schools were required to teach basic manual skills and diligence. Nonetheless, the government took over all urban schools in 1925 leaving the missions responsible for rural education. The white nationalist Rhodesia Front party, which came to power in 1962, sought further control over education. MP Andrew Skeen explained in a debate in 1969:

> We in the Rhodesia Front Government are determined to control the rate of African political advancement by controlling their education. Moreover, we wish to retain the power to retard their educational development to ensure that the government remains in responsible hands.
>
> (Cited in Ansell 2017)

Primary education was subsequently reduced from eight to seven years, black access to secondary education seriously restricted, and the churches were forced to relinquish nearly 80% of their schools (Ansell 2017).

Beyond reshaping gender relations and reinforcing racial hierarchies, education transformed the social order. New local elites emerged with different sets of values and expectations and the ability to read, write, and speak European languages. Such "civilized" people often became estranged from their own societies (Ofori-Attah 2006). Colonial administrators may have seen education as a means of social control, but Indigenous people saw it as a means of advancement. It quickly became a desirable (perhaps necessary) commodity and gained considerable status.

Due to the persistence of the association between education and elite status, the opposition of colonial authorities, and the willingness of missionaries to defend rights to education, education became a central demand in many independence struggles in the mid-twentieth century. This has generated a long-term legacy: it has proven very difficult to reform education provision in postcolonial societies where the status of those in power is shored up by their educational credentials and where colonial-style education is believed to represent a "gold standard" (Ofori-Attah 2006). Around the world, the form of education introduced in past centuries by missionaries and colonial authorities has become an immovable standard. This resilience of colonial education and its embrace by the elite is problematic. In Africa it has, according to Nyamnjoh (2012: 129), led to "a devaluation of African creativity, agency and value systems, and an internalised sense of inadequacy."

International development and neoliberalism

During the nineteenth century in Latin America and the twentieth century across much of Asia and Africa, colonialism retreated. The significance of Christian missionaries also diminished with the increasing power of independent nation states. The mid-twentieth century gave birth to a new set of global institutions and practices which perpetuated the globalisation of education in new ways. Schooling came to be seen not merely as an instrument through which to propagate religious beliefs or to manage society but as a basic human right for children worldwide. The right to free and compulsory elementary education is enshrined in the 1948 Universal Declaration of Human Rights (subsequently reinforced in the 1989 UN Convention on the Rights of the Child). Delivery of education was not to be left exclusively to national governments, but would be supported by a new set of global agencies. In particular, the United Nations Educational, Scientific and Cultural Organization (UNESCO) was established with a mandate to promote international collaboration through education. UNESCO set the global educational agenda from 1950 to 1975, seeking to expand school enrolments across the world and improve quality through curriculum change and textbook development (Gould 1993).

Another global agency established in the 1940s that rapidly became involved in shaping education was the World Bank, which invested heavily in the sector from the 1960s, exercising influence in newly independent nations through project loans and program support. The World Bank saw education not as a human right but as fundamental to economic development and modernisation. Although UNESCO had been the key agency in global education until the 1970s, the better endowed and more influential World Bank subsequently took on its mantle. In the 1980s, however, the Bank's influence on global education was far from benign. In response to the emerging debt crisis, it rescheduled many countries' debts, conditional on their adoption of Structural Adjustment Programmes. These programs generally required severe cuts in public spending on the education sector and the introduction of school fees aimed at achieving a degree of "cost recovery" (Ansell 2015). The 1980s were consequently an era in which the expansion of school enrolment diminished and in some cases went into reverse. National governments lacked resources to invest in education (even if were they permitted to do so) and since the World Bank was the major investor, governments could do little but follow its prescriptions. As a result, education policy became much more uniform and regressive in indebted countries around the world (Gould 1993).

The 1990s witnessed renewed investment in education, in large part because the World Bank reverted to its earlier view that education is essential for global economic growth. Four distinct trends emerged: the role of multilateral organisations, especially the World Bank, increased; education was increasingly seen as central to development and poverty reduction; the demands of the "knowledge economy" gained renewed influence; and the global education agenda narrowed its focus, emphasising access to primary education and readily measurable outputs.

Directing international development finance to education has thus transformed childhoods around the world. Schooling now occupies a very large amount of time for most children worldwide. Experience of schooling is highly influential in shaping young people's identities. Young people who have attended school often see themselves differently and have different expectations of their future lives compared with those who have not attended school. But while attending school shapes children's lives in many ways, it does not necessarily provide them with the formal learning that is expected.

The near-exclusive focus on enrolment has often resulted in crowded classrooms, insufficient qualified teachers, and a neglect of the form and content of education.

Approaches to enhancing learning in order to achieve improved educational outputs vary. UNICEF, for instance, recommends that in place of the traditional colonial-style education that remains particularly dominant in poorer countries, child-centered learning offers a means of democratising learning environments, while enhancing achievement and student retention (Sriprakash 2010). Social constructivist approaches that privilege active, enquiry-based learning are also favoured by development organisations. However, student-centered constructivist approaches are often resisted by teachers and viewed as Western impositions that are inappropriate to local contexts or cultural expectations. Kanu (2005), for instance, highlights challenges of cross-cultural knowledge transfer in Pakistan, where Western expatriates are involved in curriculum development. In Tanzania, efforts to shift from content-based to competency-based curricula and teacher-centered to student-centered pedagogy are confounded by the nature of exam systems, the material infrastructure of classrooms, the length and quality of teacher education programs, and cuts to teacher education (Vavrus 2009).

Another response to the perceived failures of education in poorer countries has been to focus on "learning outcomes" and to employ international measures of performance. Instruments such as the OEDS's Programme for International Student Assessment (PISA) and the International Association for the Evaluation of Educational Achievement's Trends in International Mathematics and Science Study (TIMSS) are now widely administered to 15-year-olds in order to assess the level of skills in a workforce, as they are believed to relate more closely to economic outcomes than average schooling levels. In lower- and middle-income countries, with the exception of China and Vietnam, performance is consistently below the OECD average (OECD 2013). Donors therefore believe that as investment has not raised learning outcomes, they need to look beyond inputs, and even beyond the curriculum and pedagogy, to focus on the reform of national education systems.

The interventions of international agencies in global education over recent decades is in part inspired by the idea that education serves to promote "international development," understood in terms of human rights, gender equality, and poverty reduction. They may also be understood to serve a broader neoliberal agenda. There are two key aspects to this: first, education is increasingly geared to the demands of a global economy which is promoted directly and indirectly by the World Bank and many other donor agencies, and second, education itself is becoming increasingly part of a corporate marketplace, with global corporations competing to make money from the sector in countries around the world. These two elements are not unrelated: global agencies are welcoming and facilitating private investment in education. Investment in education is founded in part on the idea that with globalisation, human capital has become much more significant in wealth accumulation and economic growth. Expansion in the global economy is focused more on knowledge-based activities than material production and labor markets are increasingly flexible, unstable, and competitive. In this context, education is seen as crucial to gaining economic advantage.

The attributes required of labor in a neoliberal global economy are not only skills of literacy and numeracy, or the obedience, punctuality, discipline, and honesty that colonial education sought to instill. A knowledge economy demands flexibility, entrepreneurship, and a willingness to take responsibility for the self. Student-centered constructivist approaches to learning may be seen as contributing to the production of these values (Vavrus 2009). Numerous examples have been explored by children's geographers in the Global North. Cairns (2013), for instance, investigates a careers education program in Canada that encourages flexibility, mobility, and self-improvement, idealising the self-reliant, future-oriented person but also encouraging students to internalise uncertainty as insecurities that need to be managed individually. Gagen (2015) examines how the introduction of Social and Emotional Aspects of Learning to schools in England and Wales used the popularisation of neuroscientific understandings of emotions to encourage a view that it is possible for individuals to manage their own emotions as a form of self-government.

Neoliberal transformation of education is having a profound impact on education worldwide. Networks involving business, social enterprise, philanthropic individuals and organisations, education consultants, transnational advocacy networks, and policy entrepreneurs are now the key actors shaping education (Ball 2012). The role of the state in determining the shape of education, even in Europe and North America, is diminishing and is shifting from "government" to "governance" – from the production of policy and delivery of services to contracting other organisations to undertake both roles. Global education problems are identified (or discursively constructed) and solutions developed and disseminated globally by "edupreneurs" and "knowledge companies". Ultimately, education (and its diverse components) are not only commodified and sold but represent an offering for financial markets to invest in and profit from.

Globally, the economisation of education continues to be driven to a large degree by the international financial institutions. The International Monetary Fund, for instance, continues to push for a reduced role for the state, while the World Trade Organization (WTO) views education as a service and is eager to create a free global market in education. Under the WTO's General Agreement on Trade in Services (GATS), countries are required to open their "education markets" to private capital. Countries may be required to allow foreign operators to provide distance education, e-learning, teaching aids and examinations, to establish universities and colleges (directly or through franchising) or other forms of training within their borders in five education sectors from preschool and primary school through higher and adult education.

One "knowledge company" that has taken advantage of the growing global education market is the UK company Pearson, which also owns Penguin Books and sells a wide range of education services. It owns the examination board, Edexcel, whose school examinations are taken in 94 countries and which claims to have marked over 5.7 million scripts across the world in the 2010/2011 academic year (Pearson 2014). Although it may not dictate the content of curricula, this involvement in assessing students' learning undoubtedly gives it power over what is taught in many schools worldwide, and impacts on children's experiences of education.

Pearson also has more direct involvement in schooling in some countries. In 2010, it paid £326 million for Sistemas do Brasil SA. "Sistemas" are integrated learning systems that include curriculum design, teacher support and training, print and digital content, technology platforms, assessment, and other services. Pearson provides these systems to both government and private preschools and primary and secondary schools, serving more than 450,000 Brazilian students. It also offers undergraduate and graduate programs to 9,000 students, as well as distance learning courses, and directly operates 31 schools in the country (Pearson 2010). In Africa and Asia, Pearson owns and operates chains of low-cost fee-paying schools. One of these, Bridge International Academies, has 130 schools in Kenya with over 50,000 students that charge $5 a month. Bridge operates a standardised curriculum and scripted lesson plans, delivered by tablet, detailing what teachers should do and say at every moment of each class. The tablets are also used to monitor lesson pacing, record attendance, and track assessment (CEI 2014). Pearson also owns Omega schools, a chain of more than 20 for-profit schools in Ghana that serve 12,000 students from nursery to Junior High School. Students pay $0.75 a day and, like Bridge, Omega operates a "school-in-a-box" approach with standardised operations manuals and teaching materials. Teachers are senior high school graduates who receive 1 week of pre-service training and 2–3 days per term of in-service training (CEI 2014). Both Bridge and Omega are among 22 private school chains supported by the Center for Education Innovations, which is funded by the British government's Department for International Development (DFID) (CEI 2014).

Bilateral donor agencies, such as the World Bank, increasingly favour the marketisation of education, and specifically the involvement of transnational corporations. Their education-related programs often facilitate the involvement of transnational capital in low-income countries around the world. DFID's Girls' Education Challenge, a £355 million program, is managed by Price Waterhouse Coopers and has Coca-Cola as one of its key partners (Curtis 2015). DFID and Coca-Cola have jointly invested in an education project in Nigeria that will promote "the economic empowerment of five million female entrepreneurs across the global Coca-Cola value chain" (cited by Curtis 2015: 8).

Educational restructuring in response to neoliberal agendas and the privatisation of school curricula are altering young people's experiences of growing up (see Jeffrey 2010). Worldwide, growing numbers of children have their education designed by companies based in Western countries and which are motivated by profit. In some respects, the situation is a little different from that which prevailed 200 years ago as colonial and missionary powers exerted their influence on children's education, but today the speed of change is rapid and the uniformity of service provision is much greater.

This chapter has demonstrated how, over the past two centuries, global actors with diverse motives have shaped education systems across the world in profound ways. It has traced four broad sets of transnational actors, each with their own motivations. Importantly, none of the actors engaged in shaping education employed a definitive set of policies or implemented a coherent education system exclusively serving their own agenda. All of the regimes represent complex, unstable, often contradictory but intersecting processes. The most recent, neoliberalism, is perhaps the hardest to pin down. Transnational actors and processes are becoming ever more salient. Not only are national governments losing control over education within their territories (in the Global North, where transnational corporations are taking on roles previously performed by the state, as well as in the Global South); international organisations, too, are no longer coherent policy-making and funding bodies. Rather, education is shaped through networks of organisations and individuals, driven largely by a profit motive but with no central locus of control.

Questions

1. Are you aware of national or international businesses, or international donor agencies, that are involved in education, in your own country or elsewhere? What kind of involvement is it?
2. Do you think large corporations are helpful where educational resources and infrastructure are lacking? What are the benefits and drawbacks?
3. What do you think are the positive or negative impacts on children of globalised educational experiences?

Further reading

Smith M.B., Laurie N., Brown E., Griffiths M. and Humble D. (2015) Education, International Volunteering, and Citizenship: Young People's Subjectivities and Geographies of Development. In Ansell N., Klocker N. and Skelton T. (Eds) *Geographies of Global Issues: Change and Threat. Geographies of Children and Young People* (vol. 8). Singapore: Springer.

Holloway, S. L., Hubbard, P., Jons, H. and Pimlott-Wilson, H. (2010) Geographies of education and the significance of children, youth and families. *Progress in Human Geography*, 34 (5), 583–600.

Tarabini, A. (2010) Education and poverty in the global development agenda: Emergence, evolution and consolidation. *International Journal of Educational Development*, 30, 204–212.

World Bank (2011) *Learning for all: Investing in People's Knowledge and Skills to Promote Development, World Bank Group Education Strategy 2020*. Washington, DC: World Bank.

The full text of this chapter is: Ansell, N. (2015) Globalizing Education from Christian Missionaries to Corporate Finance: Global Actors, Global Agendas, and the Shaping of Global Childhoods. In Ansell, N. et al. (Eds.) *Geographies of Global Issues: Change and Threat, Geographies of Children and Young People* (vol. 8). Singapore: Springer.

References

Ansell, N. (2004) Secondary schooling and rural youth transitions in Lesotho and Zimbabwe. *Youth and Society*, 36 (2), 183–202.

Ansell, N. (2015) Shaping global education: International agendas and governmental power. *International Development Planning Review*, 37 (1), 7–16.

Ansell, N. (2017) *Children, Youth and Development* (2nd ed.). London: Routledge.

Ball, S. (2012) *Global Education Inc.: New policy Networks and the Neoliberal Imaginary*. London: Routledge.

Bellenoit, H. (2016) *Missionary Education and Empire in Late Colonial India, 1860–1920*. London: Routledge.

Cairns, K. (2013) The subject of neoliberal affects: Rural youth envision their futures. *Canadian Geographer*, 57 (3), 337–344.

CEI (2014) Low-cost Private Schools. [Available at www.educationinnovations.org/topics/low-cost-private-schools.]

Curtis, M. (2015) *DfID's Controversial Support for Private Education*. Oxford: Curtis Research.

Gagen, E.A. (2015) Governing emotions: Citizenship, neuroscience and the education of youth. *Transactions of the Institute of British Geographers*, 40 (1), 140–152.

Gould, W.T.S. (1993) *People and Education in the Third World*. Harlow: Longman.

Jeffrey, C. (2010) Geographies of children and youth I: Eroding maps of life. *Progress in Human Geography*, 34 (4), 496–505.

Kanu, Y. (2005) Tensions and dilemmas of cross-cultural transfer of knowledge: Post-structural/ postcolonial reflections on an innovative teacher education in Pakistan. *International Journal of Educational Development*, 25 (5), 493–513.

King, K. (2007) Multilateral agencies in the construction of the global agenda on education. *Comparative Education*, 43 (3), 377–391.

Kong, L. (2013) Balancing spirituality and secularism, globalism and nationalism: The geographies of identity, integration and citizenship in schools. *Journal of Cultural Geography*, 30 (3), 276–307.

Lankina, T. and Getachew, L. (2013) Competitive religious entrepreneurs: Christian missionaries and female education in colonial and post-colonial India. *British Journal of Political Science*, 43 (1), 103–131.

Leach, F. (2008) African girls, nineteenth-century mission education and the patriarchal imperative. *Gender and Education*, 20 (4), 335–347.

London, N.A. (2002) Curriculum convergence: An ethno-historical investigation into schooling in Trinidad and Tobago. *Comparative Education*, 38 (1), 53–72.

Martin, C.J. (1982) Education and consumption in Maragoli (Kenya) households' educational strategies. *Comparative Education*, 18 (2), 139–155.

Nyamnjoh, F.B. (2012) 'Potted Plants in Greenhouses': A critical reflection on the resilience of colonial education in Africa. *Journal of Asian and African Studies*, 47 (2), 129–154.

OECD (2013) *PISA 2012 results in focus what 15-year-olds know and what they can do with what they know*. [Available at www.oecd.org/pisa, accessed 25 Feb 2014.]

Ofori-Attah, K.D. (2006) The British and curriculum development in West Africa: A historical discourse. *International Review of Education*, 52 (5), 409–423.

Pearson (2010) Pearson and Sistema Educacional Brasileiro agree strategic partnership: Pearson to acquire SEB's school learning systems business. [Available at www.pearson.com/news/2010/july/pearsonand-sistema-educacional-brasileiro-agree-strategic-partne.html, accessed 11 March 2004.]

Pearson (2014) International. [Available at www.pearson.com/about-us/education/intemational.html, accessed 11 Mar 2014.]

Ramirez, S.E. (2008) To serve god and king: The origins of public schools for native children in eighteenth-century Northern Peru. *Colonial Latin American Review*, 17 (1), 79–99.

Rowe, K.E. and Byong-Suh, K. (1997) The rise of women's education in the United States and Korea: A struggle for educational and occupational equality. *Asian Journal of Women's Studies*, 3 (2), 30–93.

Schendel, J. (1999) Christian missionaries in Upper Burma, 1853–85. *South East Asia Research*, 7 (1), 61–91.

Schultz, S. (2011) White teachers and the 'good' governance of indigenous souls: White governmentality and Ernabella mission (1937–1971). *Race, Ethnicity and Education*, 14 (2), 209–232.

Sriprakash, A. (2010) Child-centred education and the promise of democratic learning: Pedagogic messages in rural Indian primary schools. *International Journal of Educational Development*, 30, 297–304.

Topping, D.M. (1987) Literacy in the Pacific Islands. *Interchange*, 18 (1–2), 48–59.

UN (2015) *The Millennium Development Goals Report*. New York: United Nations.

UNESCO (2012) EFA Global Monitoring Report: Youth and Skills: Putting Education to Work. Paris: UNESCO.

Vavrus, F. (2009) The cultural politics of constructivist pedagogies: Teacher education reform in the United Republic of Tanzania. *International Journal of Educational Development*, 29 (3), 303–311.

Whitehead, C. (2005) The historiography of British Imperial education policy, part I: India. *History of Education*, 34 (3), 315–329.

Wilson, H.F. (2014) Multicultural learning: Parent encounters with difference in a Birmingham primary school. *Transactions of the Institute of British Geographers*, 39 (1), 102–114.

Wolhuter, C.C. (2007) Education for All in Sub-Saharan Africa: Prospects and Challenges in Education for All: Global promises, National Challenges. *International Perspectives on Education and Society*, 8, 337–362.

INDEX

For purposes of consistency, the index follows the spelling conventions of the United Kingdom, although spelling within the text may vary. Page numbers in *italics* refer to figures. Page numbers in **bold** refer to tables.